Politics and History in Central Asia

Series Editor
Timur Dadabaev, University of Tsukuba, Tsukuba-Shi, Ibaraki, Japan

In the past few decades, Central Asia has drawn the attention of academic and business communities as well as policy professionals because of its geostrategic importance (being located between Russia and China and in close proximity to Afghanistan, Pakistan, Iran, Turkey, and India), its international stability, and its rich energy resources. The region also faces challenges, such as post-conflict peacebuilding, impacts of the Afghan conflict, a number of recent inter-ethnic conflicts, and post-Socialist development paradigms. Approaching the problems and issues related to this region requires a multi-disciplinary perspective that takes into account political science, international relations, political economy, anthropology, geography, and security studies. The Politics and History in Central Asia series serves as a platform for emerging scholarship on this understudied region.

More information about this series at
https://link.springer.com/bookseries/14540

Timur Dadabaev
Editor

The Grass is Always Greener?

Unpacking Uzbek Migration to Japan

palgrave
macmillan

Editor
Timur Dadabaev
University of Tsukuba
Tsukuba, Japan

Politics and History in Central Asia
ISBN 978-981-16-2569-5   ISBN 978-981-16-2570-1 (eBook)
https://doi.org/10.1007/978-981-16-2570-1

Cover illustration: Tomohiro Ohsumi/Stringer

This Palgrave Macmillan imprint is published by the registered company Springer Nature Singapore Pte Ltd.
The registered company address is: 152 Beach Road, #21-01/04 Gateway East, Singapore 189721, Singapore

Acknowledgments

We would like to thankfully acknowledge the intellectual, logistical, and financial support provided by the Nippon-Foundation Central Asia-Japan Human Resource Development Project (Leader Professor Toshinobu Usuyama) at the University of Tsukuba, financial support from "The Japan Choice of Uzbek Migrants and their Positioning as New Migrants in Japan" Project (Grant-in-Aid for Scientific Research (C) 21K12400, principal investigator Prof. Timur Dadabaev), "Regional Governance of International Migration: A Comparative Perspective" Project (Grant-in-Aid for Scientific Research (B), 17H04543, principal investigator Professor Akashi Junichi), and "Perception toward the Rise of China in Comparative Perspectives: Focusing on the Post-Cold War Generation in Asia-Pacific Region" Project (Grant-in-aid for scientific research from the Japan Society for the Promotion of Science under the grant number 19H04347, principal investigator Prof. Shigeto Sonoda) at the University of Tokyo.

We would also like to acknowledge that parts of chapters constituting this volume have been particularly previously in *Acta via Serica* (2020), *Central Asian Survey* (2021), and *Europe Asia Studies* (2022) as referenced in respective parts of the chapters.

Research activities under various schemes have also received invaluable support from the Central Eurasian Research Unit at the Faculty of Social Sciences and Humanities at the University of Tsukuba for which we are deeply grateful.

Contents

Notes on Contributors

Dr. Mukaddam Akhmedova has completed her PhD thesis on Sojourning Experiences and Settlement Practices of Uzbekistani in Japan at the Doctoral Program in International and Advanced Japanese Studies of the University of Tsukuba. She published with *Europe Asia Studies* and presented her work at various conferences.

Prof. Timur Dadabaev is a Professor of International Relations and the Director of the Special Program for Japanese and Eurasian Studies at the Faculty of Social Sciences and Humanities, University of Tsukuba, Japan. He published with *Communist and Post-Communist Studies*, *The Pacific Review*, *Nationalities Papers*, *Japanese Journal of Political Science*, *Journal of Contemporary China*, *Asian Survey*, *Inner Asia*, *Central Asian Survey*, *Asian Affairs*, *Europe Asia Studies*, *Strategic Analysis*, *Journal of Eurasian Studies*, *Asia Europe Journal*, *International Journal of Asian Studies*, and many others. His latest monographic books are *Decolonizing Central Asian International Relations: Beyond Empires* (Oxon: Routledge, 2021), *Transcontinental Silk Road Strategies: Comparing China, Japan, and Korea in Uzbekistan* (Oxon: Routledge, 2019), *Chinese, Japanese, and Korean In-roads into Central Asia* (Policy Studies Series, Honolulu: East West Center, 2019), *Japan in Central Asia* (NY: Palgrave Macmillan, 2016), and *Identity and Memory in Post-Soviet Central Asia* (Oxon: Routledge, 2015). His edited volumes include *Kazakhstan, Kyrgyzstan, and Uzbekistan: Life and Politics During the Soviet Era*, (Co-edited with Hisao Komatsu), NY: Palgrave Macmillan, 2017 and *Social Capital Construction* *and Governance in Central Asia: Communities and NGOs in Post-Soviet Uzbekistan* (Co-edited with Yutaka Tsujinaka), NY: Palgrave Macmillan, 2017.

Dr. Jasur Soipov is a Researcher at the Nippon Foundation Central Asia-Japan Human Resource Development Project (NipCA Project) at the University of Tsukuba. He has completed his PhD thesis on "Changing Patterns of Student Mobility from Uzbekistan to Japan in the Post-Soviet Period" at the Doctoral Program in International and Advanced Japanese Studies of the University of Tsukuba. Along with Prof. Timur Dadabaev, Dr. Soipov has been a co-author of the award-winning paper "Craving Jobs? Revisiting Labor and Educational Migration from Uzbekistan to Japan and South Korea," ACTA VIA SERICA Vol. 5, No. 2, December 2020: 111–140 for which it has been decorated the "Silk Road Prize 2020" by Academia via Serica Society. His latest findings also appeared in coauthored paper in *Central Asian Survey* (Routledge, Taylor and Francis) in 2021.

Prof. Shigeto Sonoda is a Professor of Sociology and Asian studies at the University of Tokyo. Prof. Sonoda has taken initiatives in conducting researches including AsiaBarometer 2003–2008, Asia Student Survey 2008–2018, Tianjin Annual Survey 1997–2011. His special interest is in social stratification and globalization of cultures in Asia, and international perceptions in Asia. His latest publications include: *Global Views of China*, University of Tokyo Press (co-editor, 2021, in Japanese), *National Sentiments in Asia*, Chuo Koron (2020, in Japanese), *China Impact*, University of Tokyo Press (Co-editor, 2018, in Japanese), *Sino-Japan Relations, 1972-2012 IV*. Private Sector, University of Tokyo Press (editor, 2014, in Japanese), *Sino-Japan Relations, 1972-2012 III*. Society and Culture, University of Tokyo Press (editor, 2012, in Japanese), *China Issues: How Experts See the Future of China*, University of Tokyo Press (co-editor, 2012, in Japanese), *Emerging Middle Classes in East Asia, Keiso-shobo* (editor, 2012, in Japanese), *Social Inequality in Contemporary China, Chuo Koron* (2008, in Japanese, awarded Special Prize of 20th Asia-Pacific Award), *Where Chinese Society is Heading for?: Dialogue with Chinese Sociologists*, Iwanami Shoten Publishers (editor, 2008, in Japanese).

List of Figures

List of Tables

CHAPTER 1

Unpacking Uzbek Migration to Japan

Timur Dadabaev

Introduction

For Japanese policy officials, the Central Asian (CA) region was 'terra incognito' prior to the collapse of the Soviet Union, as their relations with states in the region began only with the independence of these states from the Soviet Union. In 30 years of post-independence development, the Japanese agenda of cooperation with CA countries has been framed by diplomatic initiatives (Silk Road/Eurasian Diplomacy, 1997; the Central Asia + Japan forum of 2004), official development assistance (ODA) or the economic penetration of the corporate communities of Japan into CA markets (Hashimoto 1997; Uyama 2015; Dadabaev 2013). Japan to some extent struggled with the issue of how to internalize the CA region into its foreign policies (see Uyama 2003; Murashkin 2015; Dadabaev 2016, 2019). As demonstrated below, one of the tasks faced by Japan was to make its engagements with CA states both effective and visible to the CA public. It also struggled with the dilemma of how to reflect their national identities in its policy engagements with their CA counterparts

T. Dadabaev (✉)
University of Tsukuba, Tsukuba, Japan
e-mail: dadabaev.timur.gm@u.tsukuba.ac.jpom

T. Dadabaev (ed.), *The Grass is Always Greener?*, Politics and History in Central Asia,
https://doi.org/10.1007/978-981-16-2570-1_1

and how to differentiate its Japanese 'self' from Chinese, Korean, Russian, etc. 'others' (Dadabaev 2019).

One approach that Japan embraced consisted of launching initiatives that would reach out to not only political leadership/corporate professionals (as is often seen in the South Korean, Chinese and Russian policy engagements with the region) but also the general public in Central Asia, where political elites and the corporate community do not necessarily speak for the general public (Dadabaev 2016, 2019).

This edited volume, through various chapters, unpacks the nature of Central Asian migration to East Asia, exemplified by the focus on Japan. This volume uses the case of Uzbekistan, the most populous country of Central Asia and demonstrates the migration channels and adaptation strategies of migrants to the realities of Japan. On par with detailing on the conditions of such migrants, this study also provides narratives of internalization of such migration by individuals involved in.

In narrowing its focus, this manuscript shed light on the notion of educational mobility and unskilled labor migration from Uzbekistan to Japan and occasionally on South Korea, and it attempts to highlight the advantages and disadvantages in this process. This focus is predicated on the fact that Uzbekistan is the largest source of educational mobility and labor migration in the CA region. While a few CA countries, such as Tajikistan and Kyrgyzstan, are well known as countries that dispatch a large number of migrant workers to Russia and other labor markets, Uzbekistan stands out in terms of both its population, which makes it the largest and the most significant country of the region, and the overall number of migrant workers seeking jobs abroad.

This study raises the following question in order to unpack the new dynamics of Japan's engagements with CA (Uzbekistan). What are the features of intensifying educational mobility and labor migration from Central Asia (Uzbekistan) to Japan in recent years? By answering this question, this study aims to detail on the social factors that play important roles in localizing foreign policy engagements and narrating them through the terms easily understood by public.

This study constructs the following arguments throughout its chapters. First, labor migration and educational mobility are becoming the next 'horizon' for the expansion of the relationship between East Asia and Central Asia. They are powered by several factors, including the efforts by Japan and to some extent South Korea to build 'original' and people-oriented policy engagements with the region and demand on the side of

CA states, such as Uzbekistan, to provide more labor opportunities to their young and growing populations.

Second, the initiatives to intensify such mobility have produced both positive and negative dynamics of movement of students and laborers from Uzbekistan to Japan which might serve as worrisome trends and impediments to such policies in the future. In particular, due to the limits of available workplaces as well as the endemic corruption, among other factors, in the process of official labor migration from Uzbekistan to Japan, there are signs that educational mobility is being increasingly abused by Uzbek students, who are turning it into a pipeline for unofficial labor migration masquerading as educational mobility.

Third, although abuse of educational migration channels for the purposes of labor migration as educational mobility is a prominent feature of mobility in East Asia (particularly from China, Vietnam and the Philippines to Japan), the patterns of Uzbek-Japanese migration demonstrates that this trend of using educational mobility for labor migration shows signs of expanding beyond East Asian countries, being found in the CA case of Uzbekistan.

Fourth, while the number of people willing to engage in such educational/labor mobility is continuously growing in Uzbekistan, there is little evidence to suggest that those engaging in such mobility consider it to be a 'side door' for permanent settlement and integration into Japanese society, as they opt to return home in the short and medium term.

Fifth, contrary to the expectation that these individuals will seek permanent or long-term settlement, our data show that the majority of those engaging in such practices do not seek long-term settlement in East Asia and regard their stay as a sojourn due to religious and identity-related differences. They define their journey along the lines of Musofir, or religious wanderers, seeking opportunities, wisdom and experience to be used back in their own society to solidify their social identity and standing.

In building and exemplifying these arguments, the second chapter by Dadabaev and Soipov spots on the notion of educational mobility and semi-skilled labor migration from Uzbekistan to Japan and South Korea and attempts to highlight the advantages and dilemmas in this process. This chapter demonstrates that as Japan and South Korea continue their engagements in an attempt to reach out to the Central Asian public, there is a new feature of intensifying labor migration. This adds new dynamics to the relations between these East Asian nations and their Central Asian counterparts, exemplified by the case of Uzbekistan in this chapter.

The third chapter by Dadabaev, Sonoda and Soipov focuses on the experiences of post-Soviet-generation Uzbek students enrolling in Japanese-language schools in Japan in an attempt to place them into the discussions of foreign student mobility and migration. It demonstrates that Japanese-language schools based in Japan not only provide great learning opportunities for Uzbek youth in terms of language education, but also at times serve as a comfortable entry strategy for Uzbeks who wish to search for better employment opportunities in Japan. In contrast with universities, entry into Japanese-language schools does not require a certain level of knowledge, passing an examination to enter the school or constantly demonstrated performance to maintain the status of a language school student. Through enrolling in these schools, these opportunity-aspiring individuals obtain a legitimate reason for entry into Japan, legal migration status at the point of entry, several years of guaranteed permission to engage in limited labor while being enrolled in the language school and, importantly, language training to enable them to engage in certain interactions with potential employers.

The fourth chapter by Dadabaev and Akhmedova demonstrates that Uzbek residents of Japan rationalize their stay in Japan largely as temporary, in line with the concept of 'sojourning'. In contrast to the previous studies which operationalize sojourning according to legal status or 'preparations to return home', this paper claims that such 'Sojourning' needs to be treated as a constantly changing socially shaped discursive category employed by respondents to mitigate challenges such as economic hardship, discrimination, and cultural assimilation. 'Sojourning' is also a culturally sensitive category that they often adopt based on ethnic or religious interpretations.

The fifth chapter by Akhmedova argues that experiences of Uzbek migrants and former students to Japan who choose to continue their professional careers in Japan are social constructed influenced, among others, by their gendered experiences.

The sixth chapter by Akhmedova then details on the role of ethnicity, religion, community in settlement practices of Uzbekistani in Japan. This chapter contributes to the understanding of sojourning experiences of Uzbek migrants of Japan by introducing the ethnic and religious perspectives into studying this topic. The sojourning concept offered by Mizukami captures several groups of settlers and sojourners. However, it does not detail the role of identity in the decisions of migrants. In legal terms, Uzbek migrants treat sojourning as the first stage in permanent residence and even naturalization in Japan. In identity terms, for them, sojourning is a safeguard against encroachments on their Uzbek identity in a largely mono-ethnic Japanese environment. While many other ethnic groups in Japan complain of not being accepted as equal to their Japanese 'hosts', even after they forego the process of permanent residence and naturalization, the Uzbek respondents in almost all interviews emphasized self-Uzbek identification as a part of their sojourning experience, which for them serves as a tool for differentiating their Uzbek self from the Japanese other. While they often state that 'no foreigner, disregarding his or her legal status is going to be accepted as one of their own' by the Japanese, the Uzbek sojourners do not dramatize such treatment from the Japanese people for the following two reasons. For the Uzbek migrants, such differentiation between someone who is similar to the self and the other is neither new nor alien partly because of the multi-ethnic structure of society in Uzbekistan where people differentiate between various ethnic groups and their behaviors. Therefore, for the Uzbek migrants, it is easy to relate to such differentiation by the local Japanese because they treat the Japanese environment as 'foreign' to their Uzbek/Russian/Tatar self. In addition, they believe that their self is different and often incompatible with their host community. In this sense, the migrant community from Uzbekistan is not socially marginalized but ideationally 'barricaded'. Due to their discursive sojourning, they do not hold an expectation of acceptance by the Japanese host community nor do they display an acceptance of Japanese values as their 'own'. In this sense, Japan is perceived as a common social space for them where they interact for functional purposes (survival, making a living, receiving an education, maintaining their educational/professional status). Japanese and Uzbek identities co-exist in this space and do not conflict with each other. This social space rarely extends into their personal space, which is largely defined by the values of the Uzbek self or a hybrid of the old self and the newly acquired self.

Chapter seven by Soipov then details on the experiences of the very specific group of individuals who use educational opportunities presented by the Japanese language schools in Japan to enter the Japanese labor market. This chapter aims to provide the narrative of how the Japanese language schools have shifted from being the institutions which educationally empowered their students into the function of 'side door' for migration practices. And the final chapter eight focuses on how educational migration provides various channels of labor migration.

What differentiates Uzbek migration to Japan from other groups

As is depicted in this book, the phenomenon of Central Asian migration to Japan, as exemplified by Uzbek migration flows, needs to be regarded as a new phenomenon that for now is dominated by education and language migration with it spilling over into professional migration. As is detailed in this volume, the literature on migration to Japan has so far covered various waves and ethnic groups ranging from experiences of Nikkeijin to experiences of migrants and students from Europe and the United States to Japan as well as numerous important studies of life experiences of various ethnic groups such as Koreans in Japan. In terms of professional occupations, the studies covered international students and various groups (lower-skill, higher-skill, and interns) of professionals entering Japan. Numerous studies considered migration from the perspective of the push and pull factors such as economic benefits, the presence of a diaspora and family or regional social networks, demographic pressures (unemployment), ecological factors, administrative factors (corruption or propiska), the way to obtain new social status and social knowledge, which can be utilized as a social remittance by migrants as well as through the prism of the trans-local connections between villages and cities.

At the same time, the literature on migration to Russia, Turkey, and other parts of the world has dominated the studies of Central Asian migration. These studies provide important inquiries into the phenomenon of outbound migration of minority groups in Central Asia, comparative studies of motivations migrants in Central Asian and European states. In addition, scholars have provided important angles to migration by analyzing transnational migration, trans-local migration, and many others.

This study builds on these important contributions to the understanding of migration from Central Asia. While the cases above in their majority analyze Central Asian migration toward Russia, Europe, and Turkey, there were few, if any, studies focusing on the increasing flows of migration from Central Asia to East Asia. In this sense, this inquiry into Uzbek migration to Japan can be considered among the first studies unpacking Central Asian migration to East Asia.

The conceptual novelty of the current study is that it attempts to grasp the complexity of the phenomenon of migration through the case of Uzbek migration to Japan. While many studies treat migration as a static phenomenon by depicting migrants as seeking access to jobs and social benefits in their migration destinations, our study demonstrates that the motivations of migrants extend far beyond these factors. In this book, we treat migration as a socially constructed and constantly changing phenomenon influenced not only by socio-economic motivations and comfort of life but also by other important factors. In line with this, we considered Central Asian migration to East Asia from the perspective of the temporality of stay (which is constantly changing) conditioned by multiple factors such as religiosity, ethnicity, and gender.

In addition to the above, we also provided adapted narration of the notion of sojourn (temporary residence with the intent to return) decorated by the experiences and self-narratives of Uzbek migrants to Japan.

The bulk of the existing literature treats sojourning as a matter of psychological inquiry, focusing more on sociocultural adjustment and the acculturation of migrants in foreign environments. We also found a number of studies that relate temporary residence with identity shifts, as the environment of residence may change an individual's values in line with those of the host society.

However, our sample of Uzbek migrants to Japan, as detailed in the following chapters, suggests additional aspects of sojourning not previously emphasized. The previous coverage of sojourning in other regional settings depicts the notion of sojourn as a static category that is not significantly influenced by socio-economic factors back home of those who migrate. In addition, the concept of sojourn is often defined by the time of one's stay in a migration destination or a possession of stable legal status for such stay.

In addition, the previous studies on sojourning did not pay significant attention to the notions of identity (religious or ethnic) when considering motivations of migrants to settle permanently or to consider their state temporary, a sojourn. In the case of Uzbeks in Japan, as described in various chapters of this book, we provided examples when it was not a legal status, access to stable income which served as the key factor in shaping the intentions to stay or depart among our respondents. Many of our respondents, as described in relevant chapters, who by their legal status had an opportunity to indefinitely stay in Japan considered their stay as a sojourn in Japan. The length of their stay and desire to return was closely related for them to the matter of comfort/discomfort related to their ethnic affiliation or religious attachment which often impacted decisions to consider migrants' stay as temporary or permanent.

And finally, this study highlights that there are several features that differentiate Uzbek migration from those of other major migrant groups in Japan.

One distinct feature is the overwhelming lack of desire to settle permanently in Japan among Uzbek migrants. While a number of studies treat migrants as people eager to exploit the socio-economic advances of the host country, our respondents in their absolute majority indicated that they considered their stay in Japan to be temporary. Temporarily of their stay was not determined by the time but it was rather connected to their ethnic identity/patterns of thinking and behavior which is radically different from the Japanese society. While our respondents displayed a desire to temporarily stay and accumulate a certain amount of financial and social wealth, they did not want to stay permanently or have their children stay in Japan permanently due to incompatibility of their own vision of self (culturally, ethnically, and religiously) with that of the Japanese hosts. In addition, such factors as the strong social pressures from back home and the expectation of parents and relatives for these migrants to eventually return to Uzbekistan shaped their plans for their future. Such outcome of our inquiry may be based on a number of accounts that are connected to the current demographic composition of migrants from Uzbekistan to Japan who represent mostly young, male-dominated groups. For these individuals, in particular, the expectation of their families and communities in Uzbekistan in choosing their Uzbek marriage partners, taking care of elderly parents, and pushing certain social roles to be played back in Uzbekistan serves as the most important factors in their decisions to stay in Japan or return to Uzbekistan. In this sense, our study rediscovered the importance of analyzing the notion of 'return' for considering their stay in Japan.

References

Dadabaev, Timur. 2013. "Japan's Search for Its Central Asian Policy: Between Idealism and Pragmatism." *Asian Survey* 53, no. 3: 506–532.

Dadabaev, Timur. 2016. "Japan's ODA Assistance Scheme and Central Asian Engagement: Determinants, Trends, Expectations." *Journal of Eurasian Studies* 7, no. 1: 24–38.

Dadabaev, Timur. 2019. *Transcontinental Silk Road Strategies: Comparing China, Japan and South Korea in Uzbekistan*. London and New York: Routledge.

Hashimoto, Ryutaro. 1997. "Address to the Japan Association of Corporate Executives." Tokyo, July 24. https://japan.kantei.go.jp/0731douyukai.html.

Murashkin, Nikolay. 2015. "Japanese Involvement in Central Asia: An Early Inter-Asian Post Neoliberal Case?" *Asian Journal of Social Science* 43, no. 1–2: 50–79.

Uyama, Tomohiko. 2003. "Japanese Policy in Relation to Kazakhstan: Is There a Strategy?" In *Thinking Strategically: The Major Powers, Kazakhstan, and the Central Asian Nexus*, edited by Robert Legvold, 165–186. Cambridge: MIT Press.

Uyama, Tomohiko. 2015. "Shin 'Great Game no Jidai no Chuou Ajia' [Central Asia in the Era of New 'Great Game']." *Gaiko* 34: 18–20.

CHAPTER 2

Revisiting Labor and Educational Migration from Uzbekistan to Japan and South Korea

Timur Dadabaev and Jasur Soipov

Introduction

In Central Asian region, Uzbekistan stands out in terms of both its large population, which also makes it the largest and the most significant country of the region, with the largest number of migrant workers seeking jobs abroad. Uzbekistan's population is estimated to be 33 million, with an estimated 10% working abroad (Kuchins et al. 2015, 3). The largest migration destinations for these migrants are Russia, Kazakhstan, the UAE, and Turkey, followed by South Korea (Seitz 2019) and, in recent years, Japan. As shown above, traditionally, Uzbek migrants and students have opted to travel to Russia and neighboring countries due to linguistic similarities and ease of communication. However, in Russia, there have been cases of aggressive discrimination against Asians in general

T. Dadabaev (✉)
University of Tsukuba, Tsukuba, Japan
e-mail: dadabaev.timur.gm@u.tsukuba.ac.jp

J. Soipov
University of Tsukuba, Tsukuba, Japan

T. Dadabaev (ed.), *The Grass is Always Greener?*, Politics and History in Central Asia,
https://doi.org/10.1007/978-981-16-2570-1_2

and CAs/Uzbeks in particular, often resulting in not only verbal insults but also physical abuse. These cases have turned the attention of these migrants to other destinations. In this sense, Japan and South Korea represent new frontiers for such migrants, and they are actively exploiting these new labor markets.

Methodologically, this chapter adopts a pilot survey that explores and occasionally compares the experiences of Uzbek migrants to Japan and South Korea, using datasets of face-to-face interviews involving 15 questions related to various aspects of life in Japan and South Korea. The interviews were conducted face to face and online (Telegram, Skype, etc.) with 66 migrants and Japanese language school students (whom this chapter treats as labor migrants masquerading as students) in Japan from November 2019 to January 2020 as well as online with 30 laborers and students in South Korea from August to September 2020 (see Appendixes 2.1 and 2.2). Once recorded, these conversations were then transcribed and thematically analyzed. The imbalance in the numbers of interviewed students was caused by limitations associated with accessing students in South Korea from Japan as well as the development of the coronavirus disease 2019 (COVID-19) situation, which made networking with potential respondents difficult. Despite these limitations, these two datasets represent a valuable source of information that was utilized for the purposes of this study.

Japanese and South Korean CA Engagements and Their Limits

For both Japan and South Korea, the independence of CA states, including Uzbekistan, was an unexpected event for which their foreign policies were poorly prepared. Both of these countries had little, if any, interaction with this region during the Soviet era due to the limitations imposed by the Soviet government and the generally limited scale of interactions between the Soviet government and these states. In addition to the limited communication of the Soviet era, there was a major geographic limitation due to the landlocked status of CA states and the lack of transportation infrastructure (railroads, highways, direct flights, etc.) other than those directed toward or through Russia. The absence of common geographic borders between both Japan and South Korea and CA states further complicated establishing a dynamic structure of relations between them.

In addition to the geographic distance of the region from Japan and South Korea, the CA region differs significantly from Japan and South Korea in terms of language, culture and religious beliefs, limiting the intercultural connection between them. Japanese foreign policy often treats the CA region as the foundation of Japanese Buddhism and emphasizes common features of worldview and the roles played by prisoners of war who worked and were appreciated in Uzbekistan in the aftermath of WWII (Dadabaev 2013, 2016). While these facts serve as powerful elements in building the narrative of Japan's presence in the CA region, they have had a limited impact on Japan's efforts to meet its future practical goals in the region (Uyama 2003). Similarly, although the Korean diaspora has been instrumental in creating a narrative of the need for South Korea to engage with the CA region and to help those sharing the same Korean roots, it has become apparent in the process that CA Koreans are different from their counterparts in South Korea in terms of culture, language and worldview, limiting the efficiency of the usage of the human resources represented by the significant number of ethnic Koreans in Uzbekistan, Kazakhstan and Kyrgyzstan (Dadabaev 2019, 138–154). Therefore, for both Japan and South Korea, the problem of how to internalize their engagements in Central Asia into their identities and foreign policy remains very acute.

Japan has attempted to approach this problem through various schemes. One of Japan's first high-level initiatives was represented by the Obuchi mission (1996) to Azerbaijan and CA countries. The mission consisted of Member of Parliament (and later PM) Obuchi, and other politicians reported to PM Hashimoto of the need to engage with Central Asia and the Caucasus as a new "frontier" in expanding Japan's presence in post-Soviet space and beyond. The mission resulted in PM Hashimoto's Eurasian/Silk Road Diplomacy speech of 1997, in which he envisioned creating a net of interdependence between Russia, China and CA states with active Japanese corporate and governmental support (Hashimoto 1997). To a great extent, this vision reflected Japan's global influence and international identity as the second most economically powerful country worldwide (Murashkin 2015). However, PM Hashimoto's vision was not implemented due to the short-lived administrations of PM Obuchi (1998–1999) and PM Mori (1999–2000). The next efforts by Japan to engage with this region were made during PM Koizumi's administration (2001–2006) (Ministry of Foreign Affairs of Japan 2002), during which FM Kawaguchi announced the establishment of the Central

Asia + Japan Dialogue Forum (2004), a set of annual interministerial and high-level talks to support regional integration in the CA region and to empower CA states by consolidating their positions in the face of growing Chinese and Russian pressures on the region. PM Koizumi was also the first Japanese PM to visit Uzbekistan and Kazakhstan. Japan's initiatives in this region saw another intensification in 2006 when Taro Aso, who was the FM at the time, later became the PM and is the current deputy PM, announced the new Arc of Freedom doctrine and Prosperity doctrine (2006), which attempted to conceptualize the CA region as a constituent part of the arc stretching from Central Asia to the Middle East (Aso 2006). However, the practical implementation of the doctrine was poor and did not entail aggressive corporate or public participation. It was only with PM Abe's 2nd administration (2013) that the CA direction of Japanese foreign policy showed signs of dynamism, with PM Abe visiting all five CA states in 2015 and announcing various infrastructure projects that offered alternatives to Chinese projects and hypothetically linked them to attempts to internationally standardize high-quality Japanese infrastructure (Abe 2015). The major achievements of these initiatives were that Japan cemented its position as one of the major regional ODA providers and created one of the most favorable environments for ODA in the region, as consistently evidenced in a range of social surveys.

South Korea's government has also attempted to construct a narrative of its CA presence in the aftermath of the collapse of the Soviet Union. The South Korean presence in Central Asia has been championed by the presence of South Korean corporations, differentiating South Korea's engagement with the CA region from Japan's, which was spearheaded by governmental initiatives. In the 1990s, South Korean corporations (Daewoo, Daewoo Unitel, Kabool Textile, etc.) were among the first to build industrial plants in the region. Additionally, the presence of the Korean diaspora offered a comparative advantage for the South Korean penetration into CA markets, and it justified the country's presence in such a remote region to South Korean taxpayers, which also differentiates South Korea from Japan. However, as stated above, the role of the diaspora was limited due to the different identities that those belonging to this diaspora have developed over their lives in the CA region.

The first governmental initiatives were articulated in the early 2000s with Roh Moo-hyun's (2003–2008) resource and corporate penetration-focused Comprehensive Central Asian Initiative (2006), which attempted to connect CA resources to South Korean technology. This initiative was followed in 2007 by the creation of the Korea + Central Asia forum, which in 2017 was institutionalized into a kind of international organization (Secretariat of Korea-Central Asia Forum, https://www.centralasia-korea.org/web/pages/gc51269b.do). Other attempts to frame South Korean strategy in the CA region include the Lee administration's New Asia Diplomacy and New Silk Road Policy (2008–2012) and the Park administration's Eurasia Initiative (2013–2017) (for the New Northeast Policy; see the Korean Institute of Economic Policy [http://www.kiep.go.kr/eng/index.do]). Among such initiatives, the most recent to have an impact on the CA region is the Moon administration's New Northern Policy (2018-present) (cf. the New Northern Policy [https://www.bukbang.go.kr/bukbang_en/]). Through these schemes, South Korea has attempted to provide a proper narrative of its policies in the CA region.

While the abovementioned initiatives of Japan and South Korea had a tremendous impact on support for CA nationhood, CA development and the decolonization of CA infrastructure by offering alternatives to Chinese and Russian projects, they had a limited direct impact on the general public while prioritizing the tasks of CA governments. The task of making their engagements more visible and accessible to the CA general public has been approached by extending diverse educational opportunities to youth and establishing throughout the region Japanese and Korean centers, which are charged with language education. However, even these centers have had little effect because those mastering the Japanese or Korean language have had very limited employment opportunities using those skills.

To address this issue, Japan and South Korea have concluded agreements on labor migration with Uzbekistan. In this respect, South Korea has been a forerunner. After the adoption of the law on migration from abroad, South Korea entered into negotiations with Uzbekistan and in 2006 signed an agreement on governmentally controlled migration. The quota decided at the time was approximately 3,000 workers per year (as of 2019, it was 3,400 available workplaces per year, with 90,000 applicants).

These migrants are preselected by the government of Uzbekistan (a labor migration center created specifically for this purpose), trained in basic language skills at home and then sent to South Korea, with their employers preselected. Uzbekistan's departments of labor migration conclude agreements with prospective applicants on their potential dispatch for employment to Japan and South Korea (and to Turkey, Russia and other countries) through the 13 "Ishga Markhamat"

(Welcome to Work) service centers throughout Uzbekistan, which also provide predispatch training lasting approximately 3 months and have a capacity to train up to 20,000 trainees per year. The announced training courses include language (Japanese, Russian, etc., depending on the country of dispatch) and professional training (welder training, etc.). Additionally, these centers provide microcredit services to those planning to be dispatched abroad so that they can cover their travel and initial expenses. These services are provided to avoid situations that occasionally occur in which those departing from Uzbekistan are taken advantage of by various companies that exploit their lack of initial financial resources for travel and document processing, lend them money under very high interest rates and then continue to demand repayment of this incurred debt out of the salary that these individuals receive from their work abroad. The interest rates of the microcredit provided by the dispatch centers are covered by funds from the government of Uzbekistan. Additionally, those dispatched through these centers are considered self-employed, and in cases in which they pay taxes, they are eligible for social payments and retirement pensions after reaching retirement age (Ministry of Employment and Labor of Uzbekistan 2020).

This scheme established by the Uzbek government allows for a degree of control over migration flows and some protection of migrants in Russia, Japan, South Korea and elsewhere. Japan has followed this example and established a training center in Uzbekistan, announcing its desire to accept foreign workers under a trainee scheme, in which foreign workers arrive in Japan as trainees who are also allowed to work during the time outside of their on-the-job training (MOFA 2019). However, these governmentally run schemes have been criticized due to various deficiencies. Regarding South Korea, the locally organized preselection has been criticized due to nepotism, corruption and the lack of proper criteria for selecting candidates, as recently reported in the press. Presently, selection is conducted through the random choice of a lottery. Regarding Japan, the scheme has been criticized because of the small number of migrants who can travel to Japan (which is in the hundreds and not the thousands, as in the case of South Korea) and because, in reality, the scheme channels poorly paid foreign labor to Japan, where trainees are paid little, as they are generally considered to be trainees, not proper workers. Their rights as migrant workers are also little protected, and their stay in Japan is heavily regulated. Due to these deficiencies, there have been several cases in which students disappeared after their arrival in Japan and joined the illegal workforce.

This situation has resulted in the latest trend of expanding educational and labor migration from Central Asia to East Asia through channels that are not controlled by the government as exemplified by language schools below. Such schools claim to be organizations dedicated to language learning in Japan and South Korea, but in reality, they create cases of labor migration in which students work 12 or more hours a day (combining several jobs) and their language studies become a part-time exercise.

Conceptualizing Educational and Labor Migration as the New "Horizon"

There are several studies that focus on the phenomenon of migration from Central Asia to international partners. Some studies emphasize the role of governments in facilitating migration flows (Bisson 2016; Liu-Farrer and Tran 2019, 235–249; Abashin 2016); however, there are many factors that facilitate and motivate migrants to travel in search of opportunities (Gel'man 2004). For instance, several studies have discussed in detail the migration of Russian-speaking populations to Russia at the outset of the collapse of the Soviet Union (Korobkov 2007). Other studies do not particularly connect these flows to interstate relations; instead, they place them in the global flows of migrants, as influenced by transnational processes (cf. Laruelle 2013; Bartolomeo et al. 2014). These studies offer both bilateral perspectives and comparisons of CA states regarding their migration experience from both the regional and gender perspectives (Portes et al. 1999; Abashin 2013; Petesch and Demarchi 2015).

Regarding the reasons for such migrations, scholars have focused on various factors that shape the flows of migrants, terming them push and pull factors (for migration from Uzbekistan to Russia, see (Urinboyev 2016), such as ethnic preferences (e.g., Kim 2014), demographic pressures and social networks (Turaeva 2013, 2014), economic factors (Kakharov et al. 2020; Kadirova 2015; Hiwatari 2016; Virkkunen 2017; Seitz 2019), ecological factors and administrative factors, such as endemic corruption or limitations imposed on mobility through domestic controls (Reeves 2012; Laruelle 2013; Schröder and Stephan-Emmrich 2016).

In addition to the factors above, some studies discuss the role of local connections not between states but between locations within the states, offering a translocal connotation of such migration (Levitt 2001a; Schröder and Stephan-Emmrich 2016; Urinboyev 2016, 28).

Among the personal motivations, the notions of "home" and "return" feature significantly in the many studies narrating the motivations of Uzbek migrants in Russia and elsewhere (Abashin 2015; Urinboyev 2016). For them, their journey is measured not purely by the amount of wealth accumulated abroad but, more importantly, by the evaluation and appreciation they receive at home, defined as a close circle of family members (Carling and Erdal 2014). The sense of community both abroad and in the home community is increasingly maintained through virtual social networking tools (Urinboyev 2017; Christensen 2012) such as Telegram, as detailed below.

To a great extent, the experiences and narratives of student-migrants to Japan and South Korea reflect the factors mentioned above and are closely related to the notions of push and pull factors in regard to seeking gainful employment abroad. However, in addition to these factors, this study emphasizes the structural problem of the poor institutionalization of official migration channels, which results in alternative tracks of labor market penetration. The lack of official channels for labor migration and the poor organization of this process combine to accelerate student-masqueraded labor mobility. In addition to the limited opportunities and number of places available for migration from Uzbekistan to Japan and South Korea, the candidate selection process is arbitrary and frequently opaque, further lowering the degree of trust in the official process and forcing these individuals to seek alternative migration channels (see Fig. 2.1).

From Central Asia to East Asia: Uzbekistan's Dynamics

Japanese Dynamics

While Chinese, Iranian, Vietnamese and Brazilian migrants attempted to take advantage of the high-speed economic growth in Japan (1955–1975) to gain employment opportunities, Uzbek migrants' entry into the Japanese employment and educational market has been slow and has largely occurred after the downturn in Japan's economic growth. This situation has influenced their understanding of the niches in Japan that they can fill. Thus, this study focuses on Uzbeks sojourning in Japan in the years of Japan's economic slump. There are several factors

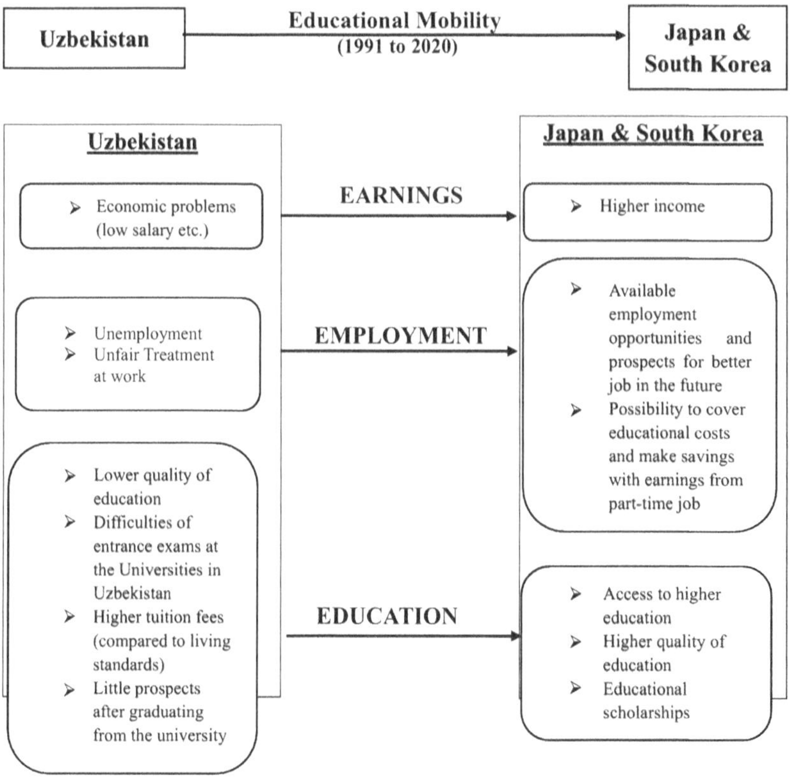

Fig. 2.1 Factors influencing Uzbek migration to Japan and South Korea

shaping the dynamics of Uzbek labor migration to Japan and South Korea (see Fig. 2.1). In addition to the domestic demand for jobs in Uzbekistan, one of the most important factors to consider is the policy of the host country with respect to migration practices, as exemplified in this chapter by Japan and South Korea (for the outline of the factors influencing migration see Fig. 2.1 above). Regarding Japan, due to cultural differences and its geographic location, historically, the country is not considered migrant friendly. Foreigners comprise just 2% of the overall population of 127 million (OECD 2018). Chinese individuals (389,117) constitute the largest foreign ethnic group in the Japanese labor market, accounting for 26.6% of foreign workers, followed by Vietnamese individuals (316,840), accounting for 21.7% of foreign workers, and Filipino individuals (164,006), accounting for 11.2% of foreign workers (Ministry of Health, Labor and Welfare 2019). The fastest growing migrant worker groups are Vietnamese (31.9%), Indonesian (21.7%) and Nepalese (18.0%) individuals. While these data do not demonstrate a significant presence of the Uzbek workforce in the Japanese labor market, the data on Uzbek citizens residing in Japan registered a 200-fold increase in their number, from as few as 20 in 1994 to 3,951 in 2018. Regarding Uzbek educational mobility, the data show that the number of people seeking educational opportunities under student visas increased from only 101 students in 2000 to 2,366 in 2018, as shown in Table 2.1.

In the interviews with 66 students conducted to clarify the purposes of their stay in Japan, the overwhelming majority (approximately 60 students) indicated that the main purpose of their stay in Japan and enrollment in language schools was to gain access to educational opportunities in Japan. While some of them indicated that they sought official travel channels to work in Japan, they also realized that gaining such employment was more complicated and difficult than the opportunities provided through educational mobility. Once enrolled in language schools, they utilized the opportunities made available to them through the permission for part-time jobs (*shikakugai katsudo kyokasho*) issued by the immigration office.

Regarding information channels, the majority of respondents replied that their choice was influenced greatly by family members, people sharing common origins (city, village, etc.) or their community (religious, professional, social).

When surveyed about the financial resources needed for their enrollment in Japan, the majority claimed to have borrowed money from family members or acquaintances (Fig. 2.2).

When asked about how important it was for them to work while studying in Japan and remit their generated income back to Uzbekistan, the majority of those enrolled in Japanese language schools replied that it was very important or relatively important, indicating that the purpose of their enrollment in educational institutions was in part if not solely to benefit from access to the Japanese labor market (Fig. 2.3).

Similarly, the number of respondents indicating that they remitted financial resources from Japan was the highest among the language school

Table 2.1 The number of Uzbek immigrants in Japan

Year	Total	Dip	Off	Pro	Art	Jou	HSP	I/BM	Res	Ins	Eng	SH/IS	Ic/T	Ent	S/L	TIT	CA	TV	Stu	Tra	Dep	PR	DA	S/ChJN	S/ChPR	LTR	WASR	TR	Oth
1994	20			2					1			1							6		9			1					
1995	22			2								1					1		7	3	7			1					
1996	29			2					1			1					1	1	10	2	10			1					
1997	47			3					1		1	1					3		27	2	7			2					
1998	80			1					2					1			3	1	55	3	11			2			1		
1999	103			2					2					1			2	4	63	3	23			3					
2000	184			5					4			1	1	15			3	33	81	3	27			8		2			1
2001	201			4					2		1	4	1	1			3	30	101	7	32			10		2	1		2
2002	262			7					2		1	8	1	12	3		2	24	122	11	45	1	4	14		3			2
2003	341			6	1				1		3	20	1	19	5		3	34	137	12	65	3	6	18		3	2		2
2004	376			6				2			3	29	2	23	1		3	41	157	9	55	5	3	27		4	1		5
2005	495			5		1		2	2	2	5	42	2	51	1		1	48	172	30	69	6	3	40	2	6			5
2006	527			5	1	1		2		1	6	52	3	12	1		5	33	219	18	92	11	5	43	2	9	9	9	9
2007	620			6		1		3			8	72	2	6	1		2	28	275	9	112	14	7	52	2	12	4		4
2008	655			8		1		2		2	8	87	2	6	1		10	19	264	8	130	15	8	63	2	12	3		4
2009	727			8		1		3		2	7	108	2	6	1		11	21	251	6	180	22	9	64	2	15	6		2
2010	832			8		1		3		4	13	123	2	4	1		8	11	286	4	232	35	6	63	3	15	8		2
2011	840			9	1	1		2	1	4	17	151	2	3	2		5	7	256	4	228	47	15	60	5	18	1		1
2012	1060	33	16	9		1		3	1	2	17	167	1	3	1		5	67	284	6	276	55	13	70	8	22			
2013	1197	26	14	11	1	1		4	1	2	19	176	3	2	1		9	50	352	1	340	74	14	63	10	23			
2014	1415	23	14	11	1	1		5		2	19	181	4	2	1		4	43	477	2	386	86	38	69	15	31			
2015	1599	24	12	11	2	1	2	8	1	2		212	4	2	1		7	59	583	2	404	115	27	68	14	38			
2016	1986	25	9	10		1	3	9	1	2		233	3		2		9	76	868	2	427	164	24	68	12	38			
2017	3068	26	14	10			10	9	1	2		280	3	1	1	17	4	106	1759	3	468	200	33	73	12	36			
2018	3951	26	16	9			12	13	1	2		395	4	2	3	9	4	136	2366	3	547	226	49	72	15	41			

Legend:

Dip: Diplomat	S/L: Skilled Labor	HSP: Highly Skilled Professional	Stu: Student	DA: Designated Activities
Off: Official	Ent: Entertainer	Ic/T: Intra-company Transferee	Tra: Trainee	S/ChPR: Spouse or Child of Permanent Resident
Pro: Professor	Ins: Instructor	I/BM: Investor/Business Manager	Dep: Dependent	LTR: Spouse or Child of Permanent Resident
Art: Artist	Eng: Engineer	TIT: Technical Intern Training	PR: Permanent Resident	WASR: Without Acquiring Status of Residence
Jou: Journalist	CA: Cultural Activities	CA: Cultural Activities	TR: Temporary Refuge	SH/IS: Specialist in Humanities/International Services
Res: Researcher	TV: Temporary Visitor	TV: Temporary Visitor	Oth: Others	S/ChJN: Spouse or Child of Japanese National

Source Ministry of Justice of Japan, http://www.moj.go.jp/housei/toukei/toukei_ichiran_touroku.html (compiled by authors using *Zairyu Gaikokujin Toukei* reports from 1996 to 2018)

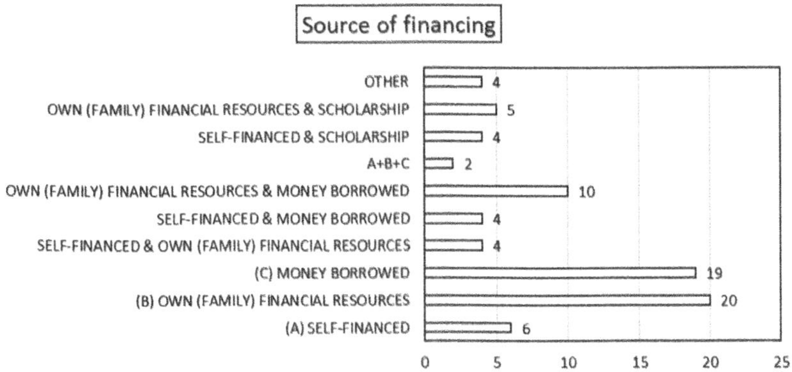

Fig. 2.2 Sources of financing for their trips (Japanese sample)

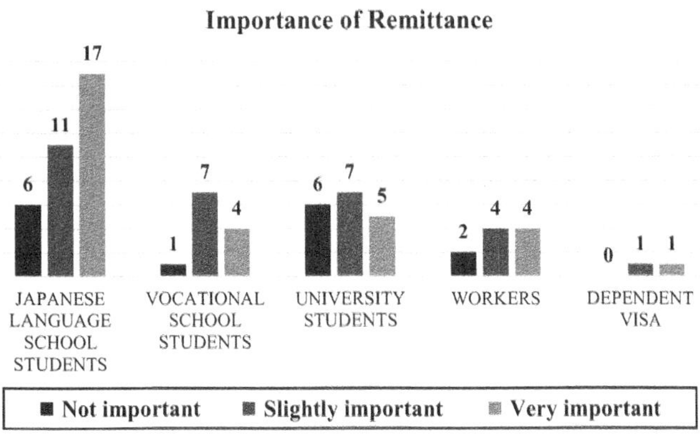

Fig. 2.3 The importance of remittances to Uzbekistan for migrants (Japanese sample)

students, while those in the other categories were inclined to downplay the practice of financial remittances (Fig. 2.4).

With respect to their plans to stay longer in Japan or even to settle down, all of the respondents indicated that they did not have intentions regarding long-term settlement and naturalization. Most of them defined the timeframe of their stay in Japan as being approximately 3–5 years to build the financial foundations for their lives back in Uzbekistan. The

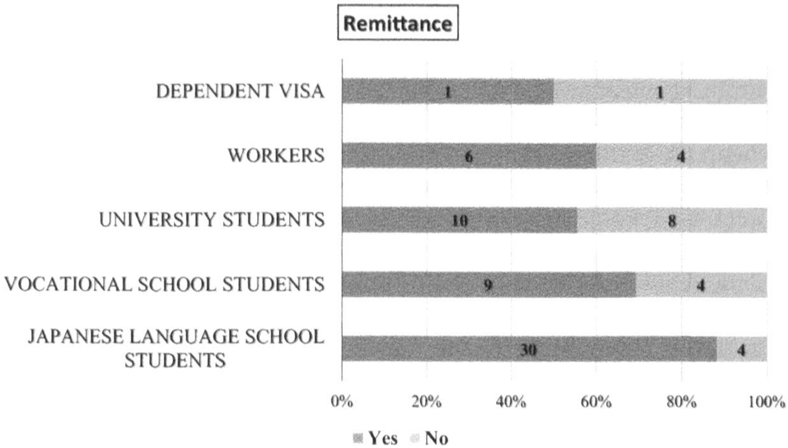

Fig. 2.4 Who remits the most? (Japanese sample)

topic of returning and building their careers back in Uzbekistan featured prominently in our conversations, and most respondents saw the value of their stay and work in Japan in relation to expected professional development and business opportunities back in Uzbekistan and not in Japan. When asked why they choose to "return" instead of building careers in Japan, some indicated a desire for further education in Japan, but they were inclined to indicate an eventual desire for return. These answers were closely connected to issues of identity (cf. Main and Sandoval 2015). The greatest reasons they desired to return were not rejection of Japanese society. Rather, they indicated that distance from their family, community and worldview (O'zbekchilik, or Uzbekness) were the reasons pulling them back to Uzbekistan. Additionally, many indicated a strong longing for religious community and Islam, which Japanese society accommodates slightly, if at all.

South Korean Dynamics

The data for South Korea demonstrate a slightly different trend. First, the number of Uzbeks in South Korea is 6 times higher than that in Japan due to the intensity of the official labor migration channel from Uzbekistan to South Korea established in 2006. As a result, in 2019, the number of Uzbek residents in South Korea reached 25,961, as shown in Table 2.2.

From a comparative perspective, Uzbek migrants are among the largest groups of incoming foreigners, ranking as the 5th largest group of foreign residents in South Korea (see Table 2.3). This group includes Uzbek Koreans who "returned" to or migrated to South Korea from Uzbekistan on business-, work- and study-related grounds.

Uzbek citizens are also the largest migrating group among those settling in South Korea from other former Soviet states, followed by individuals from Russia and Kazakhstan, both of which also host large Korean diasporas, as shown in Table 2.4.

Regarding occupations, Uzbek citizens' migration to South Korea is double layered. It is characterized by a "return" to Korea by members of the diaspora residing in Uzbekistan. On the other hand, recent years have seen very high numbers of Uzbek residents of non-Korean ethnicity resettling in South Korea for labor migration and educational purposes. As seen in the table on residence permits, the group of overseas Koreans

Table 2.2 Uzbek citizens in South Korea

Nationality	*2015*	*2016*	*2017*	*2018*	*2019*
Uzbekistan	14,246	16,151	18,486	18,818	25,961

Source The data for all the tables and graphs for South Korea have been generated using the data from the Commission for Statistics of Korea, KOSTAT at http://kostat.go.kr/portal/eng/index.action

Table 2.3 International migrants in South Korea

By Nationality	*2015 Total*	*2016 Total*	*2017 Total*	*2018 Total*	*2019 Total*
Total	372,935	402,203	452,657	495,079	438,220
China	177,001	165,494	156,848	169,336	138,653
Vietnam	30,244	40,099	47,964	55,992	61,344
United States	22,741	21,771	19,848	21,171	20,839
Thailand	20,122	28,457	71,506	80,349	53,290
Uzbekistan	14,246	16,151	18,486	18,818	25,961
Philippines	9,867	9,530	8,988	10,053	9,149
Cambodia	9,564	10,248	9,523	8,710	9,917

Table 2.4 Residents of South Korea by citizenship (selected countries of the FSU)

By Nationality	*2020. 03 Total*	*2015 Total*	*2016 Total*	*2017 Total*	*2018 Total*	*2019 Total*
Kazakhstan	178	3,534	7,711	13,356	15,724	12,469
Kyrgyzstan	53	1,385	1,759	1,688	1,898	1,622
Tajikistan	29	119	161	219	199	217
Turkmenistan	1	13	35	41	143	237
Uzbekistan	527	14,246	16,151	18,486	18,818	25,961
Georgia	1	16	12	16	19	23
Russia (Federation)	506	6,784	15,025	18,638	18,726	17,983
Ukraine	74	968	1,240	1,298	1,362	1,199

represents the largest group of Uzbek citizens in South Korea, followed by those in the unskilled employment and visiting/joining family category and those indicating education-related goals in South Korea (Table 2.5).

Table 2.5 Types of residence permits received by Uzbek citizens in South Korea

Qualification of stay	*2015 Total*	*2016 Total*	*2017 Total*	*2018 Total*	*2019 Total*
Total	14,246	16,151	18,486	18,818	25,961
Short-term visitors	1,328	1,321	1,334	1,154	1,343
Short-term employment	2	-	3	-	-
Job seeking	6	3	1	11	42
Study	343	535	1,130	1,687	2,727
Industrial trainees	220	208	282	193	98
General trainees	313	676	1,778	2,100	1,746
Trade and business	2	2	2	1	5
Professors	1	–	–	1	2
Unskilled employment	3,329	2,719	2,783	2,355	3,359
Visiting/joining family	232	1,371	2,134	2,107	3,144
Residence	15	23	36	31	132
Overseas Koreans	1,260	1,907	2,087	2,129	3,516
Marriage immigration	264	251	221	224	461
Visiting and employment	6,525	6,877	6,498	6,538	8,574

Table 2.6 The main areas of residence of Uzbek citizens in South Korea

Administrative district (Si, Gun, Gu) (1) 2013	
Gross Total	30,699
Seoul	1,480
Busan	1,313
Daegu	881
Incheon	1,494
Gwangju	730
Daejeon	272
Ulsan	729
Sejong-si	107
Gyeonggi-do	9,901
Gangwon-do	252
Chungcheongbuk-do	1,655
Chungcheongnam-do	2,414
Jeollabuk-do	908
Jeollanam-do	964
Gyeongsangbuk-do	1,748
Gyeongsangnam-do	5,789
Jeju-do	62

Similar to the case of Japan, where respondents tend to settle around major industrial cities such as Tokyo (and surrounding areas such as Kanagawa, Chiba, Saitama and Ibaraki), Osaka, and Nagoya, settlers from Uzbekistan prefer to settle around large industrial cities and economic zones with a high economic potential such as Chungcheongnam, Seoul, and Busan, as detailed in Table 2.6.

These results also demonstrate that their residence in South Korea is tightly connected to employment opportunities and the availability of jobs that provide for their social security and income for family members who depend on their remittances back to Uzbekistan.

Migrant Perceptions of South Korea and Japan

Comparing South Korea and Japan, we note that there are several similarities and differences in the way migrants treat their sojourn to Japan and South Korea. Regarding similarities, the vast majority of Uzbek student-migrants in our survey indicated that they considered their stays in Japan and South Korea to be temporary, having little desire to settle for the long/medium term or to seek permanent residence. While the lack of opportunities to settle permanently and the long- and short-term visas issued to them may have predetermined such answers, our respondents in both Japan and South Korea cited cultural differences and incompatible worldviews in regard to attitudes toward elderly people as well as religious differences as the main reasons they did not consider the possibility of staying longer in these countries. In this sense, our sample supports the findings of similar studies showing that temporary resettles in Japan and South Korea do not regard their current legal "status to be the most detrimental factor in their decision to permanently settle or 'return home'" (Dadabaev and Akhmedova 2022).

For the overwhelming majority of respondents, the projected timeframe of their stay in both countries was 3–6 years, reflecting the time within which they would be able to repay their debts for the expenses incurred to come to Japan/South Korea and build some financial and social capital that would enable them to solidify their standing back in Uzbekistan.

Among the factors significantly influencing the respondents' choices to stay or leave, family/community ties in Uzbekistan and religion (Islam) played the greatest roles in their decisions to return. Interestingly, the overwhelming majority of respondents indicated that they were fully satisfied with their lives in Japan/South Korea and therefore did not link their desire to return to Uzbekistan to dissatisfaction with their current host countries. Rather, they saw these two aspects as being not mutually exclusive. Because they lived their lives within Uzbek communes (sharing apartments with like-minded fellow citizens), they did not detach their being in Japan/South Korea from their living in a social space of "Uzbekness", and their interactions with the local communities in their host countries were purely functional. They barricaded themselves within the notions of Uzbekness and "*musofir*" (wanderer in unknown lands), and through these notions, they interacted with the host society. In their own words, their current lives are defined by their ethnic attachment to Uzbekness (*O'zbekchilik*) or by Islamic religious interpretations of their stay that are in line with their being wanderers or *musofirs* in search of not only financial rewards but also life experience, wisdom, and justice. In such a structure of self-rationalization, the eventual "return home" is the point of their judgment regarding their achievements in their host societies, where they earn the fruits of their current lives. Upon their return, the majority hope to either utilize their experience as know-how in Uzbek society (in line with the social remittance concept; see Levitt

2001b; Radjabov 2017; also Betti and Lundgren 2012) or enhance their social standing in their communities (Ruget and Usmanalieva 2011).

One feature uniting the perspectives of those pursuing opportunities in Japan and South Korea is that they see these opportunities as a choice they had to make when they had no other alternatives back home because they failed the national university entrance examinations, had no money to pay for their education or saw no prospects for work back home due to the low salary levels. Additionally, some respondents indicated that when they decided to travel to Japan or South Korea, they saw the opportunity to both study and work to save for their future after their return home. Importantly, those who considered educational mobility options or labor migration outside Uzbekistan considered Japan and South Korea to be a viable alternative to traveling to Russia, where Uzbeks are among the dominant groups of the foreign labor market but face tremendous discrimination and psychological and physical abuse.

In most of their narratives, the respondents indicated that although they appreciated the opportunities offered by their sojourn to Japan and South Korea, they had to deal with a number of challenges mainly related to the identification of "self" and their purpose while in these countries. They indicated that they were prepared to accept and deal with logistical limitations and problems in their lives in these countries because their current stays offer them an opportunity to "stand on their feet" and establish their own lives back home. Additionally, most interviews featured a discussion of the place of the respondents' sojourn in their process of maturation and increasing appreciation for their own society and, importantly, "religion". Studies of migrants in Russia and elsewhere have already raised the issue of the increasing religiosity among migrants because of the migration experience, as religious beliefs provide a proper framing for most migrants, soothing the perception of their difficulties in their host societies. In the case of Japan and South Korea, the respondents overwhelmingly emphasized that religious attachments helped them to internalize what they were going through and explain it to others. Although many indicated that they have a religious community around them, they still preferred to live in their own country, where this religious community is constituted not by random people united by their status as migrants but by close family members.

This result is connected to the respondents' high satisfaction with their stays in their host societies. That is, they have opportunities to see and learn new things that they would not be exposed back home, and any difficulties they face in their host societies are considered to be temporary and transient.

However, for both Japan and South Korea, the greatest advantage of the respondents' stays is the short-term economic benefits from their stays in the form of capital accumulation. The respondents linked this capital to the goals they plan to pursue in Uzbekistan, and the overwhelming majority of them interpreted these goals as not a pure longing for financial accumulation but as the opportunity to launch their own businesses at home. Additionally, they became aware of the opportunities available to them by learning about the social and economic institutions, schemes and enterprises present in Japan and South Korea. Many respondents indicated that they envision "copying" or "modifying" these practices to their own society in Uzbekistan. Theoretically, such behaviors can be interpreted as an attempt to socially remit practices that can potentially not only enhance the standing of these individuals but also contribute to the soft and hard power potentials of Japan and South Korea in the region because the sojourns of migrants offer channels for the transfer of business practices and work ethic and provide an opportunity for migrants to accumulate the capital needed to launch enterprises back in Uzbekistan.

In addition to the similarities between Japan and South Korea in the eyes of migrants, there are also striking differences in their perceptions of these societies. The first difference relates to the channels of their travel to these two East Asian countries. In the case of Japan, educational mobility, most commonly in the form of Japanese language training, is the most popular channel for labor migrants to travel to Japan (see Table 2.7).

Students enroll in Japanese language schools in Uzbekistan, gain a certain level of proficiency and then apply for Japanese language training in Japan, which can last from 6 months to several years, depending on the desire of the student. As indicated above, such enrollment requires a significant amount of initial investment, and these migrants borrow the funds to make this investment from their family members, friends or "brokers" who facilitate their travel to Japan. In the majority of cases, such migrants attempt to stay in Japan for several years until they accumulate enough resources to repay their debt and build the foundation of financial stability back home. Some of these individuals travel to Japan several times, enrolling in various language schools or progressing to professional training schools and, sometimes, undergraduate programs. The main reason for the popularity of this migration channel, as opposed to direct and official labor migration, is that Japan does not offer such

Table 2.7 Expenses for educational opportunities and finding part-time jobs in Japan

Fee types	*Approximate monetary amount*
Fees charged by Japanese language schools in Japan	
Tuition fee for the first year	US$6,300–7,300 (depends on the Japanese language school and its location in Japan)
Apartment rent per month	US$200–670 (depends on the location and number of people sharing a room)
Fees charged by education agencies/brokers in Uzbekistan	
Language training fee in Uzbekistan	US$ (price depends on the school and its location in Uzbekistan); even after a student obtains a visa, he/she is required to continue studying the Japanese language until his/her departure to Japan or be responsible for paying fees for the period
Processing fee for services such as preparing documents, preparing for online interviews, assisting with translation in the online interview, finding a Japanese school in Japan, paying the visa fee	US$500–1,500 (depends on the agency and individual broker); if a visa is not obtained, $300 will be retained by the agency, and the rest will be returned to the student
Airfare (one-way or two-way ticket from Uzbekistan to Japan); students' personal responsibility	US$300–720
Assistance in finding part-time jobs through people who work as brokers and live in Japan; students' personal responsibility	US$50–285 (Uzbek students in Japan are divided into three groups: Most students find part-time jobs with the assistance of their friends or relatives or by themselves; the second group of students finds part-time jobs by paying approximately $50–200 to Uzbek brokers; the third group of students finds part-time jobs by paying individual Uzbek brokers in Japan approximately $285 plus an additional 10% of their daily salary); this group of students usually uses this service in the first six months after coming to Japan (usually Japanese language school students)

migration opportunities in large numbers (per year, in the hundreds and not in thousands, as in the case of South Korea), limiting the opportunities for everybody who would like to take advantage of them (see Fig. 2.5).

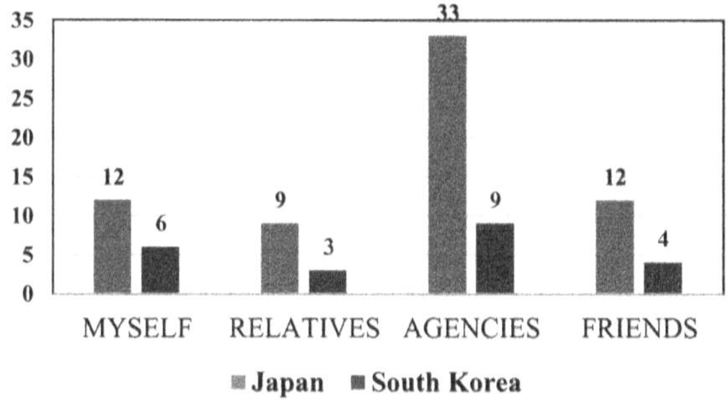

Fig. 2.5 Kind of assistance received in the process of preparing admission documents

In recent years, there has been a trend in which the areas of elderly caretaking, agriculture and certain types of manual labor (such as cargo companies) are increasing the number of foreign laborers directly employed abroad, including Uzbekistan. However, the problem with these new areas of labor migration is that they are very strictly regulated by the government, requiring applicants to have a certain level of language proficiency and certain learning skills. For instance, in the area of caretaking, applicants will need to pass a state examination a few years after their arrival in the Japanese language to qualify for a license and a longer stay. This requirement limits the opportunities for applicants interested in traveling to Japan.

In the case of South Korea, direct migration practices are more widespread, with the Uzbek Ministry of Labor establishing a special agency for labor migration responsible for facilitating the travel of such migrants to Japan and their protection. Regarding numbers, South Korea offers several thousand (approximately 3,000) spots per year for citizens of Uzbekistan. Those unable to use this opportunity then exploit the option of educational mobility for the purpose of labor migration (Table 2.8).

In regard to the logistics of their stay, the process of controlling and licensing language school students in South Korea puts additional pressures on students to properly attend to their studies, as the documents required for receiving a work permit during their studies require confirmation by the school and a review of grades, which need to be high enough to indicate that part-time work will not interfere with the students' studies. In the case of Japan, students do not feel a

Table 2.8 Comparison of expenses for educational opportunities and finding part-time jobs in Japan and South Korea

Fee types	*Japan* *Approximate monetary amount*	*South Korea* *Approximate monetary amount*
Tuition fee for the first year (it is also possible to pay every six months)	US$6,300–7,300 (depends on the Japanese language school and its location in Japan)	Nearly US$4,000 for Korean language school Approximately US$6,000 for university
Apartment rent per month	US$200–670 (depends on the location and number of people sharing a room)	US$100–350 (depends on the location and number of people sharing a room)
Fees charged by education agencies/brokers in Uzbekistan		
Language training fee in Uzbekistan	US$ (price depends on the school and its location in Uzbekistan); even after a student obtains a visa, the student is required to continue studying the Japanese language until his/her departure to Japan or be responsible for paying fees for the period	SUM120,000–200,000 (price depends on the school and its location in Uzbekistan); it is also required to finish a 6-month course in some language programs
Processing fee for services	US$500–1,500 (depends on the agency and individual broker); if a visa is not obtained, $300 will be retained by the agency, and the rest will be returned to the student; such services include preparing documents, preparing for online interviews, assisting with translation in the online interview, finding a Japanese school in Japan, paying the visa fee	US$100–500 (depends on the agency and individual broker); such services includes preparing documents, checking for mistakes in the documents, bringing and submitting them to educational institutions in South Korea
Airfare	US$300–720 (one-way or two-way ticket from Uzbekistan to Japan); students' personal responsibility	US$300–500 (one-way ticket from Uzbekistan to South Korea); students' personal responsibility

(continued)

Table 2.8 (continued)

Fee types	*Japan* *Approximate monetary amount*	*South Korea* *Approximate monetary amount*
Assistance in finding part-time jobs; students personal responsibility	US$50–285 (Uzbek students in Japan are divided into three groups: Most students find part-time jobs with the assistance of their friends or relatives or by themselves; the second group of students finds part-time jobs by paying approximately $50–200; the third group of students finds part-time jobs by paying individual Uzbek brokers in Japan approximately $285 and 10% of daily salary); this group of students typically uses such services in the first six months after coming to Japan and are considered Japanese language school students	Uzbek students in South Korea are also divided into three groups: Most students find part-time jobs with the assistance of Korean brokers/agencies by paying 10% of their daily salary; the second group of students finds part-time jobs through their friends or relatives or by themselves; the third group of students finds part-time jobs by paying approximately a $70–90 one-time fee until the agency finds suitable work for them

similar kind of pressure because Japan's immigration services entrust the task of monitoring the performance of students to the schools themselves, while part-time work permits are issued without any review of students' performance or attendance. Balancing the situation in Japan, the majority of employers require documentation from migrant workers and are frequently reluctant to offer jobs with work hours exceeding the standard defined in the labor laws. However, students attempt to "maximize" the efficiency of their time in Japan by landing part-time employment in different places with shifts that do not overlap with each other. This structure damages the efficiency of their studies, as many fall asleep while attending school. However, our respondents' priorities were defined by their financial gains through part-time employment, as opposed to their academic gains.

In regard to finding jobs, migrants to Japan largely use an informal network consisting of their fellow citizens by means of the social networking platform offered by Telegram. To do so, all respondents went online as soon as they arrived in Japan, as Telegram offers them connectivity and professional networking and they need to find jobs. In the case of South Korea, our respondents indicated various means, such as signing direct contracts with employers before arriving in South Korea, using both official agencies to find jobs for a certain fee and unofficial "brokers" who also utilize Telegram to popularize their services for a fee and relying on networks of friends. Thus, compared to those in Japan, there seem to be more options for those in South Korea to find jobs with relative ease. Interestingly, many posts in South Korea advertise jobs that offer room and board, while in Japan, jobs advertised with lodging are nonexistent. In this sense, the structure of the labor market for those coming from Uzbekistan to Japan forces them to live in communes to share the costs of lodging and food and for psychological security. Among those who arrived much earlier, there are former student-migrants and labor migrants who set up enterprises whose target audience is the student and labor migrant communities to whom they provide serves, for example, connecting them with those who can assist them with preparing documents prior to their arrival in Japan and providing money transfer services from Japan. Such services function as an underground banking system in which transfers are conducted from Japan to various cities in Uzbekistan over the phone. The money is typically brought to the office in Japan by migrants. Information on the amount to be disbursed to a relative of the person is then transmitted over the phone to an agent of the remitting service provider in Uzbekistan, and money changes hands in a matter of minutes after the call from the money pooled in Uzbekistan for this purpose. No documentation is registered, and the transaction represents an information remittance practice. In the case of South Korea, however, similar remittances are just one option that migrants use. Other alternatives are sending money through numerous businessmen who travel to South Korea for wholesale purchases or remitting money through travelers who frequently visit South Korea due to regular flights offered by Asiana Airlines and Korean Air. Migrants often exploit the fact that South Korea is a source of major industrial products, electronics and clothing for the Uzbek market and send these products to their relatives in Uzbekistan, not only remitting financial resources but also facilitating the trade business of their acquaintances and relatives back home. By doing so, they not only generate income but also help their relatives launch their own businesses in Uzbekistan.

In contrast to South Korea, Japan is not a source of products to be sent home because the prices of such products in the Japanese market are high, while many products are made elsewhere outside of Japan. Additionally, there are no direct flights between Uzbekistan and Japan, with certain flights occasionally organized by Uzbekistan Airways during the tourist season. In this sense, Japan is financially rewarding for those who can enter the labor market, with financial remittances being the main channel for supporting one's family back home.

In terms of institutional framing of their stays and job searches, they found that job searches in South Korea were easier than those in Japan for several reasons. First, compared to Japan, they generally found a more tolerant attitude toward the foreign workforce in South Korea, where employers openly search for foreigners either through agencies or through random labor markets. In Japan, our respondents indicated that such job searches are mostly informal and conducted through a network of like-minded travelers from Uzbekistan to Japan, with no official agencies used in job placement. Additionally, the strict rules of the workplace in Japan do not allow continuous, multihour shifts in the same job, forcing the respondents to seek several workplaces and shifts to maximize their profits. Those staying in South Korea, however, indicated that if they wished to work long hours exceeding those allowed by law, they could do so in the same workplace. Similarly, many respondents in South Korea indicated that their employers would arrange their place of residence and even the food provided to them. In Japan, such arrangements are rare if not nonexistent, and in many cases, the respondents were solely responsible for arranging their place of residence. The only exception to this rule is the professional trainee scheme run by the Japanese government, in which the lives of trainees are highly regulated and controlled, including their place of residence. Finally, there is a significant difference in the regulations regarding student work permits. In Japan, students are allowed to work part-time 28 hours per week during their studies and 40 hours per week during their vacations. Students can apply for work permits from the immigration authorities, and the immigration agency issues such permits, entrusting control of their study-work balance to the educational institutions in which these students enroll. In South Korea, such permits are more strongly regulated; before issuing student work permits, immigration authorities verify not only the fact of enrollment but also the academic performance of students in terms of grades and attendance.

Additionally, there were a few individuals in the Japanese sample who experienced labor migration in Russia and South Korea. They indicated that they accumulated their initial funds to travel to South Korea and Japan through seasonal work in Russia. However, the degree of discrimination faced in Russia resulted in the choice of East Asian countries to pursue a job. Comparing South Korea and Japan, they indicated that they felt that South Korea is an easier environment in which to find a job. For them, the working environment in Japan is more demanding and precise, while in South Korea, depending on the kind of job, employers often do not control the work output as scrupulously. On the other hand, some indicated that while working in Japan is more demanding, it is also more disciplining and beneficial in the long term, and such discipline and benefits are then internalized by the respondents as part of their journey to acquire wisdom and experience, as explained above.

Conclusions

This chapter makes several conclusions based on our pilot survey in Japan and South Korea. First, labor migration and educational mobility are becoming the next "horizon" for the expansion of the relationship between East Asia and Central Asia. They are powered by several factors, including the efforts by Japan and South Korea to build "original" and people-oriented policy engagements with the region and demand on the side of CA states, such as Uzbekistan, to provide more labor opportunities to their young and growing populations.

Second, the initiatives to intensify such mobility have produced both positive and negative dynamics of movement of students and laborers from Uzbekistan to Japan and South Korea which might serve as worrisome trends and impediments to such policies in the future. In particular, due to the limits of available workplaces as well as the endemic corruption, among other factors, in the process of official labor migration from Uzbekistan to Japan and South Korea, there are signs that educational mobility is being increasingly abused by Uzbek students, who are turning it into a pipeline for unofficial labor migration masquerading as educational mobility.

Third, although masquerading of labor migration as educational mobility is a prominent feature of mobility in East Asia (particularly from China, Vietnam and the Philippines to Japan and South Korea), the patterns of Uzbek-Japanese and Uzbek-South Korean migration demonstrate that this trend of using educational mobility for labor migration shows signs of expanding beyond East Asian countries, being found in the CA case of Uzbekistan.

Fourth, while the number of people willing to engage in such educational/labor mobility is continuously growing in Uzbekistan, there is little evidence to suggest that those engaging in such mobility consider it to be a "side door" for permanent settlement and integration into Japanese and South Korean society, as they opt to return home in the short and medium term.

Fifth, contrary to the expectation that these individuals will seek permanent or long-term settlement, our data show that the majority of those engaging in such practices do not seek long-term settlement in East Asia and regard their stay as a sojourn due to religious and identity-related differences. They define their journey along the lines of *musofirs*, or religious wanderers, seeking opportunities, wisdom and experience to be used back in their own society to solidify their social identity and standing.

Appendix 2.1: Survey of Respondents in Japan

#	*Pseudonyms*	*Age*	*Region*	*Gender*	*Arrival year*	*Marital status*	*Education in Uzbekistan*
Japanese language school students							
1	Said	22	Bukhara	Male	2018	Single	Incomplete higher education
2	Akmal	32	Andijan	Male	2016	Married	Undergraduate degree
3	Ali	24	Samarkand	Male	2018	Single	Undergraduate degree
4	Bilol	20	Samarkand	Male	2017	Single	Secondary vocational education
5	Feruz	19	Samarkand	Male	2018	Single	Secondary vocational education
6	Yusuf	26	Samarkand	Male	2018	Single	Academic lyceum
7	Jasur	21	Samarkand	Male	2019	Single	Academic lyceum

(continued)

(continued)

#	*Pseudonyms*	*Age*	*Region*	*Gender*	*Arrival year*	*Marital status*	*Education in Uzbekistan*
8	Doston	27	Djizzak	Male	2018	Single	Academic lyceum
9	Akram	24	Djizzak	Male	2019	Single	Undergraduate degree
10	Giyos	26	Andijan	Male	2018	Single	Secondary vocational education
11	Muhammad	20	Namangan	Male	2018	Single	Secondary vocational education
12	Ikrom	25	Andijan	Male	2018	Single	Undergraduate degree
13	Dilshod	22	Djizzak	Male	2018	Single	Secondary vocational education
14	Rustam	25	Samarkand	Male	2019	Married	Academic lyceum
15	Sardor	25	Namangan	Male	2018	Married	Academic lyceum
16	Botir	22	Namangan	Male	2018	Single	Academic lyceum
17	Javlon	23	Namangan	Male	2018	Single	Secondary vocational education
18	Sardor	20	Namangan	Male	2018	Single	Secondary vocational education
19	Inom	19	Andijan	Male	2018	Single	Secondary vocational education
20	Forhod	20	Andijan	Male	2019	Single	Secondary vocational education
21	Izzat	19	Andijan	Male	2019	Single	Secondary vocational education
22	Shuhrat	18	Samarkand	Male	2019	Single	Secondary vocational education
23	Mirjalil	20	Samarkand	Male	2018	Single	Academic lyceum
24	Abdulhamid	19	Andijan	Male	2018	Single	Academic lyceum

(continued)

(continued)

#	*Pseudonyms*	*Age*	*Region*	*Gender*	*Arrival year*	*Marital status*	*Education in Uzbekistan*
25	Sirojiddin	22	Andijan	Male	2019	Single	Secondary vocational education
26	Sardor	34	Namangan	Male	2018	Single	Undergraduate degree
27	Umid	44	Samarkand	Male	2016	Married	Undergraduate degree
28	Oybek	24	Bukhara	Male	2017	Single	Undergraduate degree
29	Said	26	Andijan	Male	2018	Single	Undergraduate degree
30	Zohid	21	Namangan	Male	2018	Single	Secondary vocational education
31	Jamshid	27	Andijan	Male	2018	Single	Undergraduate degree
32	Gilomqodir	26	Samarkand	Male	2019	Single	Secondary vocational education
33	Nadir	18	Samarkand	Male	2019	Single	Academic lyceum
34	Farruh	26	Andijan	Male	2018	Single	Undergraduate degree
Vocational school students							
35	Mirkomil	22	Samarkand	Male	2017	Single	Secondary vocational education
36	Amir	31	Samarkand	Male	2015	Single	Secondary vocational education
37	Shavkat	22	Samarkand	Male	2016	Single	Academic lyceum
38	Islom	28	Syrdarya	Male	2016	Single	Secondary vocational education
39	Botir	23	Samarkand	Male	2016	Single	Undergraduate degree
40	Mansur	22	Tashkent	Male	2016	Single	Academic lyceum
41	Aziz	25	Samarkand	Male	2017	Single	Secondary vocational education

(continued)

(continued)

#	*Pseudonyms*	*Age*	*Region*	*Gender*	*Arrival year*	*Marital status*	*Education in Uzbekistan*
42	Shuhrat	24	Andijan	Male	2016	Single	Secondary vocational education
43	Doston	22	Samarkand	Male	2017	Single	Secondary vocational education
44	Zohid	22	Andijan	Male	2018	Single	Secondary vocational education
46	Umar	26	Samarkand	Male	2017	Married	Academic lyceum
47	Feruz	25	Samarkand	Male	2016	Single	Secondary vocational education
University preparatory course students							
48	Anvar	38		Male	2016	Married	Master's degree
49	Giyos	32	Andijan	Male	2016	Married	Undergraduate degree
University students							
50	Maftuna	21	Tashkent	Female	2016	Single	Academic lyceum
51	Bahrom	26	Andijan	Male	2017	Single	Academic lyceum
52	Jumavoy	23	Fergana	Male	2017	Single	Secondary vocational education
53	I nom	23	Samarkand	Male	2017	Single	Secondary vocational education
54	Kamol	30	Tashkent	Male	2017	Single	Undergraduate degree
Workers							
55	Yusuf	25	Samarkand	Male	2018	Single	Undergraduate degree
56	Zarifa	37	Samarkand	Female	2006	Married	Undergraduate degree
57	Odilbek	36	Samarkand	Male	2016	Married	Undergraduate degree
58	Suhrob	35	Samarkand	Male	2004	Married	Secondary vocational education
59	Olim	29	Kashkadarya	Male	2016	Married	Master's degree

(continued)

(continued)

#	*Pseudonyms*	*Age*	*Region*	*Gender*	*Arrival year*	*Marital status*	*Education in Uzbekistan*
60	Mansur	32	Khorezm	Male	2008	Married	Undergraduate degree
61	Abdusamad	31	Samarkand	Male	2015	Single	Secondary vocational education
62	Nurullo	24	Andijan	Male	2016	Single	Academic lyceum
63	Bektemir	28	Samarkand	Male	2015	Single	Undergraduate degree
64	Rustam	22	Samarkand	Male	2015	Single	Secondary vocational education
Dependents							
65	Zoir	35	Samarkand	Male	2006	Married	Undergraduate degree
Spouse of Japanese national							
66	Jalil	34	Samarkand	Male	2007	Married	Undergraduate degree

Appendix 2.2 Sample Group of Respondents in South Korea

#	*Pseudonyms*	*Age*	*Region*	*Gender*	*Arrival year*	*Marital status*	*Education in Uzbekistan*
1	Miraziz	23	Andijan	Male	2018	Single	Secondary vocational education
2	Abdulhamid	25	Fergana	Male	2017	Single	Secondary vocational education
3	Boboqul	27	Namangan	Male	2018	Single	Undergraduate degree
4	Tolibbek	30	Tashkent	Male	2015	Single	Undergraduate degree
5	Turdimurodbek	28	Namangan	Male	2017	Married	Undergraduate degree
6	Ozodbek	23	Andijan	Male	2017	Single	Secondary vocational education

(continued)

(continued)

#	*Pseudonyms*	*Age*	*Region*	*Gender*	*Arrival year*	*Marital status*	*Education in Uzbekistan*
7	Abdukamol	26	Fergana	Male	2015	Single	Academic lyceum
8	Muzaffar	24	Kashkadarya	Male	2017	Single	Secondary vocational education
9	Giyos	25	Namangan	Male	2017	Single	Secondary vocational education
10	Ergashbek	21	Andijan	Male	2018	Single	Academic lyceum
11	Mavlonbek	32	Samarqand	Male	2010	Married	Undergraduate degree
12	Farhod	26	Samarqand	Male	2010	Married	Secondary vocational education
13	Hasan	29	Surkhandarya	Male	2018	Single	Academic lyceum
14	Sardor	18	Namangan	Male	2019	Single	Secondary vocational education
15	Hurshidbek	27	Namangan	Male	2013	Single	Secondary vocational education
16	Sirojiddin	24	Andijan	Male	2018	Single	Undergraduate degree
17	Shuhratbek	27	Samarqand	Male	2018	Single	Undergraduate degree
18	Abdukamol	27	Namangan	Male	2014	Single	Secondary vocational education
19	Abduganisher	43	Sirdarya	Male	2008	Married	Secondary vocational education
20	Asror	22	Tashkent	Male	2017	Single	Secondary vocational education
21	Shohruhbek	24	Namangan	Male	2020	Single	Undergraduate degree
22	Yusufbek	44	Samarqand	Male	2009	Married	Undergraduate degree

References

Abashin, Sergei. 2013. "Central Asian Migration." *Russian Politics & Law* 51, no. 3: 6–20.

Abashin, Sergey. 2015. "Vozrashcheni domoi: Semeinye i migratsionnye stsenarii v Uzbekistane" (Return Home: Family and Migration Scenarios in Uzbekistan). *Ab Imperio* 3.

Abashin, Sergey. 2016. "Migration Policies in Russia: Laws and Debates." In *Migrant Workers in Russia: Global Challenges of the Shadow Economy in Societal Transformation*, edited by Anna-Liisa Heusala and Kaarina Aitamurto, 16–34. London: Routledge.

Abe, Shinzo. 2015. "The Future of Asia: Be Innovative." Speech at the 21st International Conference on the Future of Asia, 21 May. http://japan.kantei.go.jp/97_abe/statement/201505/0521foaspeech.html.

Aso, Taro. 2006. "Speech by Mr. Taro Aso, Minister for Foreign Affairs on the Occasion of the Japan Institute of International Affairs Seminar 'Arc of Freedom and Prosperity: Japan's Expanding Diplomatic Horizons'." Ministry of Foreign Affairs of Japan. https://www.mofa.go.jp/announce/fm/aso/speech0611.html.

Bartolomeo, A. D., S. Makaryan and A. Weinar. 2014. *Regional Migration Report: Russia and Central Asia*. Florence, Italy: European University Institute.

Betti, Gianni and Lars Lundgren. 2012. "The Impact of Remittances and Equivalence Scales on Poverty in Tajikistan." *Central Asian Survey* 31, no. 4: 395–408.

Bisson, Lyubov. 2016. "Russia's Immigration Policy: Challenges and Tools." Russia/NIS Center. https://www.ifri.org/sites/default/files/atoms/files/ifri_rnv_91_lioubov_bisson_eng_january_2016_protege.pdf.

Carling, Jørgen and Marta Bivand Erdal. 2014. "Return Migration and Transnationalism: How Are the Two Connected?" *International Migration* 52, no. 6: 2–12.

Christensen, Miyase. 2012. "Online Mediations in Transnational Spaces: Cosmopolitan (Re)Formations of Belonging and Identity in the Turkish Diaspora." *Ethnic and Racial Studies* 35, no. 5: 888–905.

Dadabaev, Timur. 2013. "Japan's Search for Its Central Asian Policy: Between Idealism and Pragmatism." *Asian Survey* 53, no. 3: 506–532.

Dadabaev, Timur. 2016. "Japan's ODA Assistance Scheme and Central Asian Engagement: Determinants, Trends, Expectations." *Journal of Eurasian Studies* 7, no. 1: 24–38.

Dadabaev, Timur. 2019. *Transcontinental Silk Road Strategies: Comparing China, Japan and South Korea in Uzbekistan*. London and New York: Routledge.

Dadabaev, Timur and Mukaddam Akhmedova. 2022. "A Home Away from Home: Migration Identity and "Sojourning" in the Life of Uzbekistanis in Japan." *Europe-Asia Studies*: 1–28. (Routledge, Taylor and Francis). https://doi.org/10.1080/09668136.2021.2010660.

Gel'man, Vladimir. 2004. "The Unrule of Law in the Making: The Politics of Informal Institution Building in Russia." *Europe-Asia Studies* 56, no. 7: 1021–1040.

Hashimoto, Ryutaro. 1997. "Address to the Japan Association of Corporate Executives." Tokyo, July 24. https://japan.kantei.go.jp/0731douyukai.html.

Hiwatari, Masato. 2016. "Social Networks and Migration Decisions: The Influence of Peer Effects in Rural Households in Central Asia." *Journal of Comparative Economics* 44, no. 4.

Kadirova, Zulaykho. 2015. "Integration of Uzbekistan into International Labor Market." *Himalayan and Central Asian Studies* 19, nos. 3–4: 205–222.

Kakhkharov, Jakhongir, Muzaffarjon Ahunov, Ziyodullo Parpiev and Inna Wolfson. 2020. "South-South Migration: Remittances of Labour Migrants and Household Expenditures in Uzbekistan." *International Migration*, November 5. https://doi.org/10.1111/imig.12792.

Kim, Jaeeun. 2014. "The Colonial State, Migration, and Diasporic Nationhood in Korea." *Comparative Studies in Society and History* 56, no. 1: 34–66.

Korobkov, Andrei V. 2007. "Migration Trends in Central Eurasia: Politics versus Economics." *Communist and Post-Communist Studies* 40, no. 2: 169–189.

Kuchins, A. C., J. Mankoff, A. Kourmanova and O. Backes. 2015. *Central Asia in a Reconnecting Eurasia: Uzbekistan's Evolving Foreign Economic and Security Interests* Report of the CSIS Russia and Eurasia Program. Washington, DC: Center for Strategic & International Studies.

Laruelle, Marlène. 2013. *Migration and Social Upheaval as the Face of Globalization in Central Asia*. Leiden: Brill.

Levitt, Peggy. 2001a. "Transnational Migration: Taking Stock and Future Directions." *Global Networks* 1, no. 3: 195–216.

Levitt, Peggy. 2001b. *The Transnational Villagers*. Los Angeles: University of California Press.

Liu-Farrer, Gracia and An Huy Tran. 2019. "Bridging the Institutional Gaps: International Education as a Migration Industry." *International Migration* 57, no. 3: 235–249.

Main, Kelly and Gerardo Francisco Sandoval. 2015. "Placemaking in a Translocal Receiving Community: The Relevance of Place to Identity and Agency." *Urban Studies* 52, no. 1: 71–86.

Ministry of Employment and Labor of Uzbekistan. 2020. "Labor Which Has Value." https://mehnat.uz/en/article/labor-migration.

Ministry of Foreign Affairs of Japan. 2002. "Shirukurodo Enerugimishon [Silk Road Energy Mission]." https://www.mofa.go.jp/mofaj/annai/honsho/fuku/sugiura/af_asia02/silkroad.html.

Ministry of Health, Labor and Welfare. 2019. https://www.mhlw.go.jp/content/11655000/000472892.pdf.

MOFA Japan. 2019. "Signing of Memorandum of Cooperation Between Japan and the Republic of Uzbekistan on a Basic Framework for Information Partnership for Proper Operation of the System Pertaining to Foreign Human Resources with the Status of Residence of 'Specified Skilled Worker'." Last modified December 17. https://www.mofa.go.jp/press/release/press4e_002735.html.

Murashkin, Nikolay. 2015. "Japanese Involvement in Central Asia: An Early Inter-Asian Post Neoliberal Case?" *Asian Journal of Social Science* 43, no. 1–2: 50–79.

OECD International Migration Outlook. 2019 (2018). 'Japan', Available at: https://www.oecdilibrary.org/sites/e025d47d-en/index.html?itemId=/content/component/e025d47d-en.

Petesch, P. L. and G. Demarchi. 2015. *Gender, Mobility and Middle Class in Europe and Central Asia: Insights from Qualitative Research.* Washington, DC: World Bank Group.

Portes, Alejandro, Luis E. Guarnizo and Patricia Landolt. 1999. "Introduction: Pitfalls and Promise of an Emergent Research Field." *Ethnic and Racial Studies* 22: 217–237.

Radjabov, Bakhrom. 2017. "Social Remittances Created by Uzbek Students Studying in Kassel, Germany and Tsukuba, Japan." *Eurasia Cultura* 3.

Reeves, Madeleine. 2012. "Black Work, Green Money: Remittances, Ritual, and Domestic Economies in Southern Kyrgyzstan." *Slavic Review* 71, no. 1: 108–134.

Ruget, Vanessa and Burul Usmanalieva. 2011. "Social and Political Transnationalism Among Central Asian Migrants and Return Migrants." *Problems of Post-Communism* 58, no. 6: 48–60.

Schröder, Philipp and Manja Stephan-Emmrich. 2016. "The Institutionalization of Mobility: Well-being and Social Hierarchies in Central Asian Translocal Livelihoods." *Mobilities* 11, no. 3: 420–443.

Seitz, W. 2019. "International Migration and Household Well-Being: Evidence from Uzbekistan. Poverty and Equity Global Practice." http://documents.worldbank.org/curated/en/615721561125387061/International-Migration-and-Household-Well-Being-Evidence-from-Uzbekistan. Accessed September 1, 2020.

Turaeva, R. 2013. "Post-Soviet Uncertainties: Micro-orders of Central Asian Migrants in Russia." *Inner ASIA* 15, no. 2: 273–292.

Turaeva, R. 2014 "Mobile Entrepreneurs in Post-Soviet Central Asia." *Communist and Post-Communist Studies* 47, no. 1: 105–114.

Urinboyev, Rustam. 2016. "Migration and Transnational Informality in Post-Soviet Societies: Ethnographic Study of 'Po Rukam' Experiences of Uzbek Migrant Workers in Moscow." In *Migrant Workers in Russia: Global Challenges of the Shadow Economy in Societal Transformation*, edited by Anna-Liisa Heusala and Kaarina Aitamurto. London: Routledge.

Urinboyev, Rustam. 2017. "Establishing 'Uzbek Mahalla' via Smartphones and Social Media: Everyday Transnational Lives of Uzbek Labour Migrants in Russia." In *Constructing the Uzbek State: Narratives of Post-Soviet Years*, edited by Marlène Laruelle, 119–148. Boulder: Lexington Books.

Uyama, Tomohiko. 2003. "Japanese Policy in Relation to Kazakhstan: Is There a Strategy?" In *Thinking Strategically: The Major Powers, Kazakhstan, and the Central Asian Nexus*, edited by Robert Legvold, 165–186. Cambridge: MIT Press.

Virkkunen, Joni. 2017. "Economic Aspects of Migration from Central Asia in Russia." *Journal of Economics* 25, no. 1: 102–111.

CHAPTER 3

Uzbek Newcomers in the Japanese Educational and Labour Market

Timur Dadabaev, Shigeto Sonoda, and Jasur Soipov

Introduction

Japan has become one of the most attractive destinations for language education, and the number of Uzbek nationals enrolling in Japanese-language schools has increased rapidly in recent years. While the cumulative numbers for such enrolments in Uzbekistan are difficult to obtain, the number of Uzbek students enrolling in Japanese-language schools in Japan alone increased from only 22 students in 2010 to 1,427 in 2018 (Table 3.1). While their overall numbers relative to the dominant minority groups in Japan are still low, the number of Uzbek citizens residing in Japan grew by 200 times, i.e., from as few as 20 in 1994 to 3,951 in 2018 (Table 3.2), making them one of the fastest-growing ethnic groups (Serizawa 2018: 47).

T. Dadabaev (✉) · J. Soipov
University of Tsukuba, Tsukuba, Japan
e-mail: dadabaev.timur.gm@u.tsukuba.ac.jp

S. Sonoda
University of Tokyo, Tokyo, Japan

T. Dadabaev (ed.), *The Grass is Always Greener?*, Politics and History in Central Asia,
https://doi.org/10.1007/978-981-16-2570-1_3

Table 3.1 Number of Uzbek students by institution type in Japan

	2004	*2005*	*2006*	*2007*	*2008*	*2009*	*2010*	*2011*	*2012*	*2013*	*2014*	*2015*	*2016*	*2017*	*2018*
Graduate school	100	106	107	109	125	130	126	117	121	124	117	135	134	125	140
University (undergraduate)	25	32	32	46	50	49	57	60	59	70	121	150	172	200	292
Junior college	0	1	0	0	0	0	0	0	0	0	0	0	2	2	8
College of technology	0	0	0	0	0	0	0	0	0	0	0	0	0	0	0
Professional training college	0	0	0	11	30	44	25	13	22	22	33	50	74	111	258
University preparatoty course	2	0	0	1	0	0	0	1	1	11	3	0	1	3	7
Japanese language Institutes	–	–	–	–	–	–	22	35	28	54	84	136	258	606	1427
Total	127	139	139	167	205	223	230	226	231	281	358	471	641	1047	2132

Table 3.2 Increasing number of Uzbek immigrants in Japan

Year	Total	Dip	Off	Pro	Art	Jou	HSP	I/BM	Res	Ins	Eng	SH/IS	Ic/T	Ent	S/L	TIT	CA	TV	Stu	Tra	Dep	PR	DA	S/ChJN	S/ChPR	LTR	WAS	TR	Oth
1994	20			2					1			1							6		9			1					
1995	22			2								1					1		7	3	7			1					
1996	29			2					1			1					1	1	10	2	10			1					
1997	47			3					1		1	1					3		27	2	7			2					
1998	80			1					2					1			3	1	55	3	11			2			1		
1999	103			2					2					1			2	4	63	3	23			3					
2000	184			5					4			1	1	15			3	33	81	3	27			8		2			1
2001	201			4					2		1	4	1	1			3	30	101	7	32			10		2	1		2
2002	262			7					2		1	8	1	12	3		2	24	122	11	45	1	4	14		3			2
2003	341			6	1				1		3	20	1	19	5		3	34	137	12	65	3	6	18		3	2		2
2004	376			6				2			3	29	2	23	1		3	41	157	9	55	5	3	27		4	1		5
2005	495			5		1		2	2	2	5	42	2	51	1		1	48	172	30	69	6	3	40	2	6			5
2006	527			5	1	1		2		1	6	52	3	12	1		5	33	219	18	92	11	5	43	2	9	9	9	9
2007	620			6		1		3			8	72	2	6	1		2	28	275	9	112	14	7	52	2	12	4		4
2008	655			8		1		2		2	8	87	2	6	1		10	19	264	8	130	15	8	63	2	12	3		4
2009	727			8		1		3		2	7	108	2	6	1		11	21	251	6	180	22	9	64	2	15	6		2
2010	832			8		1		3		4	13	123	2	4	1		8	11	286	4	232	35	6	63	3	15	8		2
2011	840			9	1	1		2	1	4	17	151	2	3	2		5	7	256	4	228	47	15	60	5	18	1		1
2012	1060	33	16	9		1		3	1	2	17	167	1	3	1		5	67	284	6	276	55	13	70	8	22			
2013	1197	26	14	11	1	1		4	1	2	19	176	3	2	1		9	50	352	1	340	74	14	63	10	23			
2014	1415	23	14	11	1	1		5		2	19	181	4	2	1		4	43	477	2	386	86	38	69	15	31			
2015	1599	24	12	11	2	1	2	8	1	2	212		4	2	1		7	59	583	2	404	115	27	68	14	38			
2016	1986	25	9	10		1	3	9	1	2	233		3		2		9	76	868	2	427	164	24	68	12	38			
2017	3068	26	14	10			10	9	1	2	280		3	1	1	17	4	106	1759	3	468	200	33	73	12	36			
2018	3951	26	16	9			12	13	1	2	395		4	2	3	9	4	136	2366	3	547	226	49	72	15	41			

Legend:

Dip: Diplomat	S/L: Skilled Labor	HSP: Highly Skilled Professional	Stu: Student	DA: Designated Activities
Off: Official	Ent: Entertainer	Ic/T: Intra-company Transferee	Tra: Trainee	S/ChPR: Spouse or Child of Permanent Resident
Pro: Professor	Ins: Instructor	I/BM: Investor/Business Manager	Dep: Dependent	LTR: Spouse or Child of Permanent Resident
Art: Artist	Eng: Engineer	TIT: Technical Intern Training	PR: Permanent Resident	WASR: Without Acquiring Status of Residence
Jou: Journalist	CA: Cultural Activities	CA: Cultural Activities	TR: Temporary Refuge	SH/IS: Specialist in Humanities/International Services
Res: Researcher	TV: Temporary Visitor	TV: Temporary Visitor	Oth: Others	S/ChJN: Spouse or Child of Japanese National

The increasing popularity of Japan-based language schools among Uzbek students is related to a variety of factors. It can be attributed partly to the Japanese government's attempts to increase the number of foreign students in Japan to 300,000 by 2020, which was expected to increase the international soft-power potential of the country (Sano 2018; Serizawa 2018: 53). This phenomenon may also be a case of home countries encouraging young people to seek education abroad and return with the knowledge needed to occupy leading positions in industry and bureaucracy. An example is the Uzbek-government-run "Umid" programme, which competitively pre-selected and dispatched 466 young Uzbek specialists to internationally renowned universities from 1996 to 2003 (El-Yurt UMIDI Foundation 1996–2003). Such practices are not new for the Central Asia (CA) region. A similar successful scheme of sending students first to language schools and later to educational institutions is the "Bolazhak" programme, financed by the Kazakh government. According to observations of these programmes, the lack of opportunities at home combined with the authoritarian government's all-encompassing corruption and limited opportunities serve as "push factors" for gifted youths. Opportunities to be introduced to new educational programmes that are free of corruption and the ideological pressures of the Soviet and post-Soviet Karimov-era governments and prospects of better employment venues serve as "push factors" for such youths.

An alternative stream of studies treats the high rates of enrolment in Japanese-language schools by students from developing countries as the first stage of migration, claiming that these students will later join the official labour market by obtaining work visas and residence permits, using their studies as "side doors" to the Japanese labour market (Kajita 1995; Liu-Farrer and Tran 2019; Mochizuki 2019: 89), though some of these workers may later move to more lucrative jobs in the USA, Europe, Korea and China. Conversely, some studies have used the cases of Bangladeshi, Vietnamese and Chinese students in Japan to suggest that these students use their enrolment in language schools as a "side door" or even "back door" to Japan and eventually settle down in Japan by becoming illegal (*fuhou*) or irregular (*hiseiki*) residents (*taizaishya*) (Mochizuki 2019: 143–50). They join the group of "unfavourable foreign workers" (*konomashikunai gaikokujin roudoushya*), in counterposition to highly skilled "desired" foreign workers (Suzuki 2009).

Conceptually, this chapter stays close to the stream of studies that unpack the way educational mobility has been used to access labour markets in East Asia (Liu-Farrer 2009, 2011; Liu-Farrer and Tran 2019). However, this chapter aims to contribute to these studies by reflecting on the latest examples of this tendency by zooming in on a phenomenon of "newcomers", such as Uzbeks in Japan. In doing so, this chapter focuses on the experiences of post-Soviet-generation Uzbek students enrolling in Japanese-language schools in Japan in an attempt to place them into the discussions of foreign student mobility and migration.

What are the motivations, entry, adaptation and exit strategies of Uzbek students enrolling in Japanese-language schools in Japan? What are the problems associated with this type of educational mobility?

Research Methods and Data Collection

Methodologically, this chapter uses two datasets that we collected both in Uzbekistan and Japan. First, it uses data collected from roughly 400 university students in Uzbekistan in 2018 to demonstrate the attitude of Uzbek students towards Japan and other prospective study destinations for professional development (Table 3.3). The universities chosen for the survey are the primary institutions of education for those aspiring to international careers and similar goals.

In the second data collection, we have provided the snapshot of the survey with of 66 students (comprising 1.7% of all residents of Japan with Uzbek citizenship) enrolled in Japanese-language schools in the Kanto area of Japan (see Appendix). In treating responses of the survey, we have aimed to detail on the tendencies and practices of using the Japanese language by these students. We have presented their responses grouped around various questions. Due to space limitations, this inquiry does not include extracts of the student's voices but this and similar endeavour has been attempted elsewhere (Dadabaev and Akhmedova 2021, accepted, forthcoming). The respondents to the current survey indicated the year

Table 3.3 Details of the Uzbek university student survey 2018

Country/area	*University*	*Date of research*	*Sample size*
Uzbekistan	Uzbekistan State University of World Languages	2018.11.1–12.1	207
	University of World Economy and Diplomacy		201

of their arrival to Japan to be between 2007 and 2019, with the majority residing in Japan from 2015 to 2019 (see Appendix). The majority of the respondents maintain legal residence status in Japan; only 1 respondent indicated that they "overstayed".

By elaborating on the findings of these two datasets, this chapter demonstrates that the abuse of educational mobility for labour migration is expanding beyond East Asian countries and displays signs of launching in the Central Asian case of Uzbekistan. Japan has increasingly become another frontier for Uzbek youngsters who use educational opportunities to seek temporary employment. The main objective of this study is to present the cases of the Uzbek "newcomers" to the Japanese education and labour market from post-socialist countries that have not previously been studied.

Social Networks and "Sojourning" in the Life of Uzbek Students

There are several theoretical frameworks that could be adopted to explain the pattern of student temporary migration and the employment of Uzbeks in Japan. In regard to the logistics of migration from developing to developed countries, many studies have focused on the roles played by smugglers and their business of facilitating border transfers, as well as the labour market needs for such labour.

Smugglers are not necessarily tied to the local, regional or other contexts of migrants but operate as benefit-seeking "actors" in their own interests in the process of such migration practices. For instance, there are numerous studies of Iranian (Tsukuba Daigaku Shyakaigaku Kenkyushitsu 1994), Bangladeshi (Inaba and Higuchi 2003), and Brazilian (Higuchi and Tanno 2003) labour migrants; so-called technical interns, or *ginnou jisshyusei*, from China, Vietnam, Indonesia and Mongolia (Gaikokujin Kenshyusei Mondai Nettowâku 2006, 2009; Shukan Toyokeizai Henshubu 2014); and part-time students working in convenience stores (Serizawa 2018). These studies emphasize the role of "agents", whether they are "brokers", "facilitators" or hosting agents (Liu-Farrer 2008, 2009), such as Japanese farmers, that function under the conditions of the market economy and provide the "services" needed by those in search of jobs (Ambrosini 2016; Mahmud 2017). Similar studies have focused on networks of migrants and the abuses they experience in Eastern Europe (Elrick and Lewandowska 2008).

Different groups of studies have focused on the role of the so-called social capital of migrants and their connected networks (Massey and Espinosa 1997; Mahmud 2017). These studies emphasize the fact that temporary residents and migrants attempt to utilize their knowledge and experience, contributing both to their communities and improving their own well-being. In a somewhat similar manner, studies have analysed temporary workers, such as Nepalis (Kharel 2016) and Vietnamese (Era 2018) in Japan, and have detailed how hometown networks facilitate such migration flows. Such networks can serve their hometown customers or be middle-men minority groups (Bonacich 1973). In addition, such networks provide security and some relief from foreign cultural environments (Chavajay and Skowronek 2008).

Finally, an additional group of studies focuses on the notion of sojourners as a type of temporary migration (Siu 1952; Glick 1980; Cox 1988). Such residents do consider their stay temporary and a way to establish the foundations of future careers in their home countries. Students, who are the subject of this inquiry, often fall into this category (Mizukami 2006).

This study treats Uzbek language students in Japan as temporary workers working under the guise of being language studies students, similar to those coming from East Asia (Liu-Farrer and Tran 2019). In this sense, the theoretical frames that can be used to explain the pattern of students' entry into Japanese society and their study and work in Japan often overlap. This study emphasizes the following two aspects as the most important elements for student migrants in Japan: their home-country-related regional identity and the notion of being a "sojourner".

Local and regional identity formation has long been the focus of studies as aspects of political mobilization in regard to the politics of CA, and Uzbekistan in particular (Carlisle 1986; Tunçer-Kılavuz 2009). This study, however, demonstrates that such aspects of "belonging" are especially important in establishing networks through which entry into Japan is made possible (in line with Dadabaev and Akhmedova 2022). These networks produce "handlers" and "facilitators" who facilitate the exit strategy from the home country and the return to the home country. The core group of migrants in this study comes from Samarkand, which is one of the areas of Uzbekistan with the strongest migration networks, not only to Japan but also to Russia, South Korea and the USA. The group of migrants also includes Tashkent and Fergana Valley residents.

Their region of origin also defines the types of activities in which these people are involved in Japan, with those coming from Samarkand tending to accept lower-skilled positions and those coming from the capital city of Tashkent and the Fergana Valley tending to focus on services and higher-skilled sectors.

To come to terms with their current position in Japan, this study emphasizes the importance of "sojourning" for student migrants, who are the focus of this study (Sussman 2002). "Sojourning", defined as a temporary state of residence, resonates well with the view of student migrants being "wanderers" in search of both wisdom and economic benefits for social and religious reasons. Very few, if any, of the respondents desired to settle permanently in Japan. Rather, they saw their sojourn as an opportunity to build a foundation for future business enterprises connected to their lives back in Uzbekistan.[1]

The lack of desire to settle permanently in Japan is related to various factors, such as the drastic cultural differences from the host society, strong Islamic religious attachments and conservative and strong local family networks (Turaeva 2013, 2014, 2016), which encourage the respondents to return as soon as they can afford to do so. It follows the logic that without being a *musofir* (religious wonderer), there is no (proper understanding of) faith (*imon*) for these individuals (stated by multiple respondents in the interviews). Another reason, at least partially, relates to the ambiguous and unsettled image of the role of Japan in their future, which might be contributing to the conceptualization of their image of Japan as a place of temporary residence.

"Internationalization" of Education and Japanese-Language Schools

As has been thoroughly discussed in the previous literature, Japanese society is undergoing the ageing of its population and, thus, has difficulty attracting the younger generation to certain sectors of the economy, such as services, agriculture and industrial production (Suzuki 2009: 181–84; Gotou 2019). Thus, the Japanese Ministry of Education, Culture, Sports, Science and Technology (MEXT), along with internationalizing

[1] For the notion of home, see Abashin (2015), Urinboyev (2018)

the educational process, considers those enrolled in conventional institutions of higher learning to be a potentially significant workforce for the understaffed Japanese labour market. In 2020, there were 1.6 million foreign workers in Japan. The number of international students (with "permission to engage in an activity other than that permitted under the resident status (*shikakugai katsudo kyoka*)") with a part-time job increased dramatically from 70,833 in 2009 to 318,278 in 2020 (Ministry of Health 2009, 2020), representing 1 in 5 of all foreign workers. Youths in developing countries, such as Uzbekistan, are eager to take advantage of such opportunities (also see JETRO 2019 for alternative channels).

The student mobility data for Uzbekistan show that the greatest number of Uzbek nationals travel to Russia and other post-Soviet regions and states (Table 3.4). Knowledge of Russian and proximity to home as well as relatively low tuition fees put these countries in advantageous positions as study destinations for Uzbeks. In addition, Russia absorbs a great number of those from the Russian ethnic group who repatriate to Russia from Uzbekistan because of increasingly ethno-centric educational development.

This, to some extent, corresponds to the historical connections of the large Russian-speaking diaspora and the trend of migration from Uzbekistan to Russia, given the educational and employment opportunities it

Table 3.4 Major educational destinations for Uzbek students

Destination country	*2012*	*2017*	*% of total*	*2012–2017 trend (%)*
1 Russia	10,096	20,862	59.6	+107
2 Kazakhstan	2,898	3,818	10.9	+32
3 Ukraine	NA	2, 022	5.8	
4 South Korea	376	1,716	4.9	
5 Latvia	96	1,025	2.9	+968
6 Turkey	210	736	2.1	+250
7 Malaysia	413	666	1.9	+61
8 Germany	789	651	1.9	−17
9 Kyrgyzstan	1,544	568	1.6	−63
10 United States	471	495	1.4	+5
16 France	162	142	0.4	−12
Total	19,158	34,990	100	+83

Source Campus France, Data Sheet of Uzbek Student Mobility for 2012–2017 https://ressources.campusfrance.org/publications/mobilite_pays/en/ouzbekistan_en.pdf

offers to those with a certain level of Russian-language skill. Russia does not apply strict visa regulations to Uzbekistan and allows no-visa visits and stays for a certain period, making it an attractive destination for various types of visits (Urinboyev 2018).

However, a few "far abroad" countries, such as South Korea, Latvia, Turkey, Malaysia, Germany, the USA and Japan, are considered to be among the primary destinations for Uzbek students.

Figure 3.1 demonstrates that the most sought-after group of states in terms of educational opportunities are the USA, the UK and other English-speaking countries.

These English-speaking countries are followed by the group that includes Japan, South Korea, Germany and France, all of which require a certain level of local language proficiency other than English. In terms of ambitions for new foreign-language acquisition, many Uzbek students consider Chinese, Korean, and Japanese to be on a par with French and German, in terms of importance, which can be attributed to the economic potential of these states and future opportunities expected in relation to these languages (Fig. 3.2).

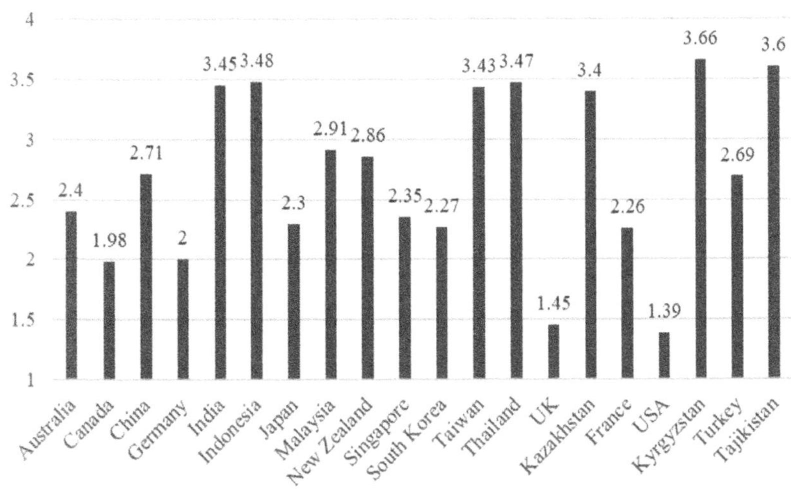

Fig. 3.1 Study destination preferences (*Note* [1] Very interested, [2] Somewhat interested, [3] Not really interested, [4] Not interested at all. *Source* Uzbek university student survey 2018)

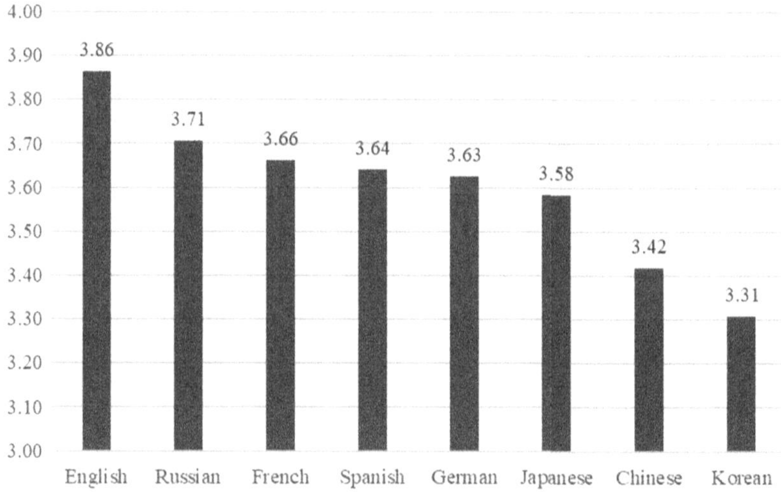

Fig. 3.2 Expectations of language acquisition (Question: "Imagine that you have a child who must pass the university entrance examination twenty years later. When he/she asks you which languages he/she should study for his/her future, do you think you will recommend the following languages to him/her? Please choose the most appropriate answer. Just bear in mind that the money and hours your child can spend in acquiring foreign languages are limited. In case the language(s) below is/are your mother tongue, please select '5 Mother Tongue'". *Note* [1] No, [2] Probably No, [3] Probably Yes, [4] Yes. *Source* Uzbek university student survey 2018)

The study destination and the desire to acquire certain language skills are not matters of improving the overall educational level of Uzbek youth. Rather, they are related to the prospects of employment either in the country of educational choice or associated with that country. Aside from domestic companies, Uzbek youth prefer to find employment opportunities in American companies, followed by European, Russian, Korean and Japanese companies (Fig. 3.3).

In terms of attitudes towards Japan, its image in the eyes of the youth in Uzbekistan is ambiguous and placed "in-between" the most desired and undesired destinations and it ranked as the second choice in terms of their preferred study abroad locations. This ambiguity towards Japan is caused by several factors. First, the corporate presence of Japanese companies in Uzbekistan is not as significant as that of other "first-choice"

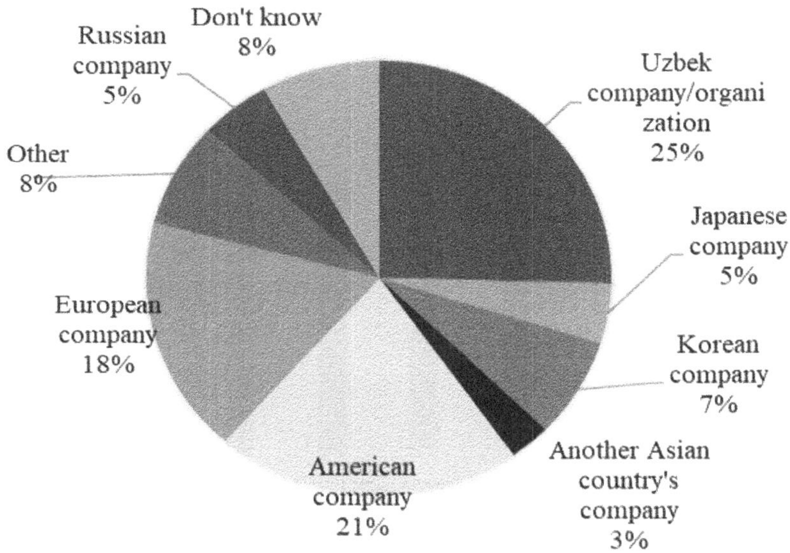

Fig. 3.3 Desire for employment in foreign companies (Question: Which company or organization would you like to work for most? Please choose the most appropriate answer. *Source* Uzbek university student survey 2018)

countries, thus representing a challenge even for those who have perfected their Japanese-language skills. Second, many young people admit that the Japanese language has the potential to be useful in their future life, but due to the lack of learning and practising opportunities, their Japanese proficiency is still poor, and the expectation towards Japanese companies as potential employers is lower when compared to that of students in Southeast Asian countries who seek opportunities for a longer stay and possibly permanent settlement in Japan.

In line with the discussion above, the increase in the number of international students in Japanese-language schools can be explained by several factors. The first is related to the promotion of the learning of the Japanese language by the Japanese government abroad. This results in an increasing interest in the Japanese language and increased motivation of foreign students to study in Japan. For those who study the Japanese language in countries where the presence of Japanese companies is not significant, as in the case of Uzbekistan, the appeal of studying in Japan after the initial period of studying at home is obvious and very natural. Students seek to enhance their basic language skills and then seek employment opportunities. Japan-based Japanese-language schools serve both purposes. For years, these schools have been used as an entry point into Japanese society for the largest groups of foreign nationals, such as Chinese (who, as of 2020, accounted for 16,512 students or 39.7%), Vietnamese (12,897 or 31%), Nepalese (2926 or 7%) and Taiwanese (1457 or 3.5%) students, followed by those from Korea (1214 or 2.9%) (Association for the Promotion of Japanese-Language Education 2020). With an increase in their well-being and economic situation, many students from some of these states (ex: China) shifted their goal from using these schools as a channel to the labour market towards regarding them as preparation for advancing to institutions of higher learning (universities or professional colleges) (Serizawa 2018: 65). However, the attitude of Uzbek students to the Japanese-language schools remains similar to those who used the language schools as pipelines for accessing the Japanese labour market.

Japan as Uzbeks' New "Virgin Lands"

The Uzbeks in Japan largely share with many of the practices, behavioural patterns, and adaptation strategies of other minority groups in Japan (Ikeguchi 2012). In addition, a significant learning effect is transmitted among language school students from various countries and then used as a model for Uzbek students' behaviour.

The largest group of Uzbek sojourners in Japan, numbering 2,366 in 2018, was those with student visas (Table 3.2), which include both students of conventional institutions of higher learning and those enrolling in Japanese-language courses (Table 3.1). The second-highest group of residents comprised those in the category of dependents, numbering 547 individuals. The third group is comprised of those in the category of specialists in humanities and international services. This visa category is normally granted to a wide range of professionals, from language specialists to those acquiring jobs in service sectors. Finally, the group of permanent residents comprised 226 individuals in 2018. The group of those with temporary visas is comprised of various individuals, many of whom were relatives of students, those employed in Japan and permanent visitors. However, some of these individuals were also those who used short-term residence permits to seek part-time employment. The definition of cultural activities and designated activities is rather blurred and often comprises activities that do not necessarily fit into other visa categories or are offered to those whose individual cases require this type of permit.

One feature that can also be traced from the data of Table 3.5 is that young males and females dominate the numbers of those visiting Japan. The most mobile group in terms of age was the group aged between 20 and 34. This again demonstrates that the most mobile and the most socially active group is those in their university years and slightly beyond. These are the years when Uzbek males and females find it easiest to travel and stay outside their country, as they seek to enhance their skills and educational opportunities abroad. In addition, many of them are not yet burdened with families and children, which significantly limit their mobility and geographic scope as well as the time available for travel as they become older.

In terms of the distribution of residents of Japan with Uzbek citizenship, the data shows that the largest number of residents from Uzbekistan was in Tokyo (2,134 in 2018), followed by the prefectures around Tokyo (Ibaraki, 109; Saitama, 268; Chiba, 301; and Kanagawa, 240).[2] This can be attributed to the fact that Tokyo is the centre of economic and educational activities in Japan, and the number of those who seek both employment opportunities and educational venues is, therefore, highest in this area. Those residing in Ibaraki have graduated from or are enrolled in the University of Tsukuba, which is one of the largest universities with a focus on hosting students from CA for regular educational degree and non-degree programmes. The university city of Tsukuba, with a great number of foreign faculties, also represents "a safe haven" for many students, former students and migrants from Uzbekistan seeking opportunities in Japan.

Despite the existence of such educational opportunities at the university level, the majority of international students, including those from Uzbekistan, choose to enrol in institutions of language learning in Japan (for details regarding the Japanese-language schools and their foreign students, see Serizawa 2018: 135–62). Student enrolment at Japanese-language schools increased from 25.622 in 2011 to 90.079 in 2020

[2] The data are obtained from the Japanese Ministry of Justice reports (*Zairyu Gaikokujin Toukei*) regarding foreign nationals residing in Japan for 1995–2018.

Table 3.5 Uzbek residents in Japan by their gender

Year	Total	Total		0~4		5~9		10~14		15~19		20~24		25~29		30~34		35~39		40~44		45~49		50~54		55~59		60~64		65~69		70~74		75~79		Over 80	
		M	F	M	F	M	F	M	F	M	F	M	F	M	F	M	F	M	F	M	F	M	F	M	F	M	F	M	F	M	F	M	F	M	F	M	F
1994	20	13	7	2	1		1	1	2			3	1	2		2	2	1		2																	
1995	22	15	7	1	1	1	1		1	1		3	1	3	1	4	1	1	1	1																	
1996	29	19	10		1	4			2			5	1	2	3	3	2	3	1	2																	
1997	47	34	13			1	1	1	1	6		11	6	2	2	4	1	4	2	2				2				1									
1998																																					
1999	103	68	35	4	2	1	2	3		2	1	29	16	19	6	4	2	3	5	1		2							1								
2000	184	126	58	6	3	1	2	4		2	5	39	24	39	11	10	7	10	4	10	1	4			1			1									
2001	201	125	76	9	3	1	2	1	1	3	3	37	37	45	18	14	9	7	2	6	1							1		1							
2002	262	151	111	9	4	2	8	1	2	5	6	44	36	50	37	26	10	5	5	6	1	1					1	1	1	1							
2003	341	193	148	8	7	9	8	3	2	4	5	55	51	64	45	29	17	6	9	8	1	6	1						1	1	1						
2004	376	202	174	11	4	5	6	2	2	6	6	49	60	73	62	37	19	10	6	4	6	5	2						1								
2005	495	259	236	10	2	8	9	3	2	5	10	72	84	87	88	54	29	12	6	4	3	4	2								1						
2006	527	308	219	9	12	11	10	1	2	11	8	90	58	103	77	54	40	19	7	7	2	1		1	1	1			1		1						
2007	620	366	254	17	16	9	12	3	4	11	6	119	69	121	89	54	40	18	9	8	2	4	2	1	2	1	1		1		1						
2008	655	396	259	21	24	6	7	5	5	6	6	115	51	143	93	66	47	17	16	11	4	2	2	4	1				2		1						
2009	727	424	303	29	39	14	10	7	6	6	3	106	55	146	90	73	65	29	17	8	4	1	3	4	5		3	1	1		2						
2010	832	493	339	47	46	17	14	9	11	17	6	111	68	156	91	87	66	35	24	8	4	1	3	4	2		1	1	1		1		1				
2011	840	506	334	43	43	17	18	11	10	14	9	99	55	172	95	95	68	38	26	10	6	3		2	2	1	1	1	-		1						
2012	1060	613	447	57	60	30	24	12	15	31	15	106	59	183	122	117	78	44	32	10	12	6	4	6	9	6	4	4	9	1	3		1				
2013	1197	720	477	74	66	34	35	15	14	54	9	120	78	182	111	147	83	56	42	13	13	9	6	2	7	7	4	5	3	2	5		1				
2014	1415	881	534	78	80	55	44	19	13	72	16	193	86	197	114	161	92	67	52	19	15	7	6	2	6	7	2	2	6	2	1		1				
2015	1599	1010	589	86	86	44	50	18	16	72	17	262	91	222	114	177	103	79	56	27	25	8	7	5	9	5	5	4	3	1	5		1		1		
2016	1986	1346	640	91	92	57	53	18	18	95	24	431	90	280	122	212	116	108	61	36	28	8	8	4	6	2	6	2	6	2	4		5				1
2017	3068	2321	747	94	101	66	60	23	28	169	31	910	110	501	137	334	117	143	78	53	35	13	13	7	9	1	10	3	6	4	5		5		1		1
2018	3951	3113	838	101	108	85	66	30	31	174	34	1360	134	684	156	402	135	177	85	69	41	11	13	9	10	3	10	6	7	2	3		4				1

Source Ministry of Justice of Japan, http://www.moj.go.jp/housei/toukei/toukei_ichiran_touroku.html (compiled by the authors using *Zairyu Gaikokujin Toukei* reports from 1996 to 2018)

(Japan Student Services Organization [JASSO] 2019). From a comparative perspective, among the total number of students (298,980), the number of students studying at Japanese-language schools (90,079) exceeded the number of students at graduate school (50,184), undergraduate school (87,806), specialized professional training schools (67,475) and preparatory schools (3,436) (Japan Student Services Organization [JASSO] 2019).

According to the Japan Student Services Organization (JASSO), incoming students from Uzbekistan have a choice of enrolling in seven types of educational establishments: basic university programmes, graduate schools, junior colleges, colleges of professional training, university preparatory courses and Japanese-language schools. The number of those who enrolled in graduate schools increased by only forty students between 2004 and 2018 (Table 3.1). The number of university undergraduates grew by nearly 12 times, from 25 students in 2004 to 292 individuals in 2018 (Japan Student Services Organization [JASSO] 2019). Those enrolled in professional training colleges during this period also increased significantly, reaching 258. However, the greatest increase in students from Uzbekistan occurred in Japanese-language schools. The data from JASSO did not include records for the period of 2004–2009 but showed a 65-fold increase in those enrolled in such schools from Uzbekistan in the period between 2010 and 2018. Many of these students see greater "potential" and "benefit" in enrolling in Japanese-language schools than in enrolling in colleges and professional training institutions.

Japanese-Language Schools and Their Uzbek Students

Uzbek students encounter the Japanese language primarily in the following three forms: first, and foremost, many of them experience Japanese-language education in their home country. Several Japanese-language courses are offered on the premises of Uzbek universities in the cities of Tashkent, Samarkand and Bukhara. One of the first centres was established at the University of Oriental Studies in Tashkent. This university has both a fully developed curriculum of Japanese-language education and native Japanese-speaking faculty members who teach at the university. In addition, there are several universities, including the University of World Economy and Diplomacy, University of Foreign Studies, and Samarkand University of Foreign Studies, where students have the chance to learn the Japanese language and interact with native Japanese speakers dispatched to those institutions through various channels, including the Japan International Cooperation Agency (JICA), Japanese partner universities or language volunteers. In addition, Japanese-language courses are offered at the Japan centres in Tashkent and Bukhara. Finally, there are local Japanese-language education initiatives similar to those in Rishtan (Rishtan Japan Centre Noriko Gakkyu), in which a grassroots organization focuses on providing Japanese-language education to those who are, for certain reasons, outside the coverage of the university educational system. Importantly, these schools, at least initially, were not established with the purpose of serving as a channel for labour migration to Japan. Rather, they aimed to provide education to those aspiring to received higher education in Japan. It was only later that languages schools discovered such profit generation opportunities.

The vast majority of those who responded to the face-to-face interviews in Japan and are reflected upon in this chapter attended the grassroots type of Japanese-language school in Uzbekistan. Due to their social standing, including financial difficulties and age limitations, many learned the Japanese language in this type of locally organized school and later decided to travel to Japan to both engage in further Japanese-language studies and seek employment opportunities while abroad. These language schools resemble to some extent similar institutions in China and Vietnam, as recently reported by Liu-Farrer and Tran (2019). However, in sharp contrast to the cases elsewhere in Asia (Liu-Farrer 2008, 2011), under the conditions of the tightly controlled society of Uzbekistan, they operate at the grass-roots level and do not advertise their services as labour migration facilitators openly due to the fear of governmental sanctions or demands of profit-sharing by those in power or connected to special services. Therefore, they often operate through personal referral and utilize the network of former "clients" and the power of social networking sites, such as the telegram, as opposed to the aggressive recruiting practices observed in China (Liu-Farrer and Tran 2019: 239). However, similar to schools in East Asia (Surak 2013), they do exploit the lack of official channels available to their clients due to the closed immigration system in Japan.

There are also some other differences when compared to East Asian operations of similar schools. One difference that stands out is the way such opportunities are framed for those students who engage in "educational migration" practices not only for the "functional" purpose of generating income but also for social capital generation (social status and religious standing after their return home). Undoubtedly, Japan-based Japanese-language schools often provide opportunities to engage in an educational process beyond high school and provide opportunities to fulfil their financial obligations towards their families. But importantly, by travelling abroad and engaging in the activities described in this chapter, they also acquire the important social status of someone who is "well-travelled", "well versed" in international affairs and "experienced" in terms of knowledge of life difficulties. They also see "merit" in their sufferings during their studies and work in Japan in a religious sense because they see themselves as and are considered by others to be a "musofir", or blessed "wanderer", whose hardships abroad make him/her wiser, more appreciative of others and protected by the almighty (Dadabaev and Akhmedova 2022). Upon their return home, they can then obtain benefits from this social capital by becoming respected members of their community who consult others and manage their communities. These factors, combined with the generally positive attitude of the general public towards Japan (Dadabaev 2016),[3] largely fuelled by old dramas such as *Oshin* or technological progress and the friendly image of the Japanese people, make Japan the perfect destination for these "wanderers" in search of education and financial opportunities.

The path towards enrolment for the majority of them started with asking their native Japanese-language instructors for information about ways to travel to Japan and find employment opportunities there. Once they arrived, many transitioned from Japanese-language schools into jobs, and some of these individuals managed to establish themselves professionally. These are the individuals who now sustain the network of "enablers" who help Uzbek students and have turned these networks into profit-generating enterprises of a semi-legal nature.

In many, if not all, cases, the students depart from their language schools after the first two to three months. As Table 3.6 shows, they start to look for jobs immediately after arrival, and by the third month, they all find such opportunities.

Under the current regulations, students may finish their school year in as little as half a year, and the requirement is that they have to attend

[3] According to the opinion poll conducted by the Ministry of Foreign Affairs of Japan in 2016, 60% of total respondents in Uzbekistan answered that they can "trust" "somewhat trust" Japan, see https://www.mofa.go.jp/mofaj/files/000159231.pdf.

Table 3.6 How much time did you spend in Japan before finding your first job?

How many months spent before first job?	
4	3 months
5	2.5 months
8	2 months
7	1.5 months
9	1 month
9	3 weeks
11	2 weeks
5	10 days
1	3 days
1	1 day

760 hours of classes a year with at least 20 hours of classes attended a week (Association for the Promotion of Japanese-Language Education 2007). It is also a responsibility of the school to verify the desire, ability and financial capacities of the students before admitting them and to vouch for them with the immigration authorities. However, many of the students do not fulfil these conditions and either partly comply with the weekly attendance requirement or leave their schools prior to completion of the requirement for graduation, as witnessed by many of our respondents.

They spend the rest of their time working. Many of those who responded to our face-to-face interviews continued to carry their student resident permits (visa permits) until they expired. Under a student permit, a student is allowed to work 28 hours per week. However, most of the respondents indicated that they worked not less than 10 hours per day, thus significantly exceeding the allowed working hours. In doing so, all the respondents indicated that they would accept jobs at several places, where they would work the night shift at one place, nap for a few hours in early morning, attend a few hours of schooling and then later work the day shift. In certain cases, they engaged in a full-time employment agreement that was not warranted by their status. This alone made their stay in Japan at least semi-legal because they did not spend the required time at educational institutions and far exceeded their allowed employment. By leaving the Japanese-language schools and relocating in terms of residence, they break the conditions of their residence permit because their student status is not properly maintained.

Table 3.7 What resources did you use to find a job?

Seeking help from......	
15	Friends
6	Relatives
6	Classmates
6	Roommates
8	Schools
7	By yourself
12	Others

In terms of channels for finding jobs, most of the respondents utilized the network of other Uzbek students or working professionals. Many of them arrived in Japan with a promised place of employment, while others sought such places during their studies through the channels indicated below (Table 3.7). In certain cases, assistance in finding a job was provided by the "enablers" free of charge. As stated above, the network of enablers among Uzbeks is premature, fluid and very informal, thus great importance is placed on the trust among individuals. The religious attachment of "enablers" and them being God-fearing and practising Muslims adds to the confidence in such enablers and, to some extent, serves as a psychological safeguard for those using these networks (for details, see Dadabaev and Akhmedova 2022).

These individuals receive payments from employers who are in urgent need of an "obedient" and undemanding labour force. However, in other instances, as indicated in Table 3.8, students who sought jobs had to pay for their positions. In such instances, the onetime payments are listed below. In 8 cases, a onetime payment of USD300 was made in Uzbekistan to a broker, with the remaining amount to be paid from the salary.

Table 3.8 What payments did you make to obtain the job? (JPY)

8	USD300 and 10% from salary each month
5	JPY20,000
16	JPY15,000
31	Free

Table 3.9 What is your preferred type of job?

18	Uber delivery service
14	7-Eleven
9	Family Mart
5	LAWSON
5	YAMATO
3	Restaurant
1	Supermarket
3	Internet café
2	Selling Turkish food

Once they find a job, they typically relocate to apartments that house many other students, who share the apartments and their corners/beds in shifts depending on their work schedule. In terms of job preference, the most popular job is Uber delivery services, which do not require high language ability, followed by convenience stores (7-Eleven, Family Mart, and LAWSON), supermarkets and restaurants, where the presence of the foreign student workforce has become a phenomenon, especially in rural settings (Table 3.9). Although the total rent paid for such an apartment is rather high, the cost for each individual resident is low because the rent is shared by everyone living there. These are similar to apartments rented by immigrants to Russia and Korea, where apartments composed of several rooms are shared by a large number of residents. The Japanese government estimates that 4,807 visa overstayers (as of July 2019, inclusive of Uzbek language school students) have overstayed their student visas, amounting to an increase of approximately 70% compared to five years ago (MOJ 2020). Starting in April 2020, Uzbekistan, along with other CA post-Soviet states, was included in the list of countries requiring enhanced screening for student visa applications in the light of an increasing number of student visa overstayers (Nikkei Shimbun 2020).

Economics of Language-Student Life in Japan

As summarized in Table 3.10, the economics of student labour are rather complex and require further elaboration. In the process of surveying the respondents of this study, they were asked questions regarding their type of job, savings, amounts sent home and their own expenses. One of the first expenses mentioned by the majority of the respondents was the initial amount spent to come to Japan. This amount includes payment for the

Table 3.10 Costs associated with travel, preparations and processing of documents (USD)

Resp.	*Tickets*	*Resp.*	*Documents*
1	$720	10	$1500
1	$700	9	$1300
11	$500	8	$1250
8	$430	2	$1200
12	$400	15	$1000
9	$370	2	$800
10	$330	8	$500
8	$300	1	$50
		5	$0

services provided by the intermediaries and the network of facilitators. One person indicated that he needed to cover only the minimal costs of postage and issuance of documents, while all other "services" were provided for free because he was close to or related to the people who provided these services. The majority had to pay approximately USD500–1500, depending not only on the degree of difficulty of processing their documents but also on the service required. Those who required merely basic instructions and document checks before submission of the documents to the Japanese-language schools and immigration authorities naturally paid less. Those who expected "full service", which included the preparation of documents, placement in the Japanese-language school, and provision of ready-to-go documents, paid more. The costs of tickets depended on the route and the timing of purchasing those tickets and varied from approximately USD300–720 (Table 3.10).

The costs mentioned above are then added to the initial living expenses (payment for dormitories for several months in advance) of the students once they arrive in Japan, as well as the tuition fees paid to the language school. The tuition fees can also differ significantly from one school to another (on average JPY650,000–700,000 according to our respondents). The schools that are less demanding in terms of acceptance requirements and the necessary documents often function as commercial enterprises and charge considerably higher tuition fees.

Thus, by the time of arrival, each of the students interviewed for this study had had to borrow USD5,500–14,000 from relatives and others willing to lend them money. Naturally, this debt served both as pressure and motivation for them to engage more actively in job hunting than in language learning to recover their initial "investment" (Table 3.11).

Table 3.11 How many months did it take you to recover the initial investment or loan?

21	During the 1st year
14	1 year 6 months
12	Between 1 and 2 years
13	Not recovered yet

While the ideal structure of their stay should be a combination of intensive language study and part-time work, in reality, what they experienced was intensive full-time work combined with some periods of language study under the pressure of their financial burdens (Table 3.12). In terms of accommodation costs, most of the respondents indicated that they spent approximately JPY10,000 (currently USD85) to 50,000 (USD450) per month, with only a few people spending more than that. In most cases, they were male residents who lived in collectively shared apartments with bunkbeds, very similar to those rented by Nepalese, Vietnamese and other immigrants (Serizawa 2018: 73). They shared their residences to save the costs, and some of them even rotated the use of those apartments in shifts (Table 3.13). In addition, a sense of security is provided by such shared living, especially in the foreign-language environment. As witnessed by the authors of this chapter, the communes of Uzbeks in Japan are formed primarily based on the regions of Uzbekistan they come from. For instance, those from the Samarkand area, who compose the largest group of Uzbek residents of Japan, prefer to reside and work together because most of them are native Tajik (Persian) speakers with many customs and norms of behaviour that are not shared by those from

Table 3.12 Financial burden of students at the time of arrival (USD)

1	$14,000
1	$13,500
2	$12,000
5	$11,000
22	$10,000
4	$9000
7	$8000
8	$7000
9	$6000
1	$5500

Table 3.13 What are the costs of living? (JPY)

Cost of rent per month		*Cost of food per month*		*Cost of other personal expenses per month*	
5	70,000	5	50,000	9	30,000
3	60,000	3	45,000	10	25,000
7	50,000	12	40,000	18	20,000
2	45,000	16	35,000	16	15,000
12	40,000	14	30,000	6	10,000
11	35,000	4	25,000		
14	30,000	3	15,000		
5	25,000	3	10,000		
1	20,000				

native Uzbek-speaking Tashkent or the Fergana Valley. In terms of occupation, the respondents often indicated that those from Samarkand were working as basic labour, generally defined as low-skilled labour.

In contrast, those from Tashkent, due to better access to education at home, sought employment in the service industry, as well as jobs generally termed high skilled by our respondents (being an officer in the trading or manufacturing companies and not having to engage into manual labour). These are generalizations mentioned by the respondents in the process of interviews, and there are exceptions to these labour divisions. However, regional identification plays a certain role in the choice of where people live and how they find their prospective jobs. Additionally, regional belonging is not merely an identity marker for these people but serves the functional purpose of maintaining contact with the homeland, transferring money and goods and safeguarding against people being overlooked in cases when some who illegally overstay in Japan are arrested.

The time of the usage of apartments depended on when the students had to show up for work, with many respondents preferring to work later hours and at night. The reason for such a choice is not pre-determined by the desire to study in the daytime and work at night, as it might initially appear. Rather, night shifts pay more and are less popular among Japanese part-time workers. Employers are also less demanding in terms of applications and are more interested in filling these positions regardless of the applicants' social backgrounds (Table 3.14). In addition to night shifts, Uber deliveries are popular as part-time jobs because the payment tends

Table 3.14 Places of employment and conditions (JPY per hour/day)

Workplaces of participants		*The payments for different jobs*	
Shop assistant at convenience store	7-Eleven	Based on destination and time, the wages are different	950–1500
	Family Mart		900–1370
	LAWSON		900–1375
	MINISTOP		900–1375
Post office	YAMATO		1000–1700
	SAGAWA		1100
	ZOZOTOWN	17:00–22:00	1000
Waiter/Waitress			950–1350
Uber delivery service		Based on order	
Filling bento boxes at plant		22:00–6:00	1000
Kitchen at family restaurant or fast-food chain		18:00–22:00	880
Supermarket		7:00–12:00	950
Internet café		22:00–6:00	1370
Hotel		9:00–12:00	950
Construction		Based on work	1300–2000
Turkish food sales		1 day	15,000

to be higher and varies depending on the service required. Although this type of job pays more than others, it is not very stable and depends on the intensity of deliveries. In this sense, it is more physically demanding than other jobs.

Other costs associated with living in Japan are food expenses and other costs. Similar to accommodation costs, many tend to share food costs by collectively preparing meals and, thus, reducing the financial burden on individual members of such small communes. While the tastes can differ, many of these student migrants are prepared to accept the limitations for a period of time to achieve higher savings and more opportunities.

In terms of savings, this study identified the following amounts as the most typical for monthly savings. The majority of those asked in the survey indicated that the maximum amount that they can save is approximately JPY50,000–60,000 per month after the payment of all their expenses (Table 3.15).[4]

[4] The data above needs to be approached as reflecting certain bias and under-reporting. First and foremost, there are reasons to believe (by following student/migrants communications on the Telegram social networking channel) that remittances are much larger (reported to be between JPY150,000 and 300,000 per month) than those reported to

Table 3.15 What are your savings (JPY per month)?

1	50,000–60,000
3	30,000–35,000
2	25,000–30,000
4	20,000–25,000
4	15,000–20,000
5	10,000–15,000
8	50,000–10,000
10	10,000–50,000
23	No answer

As indicated in our survey, over the period of a year, students can retrieve part of their initial investment in coming to Japan. According to these estimates, it takes students approximately 3 years of "education" in Japan to profit from their stay in Japan. If they opt to work more hours at the expense of their studies, which is usually the case, they can recover their initial costs in a year and begin earning a profit in the second year of their stay in Japan.

Importantly, the students widely used the financial remittance format established by the earlier generation of Uzbek newcomers to Japan. Although the students in this survey indicated that they used their "friends" in the majority of cases to transfer money, in private conversations, many indicated that in fact, by "friends", they meant the social network of money remittances through the phone established using the Telegram social network (Table 3.16).

Table 3.16 How do you transfer money?

25	Through friends
9	Through Manigram
8	Kyoday
7	On my own
9	No remittance
2	Western Union

current survey for several reasons. Migrant/students do not report their full amounts for the fear of this information being abused or used against them. The popularity of attending language schools in Japan from Uzbekistan is growing even at the time of coronavirus, implying that those incoming students see the financial profitability of this exercise, beyond the amounts indicated by our respondents.

This remittance system functions similarly to illegal banks established by Bangladeshi, Chinese, Vietnamese and other immigrants, where those remitting the money visit an office in Tokyo to pay the money. In turn, those running the system have accomplices with pooled money in Tashkent, Samarkand and Andijan from which the same amount can be retrieved in a matter of approximately 10 minutes by the relatives of students. No documentation changes hands, and the system is maintained only verbally based on trust between the remitters and the operators. In maintaining such trust, operators often appeal to their commitment to Islamic values as ones which guarantee justice and proper (halal) treatment of their clients. With the advance of social networking tools, it has become easier for student labourers to share information. On occasions when their trust has been broken, the operators of financial schemes have been shamed and held accountable by using the telegram channel popular among student migrants.

Paradoxes of Student-Work Balance

A few paradoxes, including why Uzbek students work longer hours than allowed by regulations, are associated with the nature of enrolment of Uzbek students in Japanese-language schools.

First, Japanese-language schools based in Japan provide a comfortable entry strategy for Uzbeks who wish to search for better employment opportunities in Japan. In contrast with universities, entry into Japanese-language schools does not require a certain level of knowledge, passing an examination to enter the school or constantly demonstrated performance to maintain the status of a language school student. In this sense, language schools are easy targets for those attempting to acquire a certain social and immigration status in Japanese society. Through enrolling in these schools, these opportunity-aspiring individuals obtain a legitimate reason for entry into Japan, legal migration status at the point of entry, several years of guaranteed permission to engage in limited labour while being enrolled in the language school and, importantly, language training to enable them to engage in certain interactions with potential employers.

Second, these enrolling students utilize the already developed net of social ties with Japanese-language instructors dispatched to Uzbek educational institutions to provide basic Japanese-language training in Uzbekistan. The findings of this chapter show that these Japanese-language instructors are frequently the ones who provide students with basic information about the potential Japanese-language schools in Japan and guidance in how to properly apply to these schools. That is not to say that the Japanese-language instructors were in any way involved in illegal or semi-legal labour smuggling into Japan. As described by the respondents to this survey, evil intent was not indicated by any of the actors involved in the schemes around Japanese-language schools. In contrast, everyone from the Japanese-language instructors initially providing basic information about the potential language schools to the language schools and those facilitating the Uzbek students' legal, semi-legal and illegal stays in Japan were driven by good intentions of helping those in need. Nonetheless, the way in which Japanese-language schools have been abused by Uzbek students has resulted in the creation of a whole network of informal connections through which students of the Japanese-language schools will transition into a category of labour migrant and change their migration status from legal to illegal in many cases. The same network then facilitates the "trouble-free" exit of these students. Consequently, this "well-intentioned" networking of facilitators has caused concern among immigration officials in Japan towards incoming language school students, resulting in an increasing number of visa denials for applicants (*The Japan Times* 2019).

Once enrolled in the schools, many arrive in Japan and are granted student status for the duration of their studies, which varies from 6 months to 1–2 years. The majority of students initially spend a couple of months at the Japanese-language school while searching for employment opportunities through the well-developed network of like-minded students. Once they find an employment opportunity, they combine their studies with work outside their studies. The balance gradually shifts towards prioritizing work at the expense of their studies. In such a structure, the majority, if not all, of the students far exceed the legally permitted work hours of 28 hours per week. As this chapter demonstrates, many of these students prefer to work night shifts for the reasons explained previously.

Third, the network of "enablers" of such schemes is typically composed of former students who have established themselves in Japan and often work full-time jobs while offering "assistance" on a part-time basis. They position themselves as "consultants" who provide "packaged" guidance and assistance with the applicant's "entry strategy". They provide documentation guidance to aspiring applicants, helping them navigate through peculiarities and, on occasion, offering insights into how to provide forged documents. They also provide "loans" that are to be repaid by the students once they are in Japan. The network also includes the financial arm of the underground financial operators who accept and transfer money to Uzbekistan on a monthly basis. Finally, the informal part of the network of enablers includes those who provide "guidance" regarding the "exit" of students, many of whom have become illegal by the time of their desired departure.

The interlocutors are individuals who are well aware of the Japanese immigration regulations and who often serve as interpreters for illegal migrants arrested in Japan. In our interviews, few of these interlocutors indicated that they are known to the immigration officials and provide "assistance" to those officials and to former students whose immigration status has expired.[5] According to them, they approach immigration officials to obtain permission for ex-students to voluntarily depart from Japan and, in exchange for such negotiations, receive renumeration that averages approximately 10,000 yen (roughly USD100) per person.[6]

Such cooperation between interlocutors and the Japanese immigration services can also be part of voluntary departure under the system of Written Departure Orders (*shyukoku meirei seido*), under which certain individuals overstaying their visas that fulfil the conditions of the immigration service are deported from Japan without being detained (Immigration Services Agency of Japan 2020). The Japanese immigration services are interested in cooperation from these interlocutors because if illegal foreigners do not voluntarily leave Japan, they join the number of foreigners detained at immigration centres, which stood at 1,494 at the end of June 2018 (MOJ 2018). Of that number, 704 were long-term detainees who had stayed at the facilities for six months or more (MOJ 2018).

The Japanese-language schools are in a dual position as well. In a sense, these schools are both victims and enablers of the situation. On the one hand, they benefit from the greater number of tuition-paying students. The greater the number of those paying a considerable amount of tuition (sometimes exceeding the tuition of a university), the more financial sustainability the language school can obtain. On the other hand,

[5] It is difficult to verify if these are known only by face or are employed as interpreters.

[6] It is difficult to verify if these are the payments for translation services or are documented otherwise.

they lack a mechanism to control their students once they are in Japan. In most cases, the students spend only part of the day in the school. Given the availability of the enablers mentioned above, these students quickly adapt to Japanese society and move from the places where the schools are located. While the school petitions on behalf of the students, it cannot implement the level of control required to keep them within the educational process of the school.

Conclusions

This chapter focuses on Uzbek students in Japanese-language schools in Japan. It arrives at the following conclusions based on the findings of the student survey in Uzbekistan and face-to-face interviews with 66 students from Uzbekistan who enrolled in Japanese-language schools.

First, this chapter demonstrates that Uzbek university students regard Russia and English-speaking countries to be the most preferred due to their linguistic accessibility, with Russian and English being the first and second foreign languages for Uzbeks. Japan is placed in the second tier among the most preferred destinations for study, which also include Germany, France and South Korea. As demonstrated in the chapter, the ambiguity associated with the image of Japan produces duality of its image, i.e., having great potential but also having limited corporate connections with Uzbekistan, thus, problematizing a longer stay in Japan.

Second, while the conclusion above can apply to all the youth in Uzbekistan, there is a peculiarity in the attitudes of those enrolling in Japanese-language schools in Japan. In particular, this chapter treats them as "sojourners", or a new wave of temporary residents or workers who disguise their true intentions under the pretext of seeking language education. In some instances, these student migrants do seek educational opportunities along with their employment. While the general expectation in regard to these students is that they will spend most of their time learning and some of their time earning, the reality of their life in Japan demonstrates the reverse situation. They seek employment almost immediately after arriving in Japan and stay employed at the expense of their studies, frequently leaving their studies altogether. In this sense, the Uzbek students represent similar waves of student migration seen in previous years from Bangladesh, Vietnam, China and Iran. The major difference between Uzbeks and those from other countries is that the previous waves of student migrations happened when the Japanese economy was experiencing high-speed economic growth or in the years immediately after the bubble burst, with incoming labourers seeking long-term settlement. The Uzbek student migrants, however, are attempting to enter the short-term temporary labour market at a time of economic recession, providing insights into their adaptation strategies. While there were certain instances where Chinese students entered Japan in early 2000 when the Japanese economy was also in a slump, the Uzbek students' entry into Japan under the guise of being language students demonstrates that the practice of using Japanese-language schools as pipelines for labour migration is expanding beyond East Asia into Central Asia.

Third, this chapter also demonstrates the structural problems that enable such abuse of language training schools. First, this chapter emphasizes the network of enablers who are either misled to or intentionally assist those willing to engage in student migration into Japan. The second structural problem is associated with Japanese-language schools in Japan. These schools, on the one hand, are interested in increasing the number of such students, as they depend on their tuition payments to survive. On the other hand, there are no tools for these schools to hold their students accountable for their time spent in Japan. In many cases, the Japanese schools take the "don't ask, don't tell" approach to such students and only reactively engage them when they disappear from the school or overstay their visa.

Fourth, this situation brings into the question the purpose of the existing language educational system in Japan and the attempts of the Japanese government to popularize Japanese-language education in pursuit of larger numbers of university students and Japanese soft-power potential.

The conclusions above represent a tentative outline of the current situation of Uzbek language school students in Japan. What remains to be seen however is if "sojourning" will remain the attitude of language school students from Uzbekistan in Japan as their stay extends to a longer period of time. Alternatively, "sojourning" can be a strategy of "self-persuasion", which is used by most of the newcomers in the first months and years of their stay in Japan. Once they get used to their lives in Japan, "sojourning" can fade into a philosophical category and become a very long-term goal. In this way, "sojourning" can become the first step of long-term settlement for these students. However, further research and additional data will be required to make a judgement on this subject.

Appendix: Survey of Japanese-Language School Students Conducted in 2017–2019

#	*Pseudonyms*	*Age*	*Region*	*Gender*	*Arrival year*	*Marital status*	*Education in Uzbekistan*
Japanese language school students							
1	Said	22	Bukhara	Male	2018	Single	Incomplete higher education
2	Akmal	32	Andijan	Male	2016	Married	Undergraduate degree
3	Ali	24	Samarkand	Male	2018	Single	Undergraduate degree
4	Bilol	20	Samarkand	Male	2017	Single	Secondary vocational education
5	Feruz	19	Samarkand	Male	2018	Single	Secondary vocational education
6	Yusuf	26	Samarkand	Male	2018	Single	Academic lyceum
7	Jasur	21	Samarkand	Male	2019	Single	Academic lyceum
8	Doston	27	Djizzak	Male	2018	Single	Academic lyceum
9	Akram	24	Djizzak	Male	2019	Single	Undergraduate degree
10	Giyos	26	Andijan	Male	2018	Single	Secondary vocational education
11	Muhammad	20	Namangan	Male	2018	Single	Secondary vocational education
12	Ikrom	25	Andijan	Male	2018	Single	Undergraduate degree
13	Dilshod	22	Djizzak	Male	2018	Single	Secondary vocational education
14	Rustam	25	Samarkand	Male	2019	Married	Academic lyceum
15	Sardor	25	Namangan	Male	2018	Married	Academic lyceum
16	Botir	22	Namangan	Male	2018	Single	Academic lyceum

(continued)

(continued)

#	*Pseudonyms*	*Age*	*Region*	*Gender*	*Arrival year*	*Marital status*	*Education in Uzbekistan*
17	Javlon	23	Namangan	Male	2018	Single	Secondary vocational education
18	Sardor	20	Namangan	Male	2018	Single	Secondary vocational education
19	Inom	19	Andijan	Male	2018	Single	Secondary vocational education
20	Forhod	20	Andijan	Male	2019	Single	Secondary vocational education
21	Izzat	19	Andijan	Male	2019	Single	Secondary vocational education
22	Shuhrat	18	Samarkand	Male	2019	Single	Secondary vocational education
23	Mirjalil	20	Samarkand	Male	2018	Single	Academic lyceum
24	Abdulhamid	19	Andijan	Male	2018	Single	Academic lyceum
25	Sirojiddin	22	Andijan	Male	2019	Single	Secondary vocational education
26	Sardor	34	Namangan	Male	2018	Single	Undergraduate degree
27	Umid	44	Samarkand	Male	2016	Married	Undergraduate degree
28	Oybek	24	Bukhara	Male	2017	Single	Undergraduate degree
29	Said	26	Andijan	Male	2018	Single	Undergraduate degree
30	Zohid	21	Namangan	Male	2018	Single	Secondary vocational education
31	Jamshid	27	Andijan	Male	2018	Single	Undergraduate degree
32	Gilomqodir	26	Samarkand	Male	2019	Single	Secondary vocational education
33	Nadir	18	Samarkand	Male	2019	Single	Academic lyceum

(continued)

(continued)

#	*Pseudonyms*	*Age*	*Region*	*Gender*	*Arrival year*	*Marital status*	*Education in Uzbekistan*
34	Farruh	26	Andijan	Male	2018	Single	Undergraduate degree
Vocational school students							
35	Mirkomil	22	Samarkand	Male	2017	Single	Secondary vocational education
36	Amir	31	Samarkand	Male	2015	Single	Secondary vocational education
37	Shavkat	22	Samarkand	Male	2016	Single	Academic lyceum
38	Islom	28	Syrdarya	Male	2016	Single	Secondary vocational education
39	Botir	23	Samarkand	Male	2016	Single	Undergraduate degree
40	Mansur	22	Tashkent	Male	2016	Single	Academic lyceum
41	Aziz	25	Samarkand	Male	2017	Single	Secondary vocational education
42	Shuhrat	24	Andijan	Male	2016	Single	Secondary vocational education
43	Doston	22	Samarkand	Male	2017	Single	Secondary vocational education
44	Zohid	22	Andijan	Male	2018	Single	Secondary vocational education
46	Umar	26	Samarkand	Male	2017	Married	Academic lyceum
47	Feruz	25	Samarkand	Male	2016	Single	Secondary vocational education
University preparatory course students							
48	Anvar	38		Male	2016	Married	Master's degree
49	Giyos	32	Andijan	Male	2016	Married	Undergraduate degree
University students							
50	Maftuna	21	Tashkent	Female	2016	Single	Academic lyceum

(continued)

(continued)

#	*Pseudonyms*	*Age*	*Region*	*Gender*	*Arrival year*	*Marital status*	*Education in Uzbekistan*
51	Bahrom	26	Andijan	Male	2017	Single	Academic lyceum
52	Jumavoy	23	Fergana	Male	2017	Single	Secondary vocational education
53	I nom	23	Samarkand	Male	2017	Single	Secondary vocational education
54	Kamol	30	Tashkent	Male	2017	Single	Undergraduate degree
Workers							
55	Yusuf	25	Samarkand	Male	2018	Single	Undergraduate degree
56	Zarifa	37	Samarkand	Female	2006	Married	Undergraduate degree
57	Odilbek	36	Samarkand	Male	2016	Married	Undergraduate degree
58	Suhrob	35	Samarkand	Male	2004	Married	Secondary vocational education
59	Olim	29	Kashkadarya	Male	2016	Married	Master's degree
60	Mansur	32	Khorezm	Male	2008	Married	Undergraduate degree
61	Abdusamad	31	Samarkand	Male	2015	Single	Secondary vocational education
62	Nurullo	24	Andijan	Male	2016	Single	Academic lyceum
63	Bektemir	28	Samarkand	Male	2015	Single	Undergraduate degree
64	Rustam	22	Samarkand	Male	2015	Single	Secondary vocational education
Dependents							
65	Zoir	35	Samarkand	Male	2006	Married	Undergraduate degree
Spouse of Japanese national							
66	Jalil	34	Samarkand	Male	2007	Married	Undergraduate degree

References

Abashin, Sergey. 2015. 'Возвращение домой: Семейные и миграционные сценарии в Узбекистане' (Returning Home: Family and Migration Scenarios in Uzbekistan). *Ab Imperio* 3: 125–65.

Ambrosini, Maurizio. 2016. 'Why Irregular Migrants Arrive and Remain: The Role of Intermediaries.' *Journal of Ethnic and Migration Studies* 43:11: 1813–30.

Association for the Promotion of Japanese Language Education. 2007. 'Nihongo Kyoiku Kikan Unei ni Kansuru Kijyun.' Available at https://www.nisshinkyo.org/review/pdf/index02.pdf (accessed on September 24, 2020).

Bonacich, Edna. 1973. 'A Theory of Middleman Minorities.' *American Sociological Review* 38:5: 583–94.

Carlisle, Donald S. 1986. 'The Uzbek Power Elite: Politburo and Secretariat (1938–83).' *Central Asian Survey* 5:3–4: 91–132.

Chavajay, Pablo and Jeffrey Skowronek. 2008. 'Aspects of Acculturation Stress Among International Students Attending a University in the USA.' *Psychological Reports* 103:3: 827–35.

Cox, John L. 1988. 'The Overseas Student: Expatriate, Sojourner or Settler?' *Acta Psychiatrica Scandinavica* 78:S344: 179–84.

Dadabaev, Timur. 2016. *Japan in Central Asia: Strategies, Initiatives, and Neighboring Powers*. Palgrave Macmillan.

Dadabaev, Timur and Mukaddam Akhmedova. 2022. 'A Home Away from Home: Migration, Identity and Sojourning in the Life of Uzbeks in Japan.' *Europe Asia Studies* 1–28. https://doi.org/10.1080/09668136.2021.2010660

El-Yurt UMIDI Foundation. 1996–2003. 'Official Website of the "El-Yurt Umidi" Foundation Under the Cabinet of Ministers of the Republic of Uzbekistan.' Available at https://eyuf.uz/en/wmenu?view=61 (accessed on September 24, 2020)

Elrick, Tim and Emilia Lewandowska. 2008. 'Matching and Making Labour Demand and Supply: Agents in Polish Migrant Networks of Domestic Elderly Care in Germany and Italy.' *Journal of Ethnic and Migration Studies* 34:5: 717–34.

Era, Satomi 2018. 'Koreika suru Tenkanki no Rodoshakai to Iminrodosha' (Aging Society and Migrant Workers in Transition). *Rodoshakaigaku Kenkyu* 19: 1–19

Gaikokujin Kenshyusei Mondai Nettowâku. 2006. *Gaikokujin Kenshyusei: Jikyu 300 Yenno Roudoushya* (Foreigner Interns: Workers for Hourly 300 Yen). Akashi Shyoten.

Gaikokujin Kenshyusei Mondai Nettowâku. 2009. *Gaikokujin Roudoushya Mondai to Korekarano Nihon* (The Problems of Foreign Laborers and the Future of Japan).

Glick, Clarence Elmer. 1980. *Sojourners and Settlers, Chinese Migrants in Hawaii*. University Press of Hawaii.

Gotou, Hiroyuki. 2019. *Gaikokujin to Kyousei suru Nippon he* (Towards Japan Which Co-habits with Foreigners). Kanaria Communications.

Higuchi, Naoto and Kiyoto Tanno. 2003. 'What's Driving Brazil-Japan Migration? The Making and Remaking of the Brazilian Niche in Japan.' *International Journal of Japanese Sociology* 12:1: 33–47.

Ikeguchi, Cecilia. 2012. 'Internationalization of Education & Culture Adjustment the Case of Chinese Students in Japan.' *Intercultural Communication Studies* 21:2: 170–84.

Immigration Sevices Agency of Japan. 2020. 'Shutou Shinkoku.' Available at http://www.immi-moj.go.jp/tetuduki/taikyo/qa.html (accessed on September 24, 2020)

Inaba, Nanako and Naoto Higuchi. 2003. 'Zainichi Banguradeshi jinno Shyokugyo Rireki' (Professional History of the Bangladeshi People in Japan). *Komyunikeshyon Gaku Ronshu* 19: 157–92.

Japan Student Services Organization (JASSO). 2019. 'International Students in Japan in 2018.' Available at https://www.jasso.go.jp/en/about/statistics/intl_student/__icsFiles/afieldfile/2019/04/19/data18_brief_e.pdf (accessed on September 24, 2020).

JETRO. 2019. 'Minkan Soushitsu Kikan ni Yoru Ginnou Jishyusei no Hakken Hajimaru' (Private Business-Driven Technical Interns Admission Has Started). Available at https://www.jetro.go.jp/biznews/2019/11/835ea94c3f1da621.html (accessed November 11, 2019).

Kajita, Takamichi. 1995. 'Characteristics of the Foreign Worker Problem in Japan: To an Analytical Viewpoint.' *Hitotsubashi Journal of Social Studies* 27:1: 1–26.

Kharel, Dipesh. 2016. 'From Lahures to Global Cooks: Network Migration from the Western Hills of Nepal to Japan.' *Social Science Japan Journal* 19:2: 173–92.

Liu-Farrer, Gracia. 2008. 'The Burden of Social Capital: Fujian Chinese Immigrants' Experiences of Network Closure in Japan.' *Social Science Japan Journal* 11:22: 241–57.

Liu-Farrer, Gracia. 2009. 'Educationally Channeled International Labor Migration: Post-1978 Student Mobility from China to Japan.' *International Migration Review* 43:1: 178–204.

Liu-Farrer, Gracia. 2011. *Labour Migration from China to Japan: International Students, Transnational Migrants*. Routledge.

Liu-Farrer, Gracia and An Huy Tran. 2019. 'Bridging the Institutional Gaps: International Education as a Migration Industry.' *International Migration* 57:3: 235–49.

Mahmud, Hasan. 2017. 'Social Determinants of Remitting Practices Among Bangladeshi Migrants in Japan.' *Sociological Perspectives* 60:1: 95–112.

Massey, Douglas S. and Kristin E. Espinosa. 1997. 'What's Driving Mexico-U.S. Migration? A Theoretical, Empirical, and Policy Analysis.' *American Journal of Sociology* 102:4: 939–99.

Ministry of Health, Labour and Welfare. 2009. 'The Notified Situations of Foreigners' Employment by October, 2009 (Gaikokujin Koyo Jokyo no Todokede Jokyo, Heisei 20 nen 10 Gatsu Genzai).' Available at https://www.mhlw.go.jp/houdou/2009/01/dl/h0116-9a_0003.pdf (accessed on September 24, 2020).

Ministry of Health, Labour and Welfare. 2020. 'The Notified Situations of Foreigners' Employment by October, 2020 (Gaikokujin Koyo Jokyo no Todokede Jokyo, Reiwa 2 nen 10 Gatsu Genzai).' Available at https://www.mhlw.go.jp/content/11655000/000590311.pdf (accessed on September 24, 2020)

Mizukami, Tetsuo. 2006. *The Sojourner Community: Japanese Migration and Residency in Australia*. Brill.

Mochizuki, Hiroki. 2019. *Futatsu no Nihon: "Imin Kokka" no Tatemae to Genjitsu* (Two Sides of Japan: Face and Reality of the Immigrant State). Kōdansha.

MOJ. 2018. 'Taikyo Kyosei Gyomuni Tsuite.' Available at http://www.moj.go.jp/content/001279678.pdf (accessed on September 24, 2020).

MOJ. 2020. 'Zairyu Shikakubetsu Fuhou Zairyushyasuno Suii.' Available at http://www.moj.go.jp/content/001308160.pdf (accessed on September 24, 2020).

Nikkei Shimbun. 2020. 'Japan to Tighten Foreign Student Visa Screening as of April to Cut Down on Overstayers: List of Countries.' Available at https://resources.realestate.co.jp/living/japan-to-tighten-foreign-student-visa-screening-as-of-april-to-cut-down-on-overstayers-list-of-countries/ (accessed 9 February).

Sano, Atsuko. 2018. 'Japanese-Language Schools Face Tighter Rules on Quality: Some Institutions Under Scrutiny for Being Too Quick to Help Foreign Students Find Work.' *Nikkei Asian Review*. Available at https://asia.nikkei.com/Life-Arts/Education/Japanese-language-schools-face-tighter-rules-on-quality (accessed May 31).

Serizawa, Kensuke. 2018. *Konbini Gaikokujin* (Foreigners of Convenience Stores). Shinchosha.

Shukan Toyokeizai Henshubu, ed. 2014. *Gaikokujin Roudou*. Toyo Keizai.

Siu, Paul C. P. 1952. 'The Sojourner.' *American Journal of Sociology* 58:1: 34–44.

Surak, K. 2013. 'The Migration Industry and Developmental States in East Asia.' In *The Migration Industry and the Commercialisation of International*

Migration, ed. Thomas Gammeltoft-Hansen and Ninna Nyberg Sørensen. Routledge.

Sussman, Nan M. 2002. 'Sojourners to Another Country: The Psychological Roller-Coaster of Cultural Transitions.' *Online Readings in Psychology and Culture* 8:1: 1–11.

Suzuki, Eriko. 2009. *Nihonde Hataraku Hiseiki Taizaishya: Karera wa 'Konomashikunai Gaikokujin Roudoushya' Nano Ka?* (Irregular Migrants Working in Japan: Are They Really 'Unfavorable Foreign Workers'?). Akashi Shoten.

The Japan Times. 2019. 'Japanese-Language Students from South Asian Countries See Plunge in Visa Approval Rates.' Available at https://www.japantimes.co.jp/news/2019/08/21/national/japanese-language-student-visas/#.Xp0K58gzaUk (accessed 21 August).

Tsukuba Daigaku Shyakaigaku Kenkyushitsu. 1994. *Zainichi Iranjin: Keikikotaikani Okeru Seikatsu to Roudou* (Iranians in Japan: Life and Work Under Economic Depression).

Tunçer-Kılavuz, İdil. 2009. 'Political and Social Networks in Tajikistan and Uzbekistan: "Clan", Region and Beyond.' *Central Asian Survey* 28:3: 323–34.

Turaeva, Rano. 2013. 'Post-Soviet Uncertainties: Micro-Orders of Central Asian Migrants in Russia.' *Inner Asia* 15:2: 273–92.

Turaeva, Rano. 2014. 'Mobile Entrepreneurs in Post-Soviet Central Asia.' *Communist and Post-Communist Studies* 47:1: 105–14.

Turaeva, Rano. 2016. *Migration and Identity in Central Asia: The Uzbek Experience*. Routledge.

Urinboyev, Rustam. 2018. 'Migration, Transnationalism, and Social Change in Central Asia: Everyday Transnational Lives of Uzbek Migrants in Russia.' In *Eurasia on the Move. Interdisciplinary Approaches to a Dynamic Migration Region*, ed. Marlène Laruelle and Caress Schenk. The George Washington University, Central Asia Program.

CHAPTER 4

Migration, Identity and 'Sojourning' in the Life of Uzbeks in Japan

Timur Dadabaev and Mukaddam Akhmedova

Introduction

In the 30 years since its independence, Uzbekistan has become renowned for its actively migrating population. Japan is perceived both geographically and psychologically as a distant destination for travelling Uzbek youth, with cultural and linguistic differences that serve as a barrier to their penetration of Japanese society and Japan's market. However, in recent years, Japan has increasingly become a destination for such migrants in pursuit of employment, education, professional development, and a better life.

A number of studies focus on the issues of expatriates, nikkeijins (the descendants of ethnic Japanese who migrated out of Japan) (Yamanaka 1996, 1997, 2000; Tsuda 1999a, b; Knight 2002), international students' adaptation practices (Tanaka et al. 1994; Tajima 2000, 2003), and the transitional processes of international students (Bélanger et al. 2011; Wen 2017). There are also studies focusing on the experiences of migrants and

T. Dadabaev (✉) · M. Akhmedova
University of Tsukuba, Tsukuba, Japan
e-mail: dadabaev.timur.gm@u.tsukuba.ac.jp

T. Dadabaev (ed.), *The Grass is Always Greener?*, Politics and History in Central Asia,
https://doi.org/10.1007/978-981-16-2570-1_4

students from Europe and the US (Milstein 2005; Heath 2017) in Japan, 'old' migrants who arrived in Japan during its period of rapid economic growth (1955–1975) to benefit from the various niches created by such economic performance and ethnic groups such as Koreans (Yoon et al. 2013), Chinese (Liu-Farrer 2009, 2011, 2017) and others who have been historically connected to Japan by virtue of Japanese colonial history and diasporas.

However, this chapter chooses to focus on a scarcely studied new phenomenon of temporary residence, the so-called sojourning in Japan by Uzbek citizens who constitute semi-skilled, skilled, and graduate student residents and represent a group of 'newcomers' in Japan. Uzbek citizens typically travel to Japan as a part of an educational programme and then take advantage of various policies of so-called internationalization or ***kokusaika*** to integrate into the emerging multicultural (***tabunkakyousei***) Japanese society as discussed by many authors (Vosse et al. 2014, pp. 71–90).

What are the dominating narratives of these migrants in explaining their stay in Japan? How do they rationalize their present and future in Japanese society? What kind of meaning do they attribute to their temporary stay—sojourn—in Japan?

By answering these questions, the current chapter attempts to illuminate two aspects of sojourning. The first is the mobility of smaller ethnic groups in a global migration context—examining their experiences, exploring the purposes of sojourning in a host country, and understanding the transition from sojourner to settler, which remains understudied in the migration literature due to the strong focus on mass migration phenomena (permanent or semi-permanent). The second aspect is the pattern of expectations of Uzbek migrants with respect to the post-dictatorial opening of Uzbekistan, their host country, and their perception of their 'self' and 'others'.

Methodologically, this chapter builds on semi-structured interviews with 30 individuals, including students, working individuals, spouses of working individuals, retired individuals, individuals residing currently in Japan and other types of residents in Japan from Uzbekistan. The overall number of Uzbek residents (short, long and permanent) in Japan is approximately 4000 people, and the types of experiences elaborated in this chapter are largely shared by many of them.

One of the main criteria for choosing these respondents for the purposes of this chapter is the length of their stay and their occupations.

This study follows previous studies of migrants (for instance, Mizukami 2007) by relying on Japan's Ministry of Foreign Affairs for its definition of (Japanese) long-term residents: those who reside overseas for three months or more in one calendar year. Inspired by this logic, this study has chosen its respondents from among those holding extendable resident permits of more than 6 months in Japan. As a rule, in the Uzbek case, the 6-month extendable resident permits are the type most frequently granted to Japanese language school students and, in this study, represent the minimum length of stay of respondents.

In locating these individuals, the authors have utilized various tools, including online groups such as Uzbekistani in Japan on Facebook, which has the largest number of active users, as well as members of the Uzbek Society in Japan (*Yaponiyadagi O'zbek Jamiyati*). The semi-structured interviews with members were conducted in Uzbek, Russian and, on several occasions, in English. Overall, 68 individuals were contacted, and 30 agreed to be interviewed and recorded. In terms of the representation in the sample of this chapter, the respondents consisted of men and women aged 19–39 residing in Japan (see Table 4.1).[1] In terms of ethnicity, the respondents were mainly of Uzbek ethnic origin, occasionally including representatives of Tajik and mixed backgrounds, who had resided in Uzbekistan at least until graduation from high school before travelling to Japan (see Table 4.1; Fig. 4.1).

Through analysis of these interviews, the current chapter develops the following two-fold argument. First, the findings of this chapter contradict the belief that Uzbeks in Japan, similar to other migrating diasporas, seek permanent settlement or at least long-term residence (Yamanaka 2008; Oishi 2012, 2020; D'Costa 2013; Komine 2014; Holbrow and Nagayoshi 2018) or simultaneously situate themselves as residents of both home and host societies as in other cases (Urinboyev 2018). Contrary to expectation that these individuals aspire a long-term settlement in Japan (through transnational or trans-local manners as described by Schröder and Stephan-Emmrich 2016), the respondents of this study demonstrated

[1] Given that it is more challenging to anonymize identity and personal information for a small sample of respondents (Gray et al. 2007, p. 86) and to anonymise respondents from the relatively small community of Uzbekistani in Japan and the online community of Uzbekistani (Saunders et al. 2014), snowball sampling was not actively attempted to decrease 'internal' confidentiality within this community (Tolich 2004), and respondents were not aware of the authors' contacts with other respondents.

Table 4.1 Anonymized table of respondents

#	*Pseudonym*	*Age*	*Sex*	*Ethnicity*	*Place of birth*	*Marital status*	*Education*	*Visa status*	*Period of residing in Japan*
1	Sardor	26	M	Uzbek	Chust	Single	Lyceum	International student visa	5 years
2	Bekzod	32	M	Uzbek	Tashkent	Married	Master's degree	International student visa	3 years
3	Tamara	20	F	Mixed	Tashkent	Married	High school	International student visa	3 years
4	Gulnora	30	F	Uzbek	Sirdaryo	Married	Master's degree	Family sojourn	9 years
5	Zarina	32	F	Uzbek	Rishton	Married	Medical college	Spouse of a Japanese citizen	6 years
6	Diyora	24	F	Uzbek	Andijan	Single	Undergraduate degree	Working visa	4 years
7	Osiyo	31	F	Uzbek	Tashkent	Married	Undergraduate degree	Working visa	11 years
8	Anvar	36	M	Uzbek	Samarkand	Separated	PhD	Professor	7 years
9	Oybek	32	M	Uzbek	Yangiyer	Married	MA	International student visa	6 years
10	Rustam	24	M	Uzbek	Andijon	Single	Undergraduate degree	International student visa	5 years
11	Nafisa	24	F	Uzbek	Tashkent	Married	Master's degree	International student visa	6 years
12	Tahmina	33	F	Tajik	Samarkand	Single	Undergraduate degree	Investment/Management	13 years
13	Javohir	21	M	Uzbek	Namangan	Single	Lyceum	International student visa	5 months
14	Said	20	M	Uzbek	Namangan	Single	Professional college	International student visa	5 months
15	Akmal	19	M	Uzbek	Uchqo'rg'on	Single	Professional college	International student visa	5 months
16	Bilol	35	M	Uzbek	Namangan	Married	Undergraduate degree	International student visa	5 months
17	Ilmiyaxon	39	F	Uzbek	Jalolquduq	Married	Master's degree	Permanent resident	16 years

#	*Pseudonym*	*Age*	*Sex*	*Ethnicity*	*Place of birth*	*Marital status*	*Education*	*Visa status*	*Period of residing in Japan*
18	Naima	30	F	Uzbek	Tashkent	Married	Master's degree	International student visa	8 years
19	Zohid	21	M	Uzbek	Tashkent	Single	Lyceum	International student visa	1 year
20	Abdulla	36	M	Uzbek	To'raqo'rg'on	Married	Master's degree	Instructor	8 years
21	Kamola	34	F	Uzbek	To'raqo'rg'on	Married	Master's degree	Family sojourn	8 years
22	Yusuf	34	M	Uzbek	Tashkent	Married	Master's degree	Engineer/Specialist in humanities/International services'	6 months
23	Ali	36	M	Uzbek	Ohangaron	Married	PhD degree	International student visa	4 years
24	Hamida	34	F	Uzbek	Tashkent	Married	Undergraduate degree	Family sojourn	4 years
25	Ra'no	35	F	Uzbek	Andijan	Married	PhD	Spouse of permanent resident	7 years
26	Umar	24	M	Uzbek	Chortoq	Single	Undergraduate degree	International student visa	5 months
27	Feruz	29	M	Uzbek	Tashkent	Married	Master's degree	International student visa	6 years
28	Shahlo	23	F	Uzbek	Tashkent	Married	Undergraduate degree	Family sojourn	4 months
29	Shohruh	27	M	Uzbek	Andijan	Married	Master's degree	Engineer/Specialist in humanities/International services'	13 years
30	Doston	27	M	Uzbek	Samarkand	Single	Undergraduate degree	Engineer/Specialist in humanities/International services'	8 years

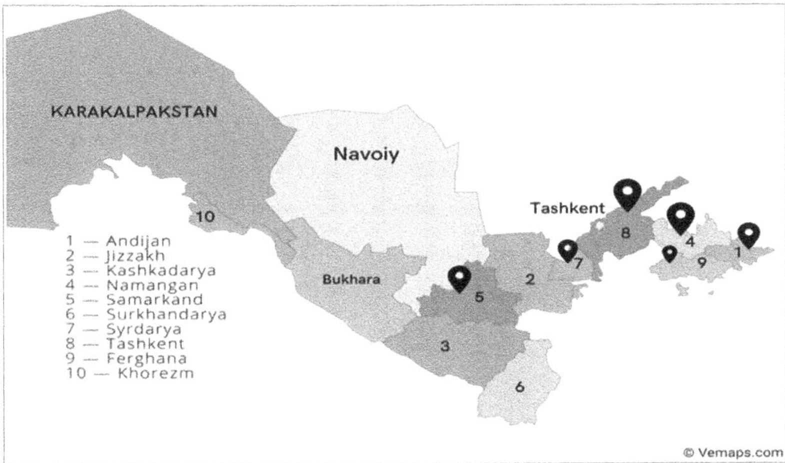

Fig. 4.1 Regions of origin of respondents in Uzbekistan (*Map source* vemaps.com. Configured and edited for research purposes)

that they treat their stay in Japan largely as temporary, in line with the concept of 'sojourning'. For the majority, if not all respondents, Japan as a migrating country was a second-choice destination, which confirms the findings of public opinion polls conducted elsewhere (Dadabaev, Sonoda and Soipov, 2021; Sonoda 2020).

Second, this chapter also argues that the concept of sojourning as articulated by the respondents of this study needs to be treated first as a constantly changing socially constructed discursive category employed by respondents to mitigate many challenges, such as economic hardship, discrimination, and cultural assimilation. Sojourning, as understood and used by these respondents, also demonstrates a pattern of departure from the conventional understanding of sojourning as employed by Mizukami. Sojourning, in the words of Uzbek migrants to Japan, is a culturally sensitive category that Uzbek migrants often adopt based on ethnic or religious interpretations of their stay in line with their being wanderers or '*musofirs*' in search of life experience, wisdom, and justice. By conceptualizing self along these lines, many come to terms with their current social status or experiences, as detailed in the sections below.

Uzbeks as New Sojourners?

It has been reported that 10% of an estimated 33 million of the Uzbekistan population work abroad (Kuchins et al. 2015, p. 3). Typical migrants from Uzbekistan, as depicted in recent studies, are mostly younger unmarried males, with a vocational educational degree that is short of a bachelor's degree, and come from a lower income family (Seitz 2019, p. 12). The largest destinations for such migrants are Russia, Kazakhstan, the UAE, Turkey and South Korea (Seitz 2019).

These patterns of migration and the movement of people from Uzbekistan and throughout the CA region have become the subject of a number of works, which have initially focused on the outbound migration of the Russian-speaking population as a result of the collapse of the Soviet Union and the migration of native CA ethnicities from CA to Russia (Korobkov 2007). Others (cf. Laruelle 2013; Bartolomeo et al. 2014) place these flows into a global framework considering the social upheavals that motivate CA people to migrate. In addition, there are also nuanced comparative studies of the motivations and experiences of migrants by comparing CA states (Kazakhstan, Tajikistan and Kyrgyzstan, in particular) with European states and highlighting not only regional but also gender-related influences (Petesch and Demarchi 2015).

Other scholars have focused on the notions of push and pull factors influencing perceptions of migrants from Uzbekistan to Russia (Bedrina and Tukhtarova 2016), outlining ethnic preferences (of non-titular ethnic groups to move from Uzbekistan to Russia, South Korea, Kazakhstan) (for instance, Kim 2014), demographic pressures (such as economic growth and lack employment), economic factors (over-supply in the workforce), ecological factors (urban–rural imbalance or environmental events such as the Aral Sea disaster as a push factor for those residing in nearby areas) and administrative factors (endemic corruption or limitations imposed on mobility through domestic residence registration or *propiska*) (for instance, see Radnitz 2006). In addition, the closed political system of the country under the rule of its first president, Islam Karimov, has served as a push factor for many in search of more transparent and merit-based societies.

This latter group of studies refers to so-called pull factors for migrants from Uzbekistan, such as administrative (absence of a visa regime between Russia and Uzbekistan), economic (higher income in the migration destination; demand for a less skilled labour force; contribution to the household, etc.) (Kakharov 2012; Hiwatari 2016; Virkkunen 2017; Seitz 2019), and socio-linguistic factors exemplified by historical ties and language fluency, the presence of the diaspora and family/regional social networks (Turaeva 2013, 2014, 2018) and the value of migration as a way to obtain new social or societal (for instance, for women, freedom from stereotypes) status. Accordingly, some migrants residing abroad use or aspire to using their social status to impact their home societies through political or economic influence or social remittance, which highlights the issue of migration from the perspective of transnationalism (Peggy 2001; Ruget and Usmanalieva 2011). The translocal connections between villages and cities further illustrate how transnational migration is facilitated and promoted by connecting the local places, villages and cities through which migrants abroad relate to their home communities (Schröder and Stephan-Emmrich 2016; Urinboyev 2018, p. 28). In addition to the above, migration can also be influenced by government facilitation of such processes through intergovernmental agreements, as seen between Uzbekistan and Russia, South Korea and Japan (also see Kim 2017).

In terms of personal motivations, contribution to one's family and the notion of 'returning home' are prominently featured in the decisions of most Uzbek migrants, as is very precisely captured by scholars supporting the narratives of transnationalism in migration (Abashin 2015; Urinboyev 2018). The importance of family ties and societal norms for typical Uzbek migrants tends to dictate the patterns of behaviour for individuals such as the only son in an Uzbek family, a father, a mother, or a son acting as a father.

While the above studies each provide important perspectives through which to understand the motivations of various groups, they do not reflect upon the subjectivity of migrants' rationalization of their stay and how they discursively mediate various pressures from their home country and in their host societies.

As outlined below, the notion and the concept of sojourning offers a possible response to the need to reflect on how migrants rationalize their self and the others and how they subjectively narrate both their own intentions and the expectations of society around them.

A bulk of the previous literature on the subject matter treats the notion of sojourning as a matter of psychological enquiry, focusing more on the notions of socio-cultural adjustment and the acculturation of migrants in foreign environments (Church 1982; Rohrlich and Martin 1991; Ward and Kennedy 1993; Hunsley et al. 2004; Pedersen et al. 2011; Wilson et al. 2017). There are also studies that relate temporary residence with identity shifts, as the environment of residence inevitably influences one's understanding of values (Sussman 2002).

The initial inquiries into sojourning (Siu 1952) referred to migrants travelling from a developing country to a developed country, primarily motivated by a search for better employment opportunities. It treats such sojourners as marginalized people with limited socio-cultural adaptation skills and linguistic ability who prefer to stick to their ethnic community outside of their professional activity.

This notion has been complemented by other studies (see, for instance, Bonacich 1973) that attempt to integrate the perceptions of both the marginalized worker and the host community to explain the behavioural patterns and motivations of certain migrant communities. They elaborate on the importance of two main categories for sojourners, which are based on the intention to return home, and the importance of the host community, which can, to a great extent, empower the sojourner.

Subsequent studies then further developed the notion of sojourning by emphasizing that there are no clear lines between sojourners and settlers. These introduced the notion of a 'permanent sojourner' (Uriely 1994), exemplifying this with the case of migrants from Israel to Chicago. The main idea behind these types of studies, which this chapter stays close to, is that sojourners do not have to be isolated or marginalized in their own community to qualify as a sojourner. In addition, the temporality of sojourning and the time frame criteria for being branded as sojourner can also be relative, according to this strand of works.

In his attempts to attribute clear definitions to various groups, Mizukami divides migrants into sojourners, settlers, consequent sojourners and consequent settlers. These categories are divided into two groups—permanent residence and non-permanent residence—taking into consideration Uriely's studies with regard to the permanence and temporality of sojourning (see Fig. 4.2).

Mizukami uses the intention to return home as one of the markers that differentiates sojourners from others (Table 4.2).

Mizukami's understanding of sojourners is informed by Uriely's typology as he makes judgements about the temporality of stay according to legal status (permanent resident/temporary resident), expressed intentions to stay and the availability of preparations to facilitate leaving. As a result, he creates nuanced categories of settlers, consequent sojourners

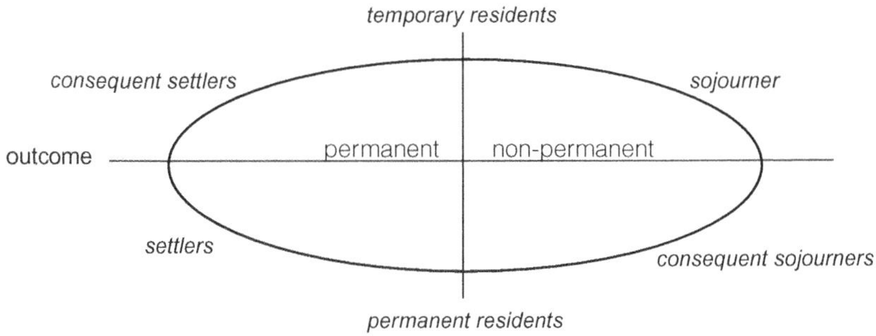

Fig. 4.2 Basic patterns of residency by Mizukami (2007)

Table 4.2 Uriely's (1994) modified typology of sojourning intentions by Mizukami (2007)

	General intentions to return to the Homeland	*Concrete plans to return to the Homeland*
Sojourner	Yes	Yes
Permanent sojourner	Yes	No
Settler	No	No
Reluctant returnee	No	Yes

(permanent residents with intentions and preparations to return), consequent settlers (sojourners who eventually stay) and sojourners (temporary residents with an intention to leave).

Despite the attempts above to clarify the notions around sojourning, the concept of sojourning remains largely blurred. There are several areas where this chapter problematizes Mizukami's framework and offers a new understanding of sojourning.

This study adapts the concept of sojourning to Uzbek migrant experiences in Japan and develops Mizukami's concept of sojourning in three ways.

First, as shown in the narratives of the interviews, many Uzbek residents in Japan do not consider their current legal status to be connected to their future. Some with relatively short-term residence permits (6 months or more) are hoping to change their legal status to a longer one, and some with long-term permits are hoping to obtain permanent residence permits. However, they do not consider longer-term permits and even naturalization to be an indication of their commitment to stay in Japan for the duration of their lifetime. Rather, they view these permits as a functional tool simplifying their stay in Japan. In this sense, they do not regard their legal status as the most determining factor in their decision to permanently settle or return home.

Second, the sojourning concept offered by Mizukami captures several groups of settlers and sojourners. However, it does not detail the role of identity in the decisions of migrants. In legal terms, Uzbek migrants treat sojourning as the first stage in permanent residence and even naturalization in Japan. In identity terms, for them, sojourning is a safeguard against encroachments on their Uzbek identity in a largely mono-ethnic Japanese environment. While many other ethnic groups in Japan complain of not being accepted as equal to their Japanese 'hosts', even after they forego the process of permanent residence and naturalization, the Uzbek respondents in almost all interviews emphasized self-Uzbek identification as a part of their sojourning experience, which for them serves as a tool for differentiating their Uzbek self from the Japanese other. While they often state that 'no foreigner, disregarding his or her legal status is going to be accepted as one of their own' by the Japanese, the Uzbek sojourners do not dramatize such treatment from the Japanese people for the following two reasons. For the Uzbek migrants, such differentiation between someone who is similar to the self and the other is neither new nor alien partly because of the multi-ethnic structure of society in Uzbekistan where people differentiate between various ethnic groups and their behaviours. Therefore, for the Uzbek migrants, it is easy to relate to such differentiation by the local Japanese because they treat the Japanese environment as 'foreign' to their Uzbek/Russian/Tatar self. In addition, they believe that their self is different and often incompatible with their host community. In this sense, the migrant community from Uzbekistan is not socially marginalized but ideationally 'barricaded'. Due to their discursive sojourning, they do not hold an expectation of acceptance by the Japanese host community nor do they display an acceptance of Japanese values as their 'own'. In this sense, Japan is perceived as a common social space for them where they interact for functional purposes (survival, making a living, receiving an education, maintaining their educational/professional status). Japanese and Uzbek identities co-exist in this space and do not conflict with each other. This social space rarely extends into their personal space, which is largely defined by the values of the Uzbek self or a hybrid of the old self and the newly acquired self.

Third, as is also discussed and pointed in the previous chapters, there is little discussion, if any, in the literature in regard to the way in which sojourning transitions from being a temporary explanation of one's stay in Japan to a permanent category of rationalization of one's lifetime in Japan. Sojourning, in the words of Uzbek migrants to Japan, is a culturally sensitive category that Uzbek migrants often adopt through ethnic attachment to Uzbekness (*O'zbekchilik*) or Islamic religious interpretations of their stay in line with their being wanderers or *musofirs* in search of life experience, wisdom, and justice. In such self-rationalizing, the sufferings encountered in the course of sojourning only enhance one's standing in the home society and increase one's social status and professional potential. As such, the concept of the return home cannot be detached from being a sojourner because it justifies the very purpose and 'sacrifices' made in the process of sojourning.

The social status at 'home' for Uzbek migrants in Japan is not defined in terms used by transnationalism (Uzbekistan as a whole) or translocalism (particular locality). Uzbek sojourners in Japan, in contrast to the depictions of transnationalism studies (Ruget and Usmanalieva 2011, p. 51), do not necessarily aspire to play any social, public or political roles at home. In addition, aside from few instances of higher skilled professionals (Radjabov 2017), social remittances expected by scholars of transnationalism (Peggy 2001) from these migrants back to Uzbekistan (if they exist) are currently difficult to define and identify. Aside from using their origin as a tool of initial information gathering about their travels to Japan and their modes of financial remittances, these migrants in Japan are not as intricately connected by the cities/localities/villages of their origin as depicted in trans-local studies on CA migrants in China, Egypt (Schröder and Stephan-Emmrich 2016, pp. 422–425) or evidenced in the case of Uzbek migration to Russia (Urinboyev 2018, p. 30). Rather, Uzbek sojourners in Japan define the importance and status of their residence in Japan in religious terms or through the eyes of their immediate family circles and immediate neighbours.

By conceptualizing the self along these lines, many come to terms with their current social status or experiences. As stated above, Uzbek sojourning in Japan does not seem to have a timeframe or limitation as described in Mizukami or a relation to legal status. Although conventionally, sojourning is defined as a temporary state of residence, for many respondents, temporality of their stay in Japan can be defined in terms of their Uzbek belonging. Thus, they see their sojourning status as long term or even lifelong, at which point the permanent return home just becomes the 'horizon' that one never reaches. On the other hand, Uzbek respondents do experience many temporary returns home, and during those returns, they become sojourners in their own country because they are always preparing to return to Japan. In this sense, Uzbek migrants are in a constant state of sojourning in both Japan and Uzbekistan, with essentially no home to return to.

Uzbeks in Japan

Out of 127 million of Japan's population, the number of foreign residents (excluding illegal immigrants and short-term visitors) holds at just 2.6 million, comprising 2% of the overall population (OECD International Migration Outlook 2019). The top three countries of origin for newcomers to Japan are China, Vietnam and the Philippines (OECD International Migration Outlook 2019). While Chinese, Iranian, Vietnamese and Brazilian migrants attempted to take advantage of the high speed economic growth in Japan to gain employment opportunities, Uzbek migrants' entry into the Japanese employment and educational market has been slow and largely after the downturn in Japan's economic growth.

Compared to the cases of the many low-skilled minority groups in Japan, Uzbek newcomers in Japan can be categorized as semi-skilled migrants as they have certain educational degrees and have completed their basic and, in many instances, higher education prior to their arrival (for details see Dadabaev, Sonoda, Soipov, 2021).

When contrasted with other CA states' citizens in Japan, those residents holding Uzbek citizenship make up the largest group among them (see Fig. 4.3).

These numbers have increased by a multiple of twenty-five since 2006, turning Uzbeks into one of the fastest growing minority groups in Japan (Serizawa 2018, p. 47). Such growth dynamics are facilitated by intense educational mobility and intergovernmental agreements on labour mobility between the two countries as well as by an increase in the number enrolling in short-term Japanese language schools in recent years. According to statistics, in terms of their gender distribution, Uzbek residents in Japan are predominantly males in the 20–40 age group (see

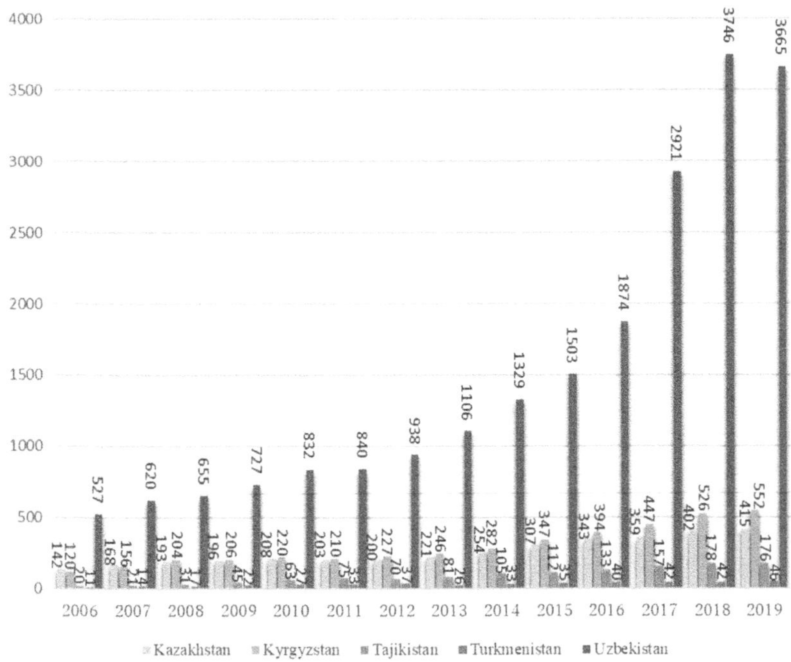

Fig. 4.3 Number of Central Asian citizens in Japan (Source : Compiled by authors using the data from 'Statistics of Foreign Residents (Formerly Registered Foreigners) (2006–2020)', Immigration Services Agency of Japan, available at:http://www.moj.go.jp/housei/toukei/toukei_ichiran_touroku.html, accessed 5 October 2021) (*Source* MOJ)

Dadabaev, Sonoda, Soipov 2021). Thus, the most mobile and the most socially active group is those in their university years and slightly beyond. The dominance of males in the group of residents in Japan also reflects a conservative trend, in that the families of male migrants are more likely to allow them to travel than the families of female students (see Fig. 4.4). This again is in line with the social roles attributed to males and females in Uzbek society as described by Abashin (2015) and others. As of 2019, women constitute 21% of total Uzbekistani residents in Japan.

However, one must also note that strong females stereotypes are changing as gender roles in Uzbek society are undergoing transformation, and these figures may change in future years.

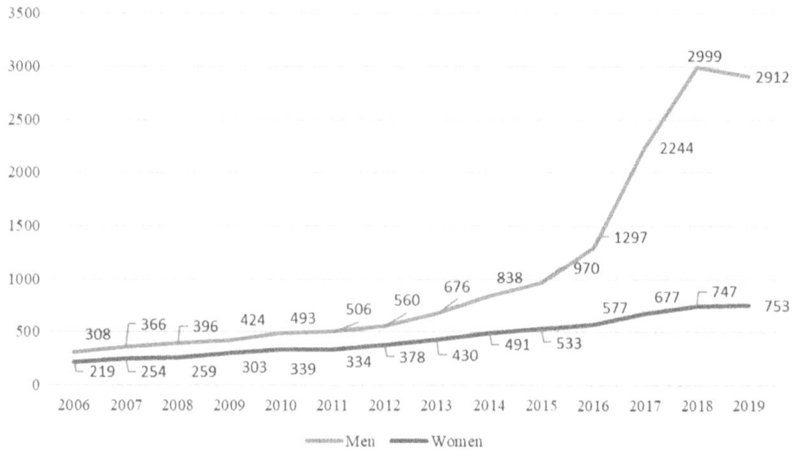

Fig. 4.4 Uzbekistani residents' gender ratio in Japan (Source : Compiled by authors using the data from 'Statistics of Foreign Residents (Formerly Registered Foreigners) (2006–2020)', Immigration Services Agency of Japan, available at:http://www.moj.go.jp/housei/toukei/toukei_ichiran_touroku.html, accessed 5 October 2021)

In relation to the legal status of residence that Mizukami uses as a marker for sojourners, the five most common legal statuses used by Uzbek citizens are 'international student' [ryūgaku], 'family residence' [kazoku taizai], 'school enrolment' [shūgaku], 'spouse of Japanese citizen' [nihonjin no haigūsha] and 'permanent resident' [eijūsha] permit holders.

In terms of the dynamics among these groups, the number of international students grew from 172 in 2009 to 2180 in 2019 while the total number of Uzbekistanis in Japan in 2019 was 3665. Permanent residents increased from 22 in 2009 to 236 in 2019. The group of 'dependents'—inclusive of spouses, children and the immediate family of temporary resident permit holders—increased from 92 in 2006 to 571 in 2019 (Fig. 4.5).

Proportionally speaking, international students (62%) comprise the largest group of Uzbek residents living in Japan, followed by dependents (16%) and specialist visa holders (13%). Permanent resident permit holders account for a fraction (7%) of Uzbek residents, with the spouse

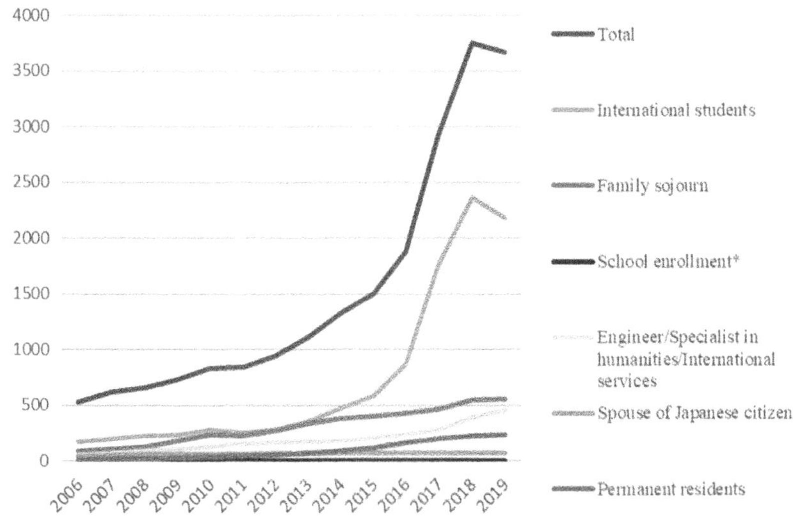

Fig. 4.5 Uzbekistani population in Japan by residence status

of Japanese national (2%) group being even smaller (Immigration Services Agency of Japan, 2020) (Fig. 4.6).

One feature of dependents is that they typically accompany the main breadwinner, whose professional occupation and affiliations in Japan are stronger. This is related to the fact that it is increasingly difficult for foreign residents of Japan to invite their family members to Japan if they do not have sufficient earnings to prove to the immigration authorities that they are capable of supporting themselves and their dependents. While the amount needed as such proof of earnings is not made official by the Ministry of Justice, information inquiries indicate the amount to be equal to 200.000 yen for main earner to be allowed to invite a spouse.

The category of 'engineer/specialist in humanities/international services' permit holders increased from 52 people to 460 over the same period. Finally, the spouse of Japanese citizen category registered an increase from 43 in 2006 to 75 in 2019, representing a rather small group in overall numbers of Uzbek nationals residing in Japan.

As these individuals differently interpret and rationalize the nature of their stay in Japan, there are four types of traits that can be traced thematically and in terms of content in these narratives. These traits

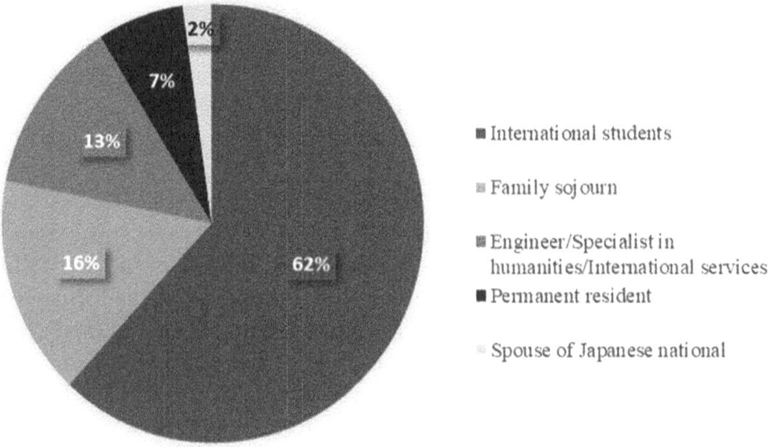

Fig. 4.6 Five largest groups of Uzbekistani residents in Japan by type of permit in 2019 (Source : Compiled by authors using the data from 'Statistics of Foreign Residents (Formerly Registered Foreigners) (2006–2020)', Immigration Services Agency of Japan, available at: http://www.moj.go.jp/housei/toukei/toukei_ichiran_touroku.html, accessed 5 October 2021)

are perceptions of the temporality of sojourning as a relative and flexible concept, the pattern of transition from a consequent settler into a sojourner, a gendered perspective on sojourning as a type of 'escape', the identity relevance of sojourning and the concept of the return home and are essential to making sense of the meaning of self in sojourning.

Temporality of Sojourning and Its Relativity

One pattern of thinking clearly expressed in the interviews is the perception that the sojourning experience for many is largely socially constructed and influenced by many factors. The intentions of respondents towards living in Japan have changed over time, and it would not be entirely appropriate to consider the length of their stay, legal status or preparations to leave as an indication of their lack of commitment to a longer stay in Japan.

In most cases, the initially planned stay period was set at approximately 5 years or more depending on the circumstance of labour. The expected length of stay to a large extent depended on the type of activity the migrant was planning to engage in, his or her marital status, the area of residence in Uzbekistan and the expectations of the remaining family members. For instance, those coming in the guise of language school students and mainly aiming to engage in work describe their expectations in the following way.

As symbolized by the following statement, the initial idea was 'I got to stay in Japan working. I wanted to work for 5–10 years at the longest, earn better money and then go to Uzbekistan' (Sardor 2018). Others initially indicated the time frame needed to repay the debts incurred for the cost of travel to Japan. As some state, they naively regarded Japan as a 'virgin land' (in comparison to Russia and other migration destinations of Uzbeks) 'having an opportunity to work with no limits to working hours and earn money quick enough to cover their debts'. Some others say that their design for the length of their stay did not necessarily have a time frame but was rather dictated by outcomes such as 'working, gaining experience, creating a network, learning a language to some extent...and then either to return to homeland, or to look for other possibilities, as there were not so many opportunities for development and for experience in my specialization in my country at that time' (Anvar 2018). Tahmina, a female respondent, looking back at her initial plans describes them as short-term plans oriented primarily towards her studies. However, her positive experiences in Japan and professional networking (not community-based networking) have shaped her decision to stay longer. As she puts it:

> I was not thinking about staying here longer or working here. I thought I would stay only one year. And living in Kobe, I really loved Japan, and people were super-friendly, curious. So, I had only good experiences the first year, and I was also searching for opportunities to build my career in Japan. [...] So, I wanted to find a job in Japanese company. (Tahmina 2018)

Even those individuals who planned for longer stays indicate that their initial plans were defined by a lack of opportunities back home (Anvar, Javohir and Ilmiyaxon, who initially planned to stay for approximately 6 years), influenced significantly after their arrival in Japan. This again contrasts with the experiences of sojourners explained by Mizukami and Uriely.

As indicated by the interview above, some of these individuals were inspired to pursue long-term careers, while individuals such as Anvar indicate that they are considering their stay in Japan to be 'transitional sojourning', implying that they do not necessarily intend to return home after their stay in Japan but perhaps will attempt to build the foundations for moving to a third country. Others have made several returns home after their study in Japan. For example, Osiyo re-entered Japan having been 'pushed' out of Uzbekistan by the lack of opportunities, the indifference of local officials to her knowledge and the bureaucracy, which literally 'depressed' her at home. Her stay in Uzbekistan was a sojourning experience of its own, as she constantly thought of returning to Japan and felt like an 'alien' in her own country. She utilized professional networks in Japan developed over the period of her stay that offered new opportunities, as exemplified below.

> When I came back for the second time, I thought about my goal: It's done, I'm in a master's programme. I will work after graduation, at least after graduating from the PhD [programme]. I will find a good job. (Osiyo 2018)

She later became a *reluctant returnee* in 2011 after the Tohoku/Great Western Japan Earthquake and consequent Fukushima nuclear incident. She again describes the features of being a sojourner in her own country by referring to being depressed and isolated, with no place for herself in Uzbekistan because of her interrupted stay in Japan. She then returned for a third time on a visitor's visa and sought job interviews.

When she looks back at her third attempt to come to Japan, she observes that she did not have any idea about the job-hunting system or job-hunting length in Japan. Her 3-month job-hunt was unsuccessful, and she returned to Uzbekistan, once again a *reluctant returnee* due to the visa regime between the two countries. She eventually received a job offer on her fifth return to Japan, but what her case demonstrates about the sojourning experiences of Uzbeks in Japan is that sojourning experience to a great extent influences one's ideas regarding home and the host society. As is the case with Osiyo, it can shift the individuals understanding of their self to the extent that they consider themselves to be sojourners both in the host country and in their home country. Their sojourning expresses itself in the conditions of their sojourn in the host country and during their return to Uzbekistan. Eventually, such individuals may transit to a third country or, as is the case with Osiyo, who choose to marry a Turkish citizen, 'stabilize' their status as sojourner in both Japan and Uzbekistan while working in Japan.

From Consequent Settler to Sojourner

Another aspect of the social construction of sojourning comes with the narratives of how Uzbek 'consequent settlers' become sojourners. This process is, to a great extent, influenced by Uzbek migrants' domestic origin, access to education prior to arrival in Japan, occupational background and pressure from families at home.

In terms of the origins of respondents, many of them, especially those coming from areas outside of the capital city of Tashkent, experienced being consequent settlers in various locations in Uzbekistan and elsewhere prior to their sojourn in Japan (Sardor, Gulnora, Diyora, Anvar, Oybek, Abdulla, Kamola, Doston).

Therefore, as seen in the interview with Said below, they consider their move to Japan to be a part of their consequent settler experience, which only later turned into sojourning. For them, the move to Japan is a continuation of the search for better opportunities, and in their case, sojourning in Japan needs to be considered along these lines. In addition, for them, resettlement in their home country or in Japan is to a great extent related to the expectations of family members, which is also in line with Abashin's findings with respect to the social roles of migrants in their home societies.

> I can't say that our family situation is bad, but it [going outside of Namangan] still needs a lot of money. Tashkent [where he initially travelled] is like Japan – it is more expensive than Namangan and the [Ferghana] valley. Everything is expensive… My cousin said, 'I'm going to Japan to study, such and such conditions, such and such is the education there'. And my father said, 'You are going to Japan to study, too.' I was surprised, to be honest. I didn't think I'd go abroad, I didn't think I'd study abroad, I didn't imagine it, to be honest. I am the youngest, second child. Maybe because I was a pampered child, it had a different effect on me. (Said 2018)

Those who used their networking opportunities to move to the capital city of Tashkent from, for instance, Samarkand, then developed ties in

Tashkent to move to Japan and moved to search for a better way to improve their skills (Anvar).

In line with this, many respondents first moved from provincial cities to Tashkent and then had the opportunity to experience living in the US, UK or Germany before arriving in Japan (Bekzod, Ilmiyaxon, Anvar, Ali, 2018). Some others looked into the US, Australia (Diyora), Canada, England and Australia (Nafisa), and Dubai (Sardor) as their choices for relocation.

> I first went to study in Dubai. In Dubai, I expected to work and study, but, firstly, tuition fees were very expensive, and then the education was not as good as I thought it would be... in my field, in law. So, in six months I both worked and studied, but I did not want to study. I withdrew from the law degree and headed to Japan.

Some respondents were influenced by friends and to a great extent mimicked their behaviour.

> The first goal of choosing Japan was... at first, I wanted to go to England or America, but when I was looking for options in Uzbekistan, my friends went abroad [and advised I'd do the same]. One or two of my classmates went to Japan and one or two to the UK. I talked to everyone. Then one of my close friends said, 'You should come to Japan.' (Rustam 2018)

Our interviews confirmed in this sense that Japan is not a primary choice as a resettlement destination, a finding that supports the conclusion of other studies (see Dadabaev, Sonoda, Soipov, 2021; Sonoda 2020).

In terms of educational background, those who focused on Japan and Japanese language during their undergraduate studies were naturally predisposed to travel to Japan for study or work as exemplified by the comments below.

> I chose the Japanese language in the beginning [because] I know a Western language—English, so, I wanted to try an Eastern language, too. But I think my scholarship played a big role, too ... I won a Monbusho [Japanese Ministry of Education (MEXT)] scholarship for the second time [as it is very rare for applicants to be awarded MEXT scholarship twice unless he/she displays particular excellence] ... I won a big scholarship, but I didn't apply anywhere else, I only applied for ascholarship here. (Gulnora 2018)

In terms of family and friends' networks, many mentioned the influence of their relatives as opposed to rational choices when making decisions to resettle. In doing so, the notion of belonging to the Uzbek group and looking out for each other in an alien environment played a certain role as indicated below. It is only later that they come to appreciate the option of settling down in Japan.

> The reason I came to Nagoya was because my parents 'friends' family lived in Nagoya, and they had their daughter there. We had attended the same school in Tashkent. So they were, like, if you come to Nagoya, we can help you and an apartment close to us, so we can help you. Helping each other isan Uzbek tradition. And then help and you a school ... That's how I ended up in Nagoya. (Tamara 2018)

Others were directly guided by relatives who had already navigated their way through the immigration system and the system of school admissions.

> My relative studied in Japan. He came to Tsukuba for a year, then he completed his master's degreeat Waseda and now works for Panasonic. He suggested I study in Japan, so I researched Japan. He directed me to the Japanese Student Centre, the Nagoya business centre, in Tashkent. So, I went there, gathered information. As I don't really like noisy places, I chose Tsukuba, not Tokyo. (Sardor 2018)

Gendered Sojourning: Escape

Another feature of sojourning that can be traced in the narratives of the informants is considering sojourning to be an escape from the problems associated with social status, imposed gender roles and the high expectations of parents.

As in the case below, traditional Uzbek values, defined through O'zbekchilik (Uzbekness), represent a set of unwritten rules and patterns of behaviour that serve as the criteria for judging 'real' Uzbek belonging as contrasted to 'nominal' belonging. These rules have a strong tendency to favour collective interests as opposed to individual interests and to voice strong support for authority, especially authority entrusted to men rather than women.

In terms of gender, these values often dictate that while girls are expected to seek certain social roles in society, their main contribution to society remains in the private domain. Therefore, the traditional expectation, which in recent years shows signs of deviation, is that girls are married relatively early (by mid-20s), and those who do not accept such expectations seek alternative paths, among which sojourning offers an escape, as exemplified in the chapter on gendered migration by Mukaddam Akhmedova in this volume.

For such individuals (see experience of Osiyo in the later chapter), Japan offers both a refuge from the pressures of the family at home and at the same time, an opportunity to prove to her parents that her choice of professional development is also a worthy option.

Tahmina, on the other hand, gave in into parental pressure and entered into an arranged marriage that ended in divorce. Divorce puts extensive pressure on females, as in many cases, they are left with no financial support, at the mercy of their parents and with few social and professional skills. The chances of re-marrying for a divorcee are not as high as those of a first marriage because the traditional male perspective of divorcees is that they have had a traumatic experience with a cause often assumed to be rooted in their 'improper' behaviour and not their husband's. Additionally, traditional Uzbek values perceive women as entitled to one husband in a lifetime, while men quite hypocritically consider themselves to be in a position to even seek a second concurrent wife if it is affordable.

Takhmina attempted to escape her post-divorce societal pressures and develop her professional skills by moving to Japan (as also detailed in the chapter on gendering migration in this volume). Although she had been exposed to the Japanese language from early childhood, as she grew up in an area visited by Japanese tourists, her unsuccessful marriage was the main reason she resettled in Japan.

A slightly different but also gendered perspective is given by Nafisa, who was a master's student at the time of the interview. Similar to Tahmina, she accommodated her parents' wish for her to get married and then persuaded her husband to seek opportunities in Japan. She also felt as if she was sojourning in her own society when she first returned from Japan after her initial period of study. She did not feel fulfilled in her own society, as her first trip to Japan had reshaped her expectations with respect to her home society, as stated below.

> When I first came here [Japan], I wanted to get a bachelor's degree, a master' degree, and build my career in Japan. But my parents wanted me to return to Uzbekistan after earning a BA degree. 'You've lived four years away from us. Now come back', they said. 'May be you will have a career in

> Uzbekistan.' I went home and got a job, but I realised that it was difficult for me to adapt to Uzbekistan after living here in Japan for four years. Then my family wanted me to get married ... I got married when I was 22 years old. Then I came to Japan with my husband ... My current goal in Japan is to get a job in a big foreign company in Japan after graduating from the master's programme and continue my career here. (Nafisa 2018)

Ilmiyaxon, by contrast, returned from Japan for the first time to stay and work in Uzbekistan, building a career there. After she returned home, she married and had a baby. She recalls her experience of trying to find a job at mayoral office in Uzbekistan after her graduation from Japanese University to no success.

> I have such [great] ideas, I have such [great] thoughts. 'If you can help me, if you can motivate me, I want to do these things, I told them [at the job fair at the city of ce in Uzbekistan] about things I wrote in my research [in Japan]. 'Yes, that's fine. Great ideas, great thoughts, we'll get back to you', they replied and nobody ever got back to me. (Ilmiyaxon 2018)

Feeling excluded from participation in Uzbek society, Ilmiyaxon moved back to Japan with her partner. She stated her relief at fulfilling the dreams of her parents for her to have a family of her own while also finding a partner who understood her desire to seek opportunities in Japan.

She sought help from her Japanese host father by first coming with a visiting visa and later switching to a specialist visa. Although her plans at the time consisted of staying for a few years until her husband graduated, she eventually stayed, received an academic position and now holds a permanent visa permit.

At the same time, she still does not consider her stay to be permanent and sees her permanent residence permit as a comfortable accommodation rather than a commitment to stay for life. She also indicated that she contemplated naturalization in Japan, but even her naturalization plans were more related to the fact that she would not have to deal with Uzbek bureaucracy and receive exit/departure permits from Uzbekistan every two years, which were applied to all citizens during the Karimov era and arbitrarily issued by security services. Therefore, her naturalization plans did not indicate a lifelong commitment to Japan, and she still hopes that one day they will return to the place where she was born and that she will be able to contribute there.

Identity and Sojourning

Despite the comfort, opportunities, and escape from pressures that Japan offers to many respondents, they consider their sojourn and eventual return to Uzbekistan or transition elsewhere to be connected and primarily a product of their identity bonds. There are two aspects that serve as markers of temporality for respondents staying in Japan. These are namely the notion of Uzbekness (O'zbekchilik) and that of being a musofir or a wanderer, which provides a religious rationalization of their stay in Japan for many respondents.

In terms of rationalizing their stay as only temporary, many respondents refer to the notion of Uzbekness (O'zbekchilik). Even those who claim that they 'don't have extra time for Uzbeks. [...] and do not live in Uzbek society...' (Nafisa), used this category of identification as a point of departure.

Therefore, those who eventually hope to return to Uzbekistan indicate that their reasons for eventual return do not lie in the area of legal constraints or professional limitations for growth in Japan. Rather, they see the limits of their stay in Japan as set by the limitations of their Uzbek identification.

This is especially true for parents with children who hope to bring them up in the Uzbek and Islamic traditions and even consider their children's marriage options from their early years.

> When I returned to Japan, I thought, 'My child is still young, my husband was studying at that time, he was studying for a master's degree. We thought that if my husband graduated, if we lived in Japan for 1-2 more years, then we would return to Uzbekistan. (Ilmiyaxon 2018)

While many consider their stay to currently be reconcilable with their identity, they feel that their desire for their children to marry an Uzbek or Muslim person and have a traditional Uzbek family may not be quite possible while living in Japan. Others state that they do not want to stand out or be considered alien and thus believe that return to the place where they grew up and 'belong' is a valid choice for their future. In stating this, respondents display a great degree of understanding of why

Japan does not offer them inclusivity, and they do not blame Japanese for differentiating between Japanese and ethnic others.

> Life in Japan is good, peaceful, safe, but as I said earlier, socialising with people is rare. We've lived with Japanese, for example, outside the campus. I know the Japanese language, I have ikkyu level [Level 1, the highest grade of the Japanese Language Proficiency Test] of proficiency, I work with Japanese people. But it's still difficult with the Japanese, somehow. In my opinion, because it is one nation [country], 97% of them are Japanese, they don't consider foreigners as their own [people].You have a good relationship with them, but you feel like a stranger. (Gulnora 2018)

As stated in the section on sojourning, for Uzbek citizens, such differentiating is not alien as they apply the same logic in Uzbekistan when differentiating between the behaviour and lifestyle patterns of various ethnic groups. They are typically very positive of the Japanese people and culture, as they enjoy their interactions with Japanese in social spaces and do not feel any sense of isolation, whatsoever. However, they also imply that they associate their self primarily with Uzbeks and do not want to assimilate with the Japanese other, as exemplified by the following narration.

Similarly, some others emphasize that, for them, co-existing in the Japanese setting is not a problem. However, the pattern of communication in Uzbekistan when one talks about his or her problems with friends and seeks advice from them is not something that is common in the Japanese community. One respondent even indicated that once she started talking about her problems, she immediately started losing Japanese friends. She indicated that in Uzbekistan, people share their problems to obtain psychological relief while in Japan people tend to share their successes with friends. Thus, for Uzbek residents in Japan, the ultimate choice is either to seek socialization through their Uzbek/Russian/other identity or maintain social ties in the international (rather than cosmopolitan) setting.

In addition to Uzbekness, there is another category that is often explicitly mentioned or at least implied by our respondents related to their religious self, which is largely Muslim. For many of the respondents, especially those who migrated to attend Japanese language schools and reside in 'communes' of 8 or more people, their current stay in Japan is connected with their learning experience, their identity as a musofir (a wanderer in alien lands) and their maturing process. Such migrant experiences bear a certain similarity to other cases of migration such as in Russia (Urinboyev 2018, p. 37). They regard their musofir lives as a test that they must complete with dignity to be rewarded later after their return home. They often speak of other countrymen who engage in 'haram' activities by 'enjoying night life' or 'exploiting the circumstances of needy countrymen by making introductions for jobs that pay money' in big Japanese cities such as Tokyo (Javohir 2018). They are also deeply religious in terms of their practices, and they maintain ties with others in Japan through social networks such as Telegram. Those who share rooms with others are happy that most of their roommates are practising Muslims as they did not engage in such 'haram' activities and were 'Allah-fearing' regularly praying people (Akmal 2018).

In many cases, these migrants come from conservative areas in Uzbekistan and were brought up in strict religious traditions. Returning to Uzbekistan for such individuals brings with it a social status based on being a person who has experienced the hardships of life abroad and who is now able to consult others. Therefore, their sojourn is not defined by time or legal status but is rather conditioned by the savings that will 'empower' them after their return and will bring the social status they seek. 'Saving' enough to start a business seems to be closely connected to the social status they will acquire after return because their economic gains will ultimately be a symbol to their community and family members that they were good musofirs who worked hard in Japan, saved their earnings and did not give in to the temptations of haram.

There is another group of respondents who do not subscribe to these sentiments and attachments with respect to ethnicity or religion. Rather, they negate such values and suggest that their sojourning in Japan is a search for a more inclusive cosmopolitan identity that is currently neither present in Japan nor offered by the notion of Uzbekness back home. This attitude can be seen both among Uzbeks who consider Uzbekness as too constraining for them and among those who are not ethnically Uzbek, such as Russians, Tatars, Jews, Koreans and so on. However, they believe that Japan also does not offer them the desired inclusivity of cultures, which serves as a ground for them to think of their future departure from Japan (see, for instance, Tahmina, who divorced her Uzbek husband, met her non-Uzbek partner and started her own business and now contemplates shuttling between Japan and Europe).

Understanding the motivations of temporary Uzbek residents of Japan along the identity dimension adds to Mizukami's concept of sojourning. As shown above, there is an obvious nexus among mobility, gender, and cultural norms and values. For those who reject the assumptions of O'zbekchilik, Japan serves as an escape while, for those who reluctantly accept them, Japan presents an opportunity to transform the notion and use only the positive aspects associated with it while ignore its constraining aspects.

Interestingly, the idea of O'zbekchilik has a counterpart in Japanese society that is referred to as Nihonjinron (or Japaneseness), which resembles O'zbekchilik in terms of the existence of unwritten rules and the necessity for 'reading between the lines' with regard to that which differentiates the Japanese way of doing things. In this sense, O'zbekchilik is also a kind of translation tool adopted by many Uzbek settlers in Japan when they attempt to come to terms with their Japanese societal environment.

Return Home

Despite such cultural differences, one aspect that is widely appreciated by the majority of respondents and to a great extent serves as a pull factor for their continuous stay in Japan is that ethnic, cultural and linguistic 'othering' in Japan does not turn into structural discrimination in terms of the associated procedures, legal treatment, access to services and bureaucracy.

> If we talk about the bureaucratic part ... It is a very effective bureaucracy. Naturally, there is no question of corruption here, which, of course, is a reason why it is comfortable to live here, especially for those who come from countries with a high level of corruption. Bureaucracy is quite effective, it takes a lot of time, for example, making enquiries, getting documents, referrals, anything, but if a person goes through all stages in an organised and consistent manner, then the bureaucracy, I would say, is quite effective. (Anvar 2018)

For many, this is one aspect that outweighs the benefits of returning home because they realize that their return to Uzbekistan would entail dealing with many issues just to achieve the level of well-being they enjoy now in Japan.

In terms of the format of the return home, the views differ significantly from one person to another, depending on the types of activities they are involved in. Interestingly, those who came under the guise of Japanese language studies mostly worked to maximize their earnings over the time of their stay in Japan to demonstrate their success upon their return home. As some of them say,

> Family members and neighbours are all watching to see what will happen to me. If I do not achieve something, they will judge that I have wasted all this time abroad and returned with nothing. I do not want to shame my parents and family, so, I should go through this with dignity and diligence and try hard. (Said 2018)

The types of preferred business ventures diverge significantly, displaying the pattern of a social remittance when respondents discuss their intentions to export the type of business they considered to be effective and successful in Japan to Uzbekistan, as exemplified by the cases below.

> I thought of my specialization in college — it was automotive industry. Uzbekistan, for example, has a joint venture with Korea – Asaka. And to make such a joint venture, even if it produces a small simple, for example, a headlight, or an engine, it will be very useful for Uzbekistan. It will be useful. We have a lot of vacant land, we could build factories in Uzbekistan and do a lot of work there, I thought. That's what I came here for. (Said 2018)

Some others state that they considered their sojourning in Japan to be intricately connected to engaging in entrepreneurial activities from the very beginning of their sojourning.

> When I arrived, my plans were to study first—for a year, go to school, then get a work visa and work in a good place. And if the work went well, I wanted to open a joint venture in Uzbekistan. That was the plan ... Initially, I wanted to reach my goals here and bring what I had achieved back to Uzbekistan. That was my goal. (Bilol 2018)

Those coming to Japan to study and later acquire jobs in academic and corporate environments emphasize the path through which they plan to join the public service. In doing so, they hope that their academic and work experiences in Japan will be appreciated. However, some of them also consider using their social connections or their parents' ties to seek opportunities. While they do appreciate the corruption-free merit-based society of Japan, they believe that Uzbekistan currently does not provide for such meritocratic professional growth, forcing them to seek other opportunities.

> I am planning to stay here only for another two to three years, and then I will use my home network to get a job [back in Uzbekistan]. I will need to save some money rst because salaries back homeare miserable … But I do have some options back home. One is to be employed by the national security services like my father, who made a career in the taxation agency. 49 He has a closefriend who promised to help me. Aside from him, we also have someone who can help me to get into the Ministry of Defence … He retires soon, in two years [so I need to return before heretires so he can still help]. (Sardor 2018)

As is seen in the testimonies above, the return home, is one of the most important categories for all the respondents in this survey. Those who experience hardships rationalize their difficulties through the return home, while those who enjoy their life in Japan consider their 'return' as an instance of differentiation between their current successful lives and the lives that would have had or the lives that they want to escape from.

Conclusion

This chapter demonstrates that the concept of sojourning as articulated by the respondents of this study must be treated first as a socially constructed and constantly changing discursive category employed by the respondents to mitigate many challenges such as economic hardships, discrimination, and cultural assimilation.

The following conclusions can be made based on the discussion of the sojourning experiences of Uzbek residents of Japan. First, as shown above, in contrast with other migrants, Uzbek residents of Japan do not necessarily seek permanent settlement in Japan. They consider their experiences in Japan to be a form of sojourning, which is defined as a way to escape from economic or gender-related pressures or seek professional development. As such, Uzbek sojourning in Japan is not framed by certain period of time or the type of residence in which one lives. Rather, it is localized through notions of identity (ethnic or religious), which either serve as the primary reason for wanting to return to Uzbekistan or are strongly rejected in search for a type of cosmopolitan society that is present in neither Uzbekistan nor Japan. In both cases, however, Japan is not considered by the respondents to be the country of their permanent stay but rather a place where they prepare for departure.

With the above rationalization, multiple instances of sojourning in Japan turn into a long-term rather than a short-term prospect. For many, especially those with permanent resident permits or who are contemplating naturalization in Japan, the temporality of their sojourn in Japan ceases to be measured in terms of time. As such, sojourning can be understood as an indefinite and everlasting process. Thus, this chapter concludes that in Uzbek migrants' rationalization of their stay, sojourning has shifted from a term defining the length and purpose of their stay to a discursive accommodating category used to suggest that whatever issues or problems they currently face are temporary and will end with the end of their sojourn in Japan.

References

Abashin, S. (2015) 'Возвращение домой: Семейные и миграционные сценарии в Узбекистане [Returning Home: Family and Migration Scenarios in Uzbekistan]', *Ab Imperio*, 3, 125–165.

Bartolomeo, A. D., Makaryan, S. & Weinar, A. (2014) *Regional Migration Report: Russia and Central Asia* (Florence, Italy, European University Institute).

Bedrina, E. B. & Tukhtarova, E. H. (2016) 'Мониторинг факторов формирования миграционных потоков из Узбекистана в Россию [Monitoring of Migration Formation Factors Flows from Uzbekistan to Russia]', *Bulletin of Ural Federal University. Series Economics and Management*, 15, 4.

Bélanger, D., Ueno, K., Hong, K. T. & Ochiai, E. (2011) 'From Foreign Trainees to Unauthorized Workers: Vietnamese Migrant Workers in Japan', *Asian and Pacific Migration Journal*, 20, 1, 31–53.

Bonacich, E. (1973) 'A Theory of Middleman Minorities', *American Sociological Review*, 38, 5, 583.

Church, A. T. (1982) 'Sojourner Adjustment', *Psychological Bulletin*, 91, 3, 540–572.

Dadabaev, T., Sonoda, S., & Soipov, J. (2021). A guest for a day? An analysis of Uzbek 'language migration' into the Japanese educational and labour markets. *Central Asian Survey, 40*(3), 438–466. https://doi.org/10.1080/02634937.2021.1942788

D'Costa, A. P. (2013) 'Positioning Indian Emigration to Japan: The Case of the IT Industry', *Migration and Development*, 2, 1, 16–36.

Gray, P. S., Williamson, J. B., Karp, D. A. & Dalphin, J. A. (2007) *The Research Imagination: An Introduction to Qualitative and Quantitative Methods* (New York, NY, Cambridge University Press).

Heath, D. (2017) *Long-Term Western Residents in Japan: Hidden Barriers to Acculturation*. Master's Thesis (Stockton, CA, University of the Pacific).

Hiwatari, M. (2016) 'Social Networks and Migration Decisions: The Influence of Peer Effects in Rural Households in Central Asia', *Journal of Comparative Economics*, 44, 4, 1115–1131.

Holbrow, H. J. & Nagayoshi, K. (2018) 'Economic Integration of Skilled Migrants in Japan: The Role of Employment Practices', *International Migration Review*, 52, 2, 458–486.

Hunsley, J., Navara, G. S. & Alles, M. (2004) 'Marital, Psychological, and Sociocultural Aspects of Sojourner Adjustment: Expanding the Field of Enquiry', *International Journal of Intercultural Relations*, 28, 2, 111–126.

Kakharov, J. (2012) 'Labor Migration from Uzbekistan', *Himalayan and Central Asian Studies*, 16, 3–4, 104.

Kim, E. V. (2017) 'Особенности процессов трудовой миграции в Центральной Азии (на примере республик Узбекистан и Казахстан) [Features of Labor Migration in Central Asia (on the Example of the Republic of Uzbekistan and the Republic of Kazakhstan)]', *Vestnik Tomskogo Gosudarstvennogo Universiteta*, 419, https://doi.org/10.17223/15617793/419/17.419.

Kim, H. H. S. (2014) 'Immigrant Network Structure and Perceived Social Capital: A Study of the Korean Ethnic Enclave in Uzbekistan', *Development and Society*, 43, 2, 351–379.

Knight, W. A. (2002) 'Conceptualizing Transnational Community Formation: Migrants, Sojourners and Diasporas in a Globalized Era', *Canadian Studies in Population*, 29, 1.

Korobkov, A. V. (2007) 'Migration Trends in Central Eurasia: Politics versus Economics', *Communist and Post-Communist Studies*, 40, 2, 169–189.

Komine, A (2014) 'When Migrants Became Denizens: Understanding Japan as a Reactive Immigration Country', *Contemporary Japan*, 26, 2, 197–222.

Kuchins, A. C., Mankoff, J., Kourmanova, A. & Backes, O. (2015) *Central Asia in a Reconnecting Eurasia: Uzbekistan's Evolving Foreign Economic and Security Interests* (Report of the CSIS Russia and Eurasia Program) (Washington, DC, Center for Strategic & International Studies).

Laruelle, M. (2013) *Migration and Social Upheaval as the Face of Globalization in Central Asia* (Boston, MA, Brill).

Liu-Farrer, G. (2009) 'Educationally Channeled International Labor Mobility: Contemporary Student Migration from China to Japan', *International Migration Review*, 43, 1, 178–204.

Liu-Farrer, G. (2011) *Labor Migration from China to Japan: International Students, Transnational Migrants* (New York, NY, Routledge).

Liu-Farrer, G. (2017) 'Immigrants in a Non-immigrant Society: Recent PhD Dissertations on Migration in Japan', *Social Science Japan Journal*, 21, 1, 117–127.

Milstein, T. (2005) 'Transformation Abroad: Sojourning and the Perceived Enhancement of Self-Efficacy', *International Journal of Intercultural Relations*, 29, 2, 217–238.

Mizukami, T. (2007) *The Sojourner Community* (Leiden, The Netherlands, Brill).

OECD International Migration Outlook (2019) 'Japan', available at: https://www.oecd-ilibrary.org/sites/e025d47d-en/index.html?itemId=/content/component/e025d47d-en.

Oishi, N. (2012) 'The Limits of Immigration Policies', *American Behavioral Scientist*, 56, 8, 1080–1100.

Oishi, N. (2020) 'Skilled or Unskilled?: The Reconfiguration of Migration Policies in Japan', *Journal of Ethnic and Migration Studies*, https://doi.org/10.1080/1369183x.2020.1731984.

Pedersen, E. R., Neighbors, C., Larimer, M. E. & Lee, C. M. (2011) 'Measuring Sojourner Adjustment among American Students Studying Abroad', *International Journal of Intercultural Relations*, 35, 6, 881–889.

Peggy, L. (2001) *The Transnational Villager* (Berkeley, CA, University of California Press).

Petesch, P. L. & Demarchi, G. (2015) *Gender, Mobility and Middle Class in Europe and Central Asia: Insights from Qualitative Research* (Washington, DC, World Bank Group).

Radjabov, B. (2017) 'Social Remittances Created by Uzbek Students Studying in Kassel, Germany and Tsukuba, Japan', *Eurasia Cultura*, 3(September), 57–88.

Radnitz, S. (2006) 'Weighing the Political and Economic Motivations for Migration in Post-Soviet Space: The Case of Uzbekistan', *Europe-Asia Studies*, 58, 5, 653–677.

Rohrlich, B. F. & Martin, J. N. (1991) 'Host Country and Reentry Adjustment of Student Sojourners', *International Journal of Intercultural Relations*, 15, 2, 163–182.

Ruget, V. & Usmanalieva, B. (2011) 'Social and Political Transnationalism Among Central Asian Migrants and Return Migrants', *Problems of PostCommunism*, 58, 6, 48–60.

Saunders, B., Kitzinger, J. & Kitzinger, C. (2014) 'Anonymising Interview Data: Challenges and Compromise in Practice', *Qualitative Research*, 15, 5, 616–632.

Schröder, P. & Stephan-Emmrich, M. (2016) 'The Institutionalization of Mobility: Well-Being and Social Hierarchies in Central Asian Translocal Livelihoods', *Mobilities*, 11, 3, 420–443.

Seitz, W. (2019) 'International Migration and Household Well-Being: Evidence from Uzbekistan. Poverty and Equity Global Practice', available at: http://documents.worldbank.org/curated/en/615721561125387061/International-Migration-and-Household-Well-Being-Evidence-from-Uzbekistan, accessed September 1, 2020.

Serizawa, K. (2018) *Konbini Gaikokujin (Foreigners of Convenience Stores)* (Tokyo, Japan, Shinchosha).

Siu, P. (1952) 'The Sojourner', *American Journal of Sociology*, 58, 1, 34–44.

Sonoda, S. (2020) 'Daigakusei Chosa kara Miete Kuru Kokumin Kanjyo (Public Sentiments as Seen in the University Students' Survey)', paper presented at the *Chugoku no ittai ichiro to Chuou Ajia shyokoku ni okeru kokumin kanjyono kosatsu kenkyukai (Seminar on BRI and Central Asian Sentiments)* (University of Tokyo).

Statistics of Foreign Residents (Formerly Registered Foreigners). (2020). *Immigration Services Agency of Japan*, http://www.moj.go.jp/housei/toukei/toukei_ichiran_touroku.html

Sussman, N. M. (2002) 'Sojourners to Another Country: The Psychological Roller-Coaster of Cultural Transitions', *Online Readings in Psychology and Culture*, 8, 1, 1–11.

Tajima, J. (2000) 'A Study of Asian Immigrants in Global City Tokyo', *Asian and Pacific Migration Journal*, 9, 3, 349–364.

Tajima, J. (2003) 'Chinese Newcomers in the Global City Tokyo: Social Networks and Settlement Tendencies', *International Journal of Japanese Sociology*, 12, 1, 68–78.

Tanaka, T., Takai, J., Kohyama, T. & Fujihara, T. (1994) 'Adjustment Patterns of International Students in Japan', *International Journal of Intercultural Relations*, 18, 1, 349–364.

Tolich, M. (2004) 'Internal Confidentiality: When Confidentiality Assurances Fail Relational Informants', *Qualitative Sociology*, 27, 1, 101–106.

Tsuda, T. (1999a) 'The Motivation to Migrate: The Ethnic and Sociocultural Constitution of the Japanese-Brazilian Return-Migration System', *Economic Development and Cultural Change*, 48, 1, 1–31.

Tsuda, T. (1999b) 'The Permanence of "Temporary" Migration: The "Structural Embeddedness" of Japanese-Brazilian Immigrant Workers in Japan', *The Journal of Asian Studies*, 58, 3, 687–722.

Turaeva, R. (2013) 'Post-Soviet Uncertainties: Micro-orders of Central Asian Migrants in Russia', *Inner ASIA*, 15, 2, 273–292.

Turaeva, R. (2014) 'Mobile Entrepreneurs in Post-Soviet Central Asia', *Communist and Post-Communist Studies*, 47, 1, 105–114.

Turaeva, R. (2018) *Migration and Identity in Central Asia: The Uzbek Experience* (New York, NY, Routledge).

Uriely, N. (1994) 'Rhetorical Ethnicity of Permanent Sojourners: The Case of Israeli Immigrants in the Chicago Area', *International Sociology*, 9, 4, 431–445.

Urinboyev, R. (2018) 'Migration, Transnationalism, and Social Change in Central Asia: Everyday Transnational Lives of Uzbek Migrants in Russia', in Marlene, L. & Caress, S. (eds) *Eurasia on the Move.Interdisciplinary Approaches to a Dynamic Migration Region* (Washington, DC, The George Washington University, Central Asia Program).

Virkkunen, J. (2017) 'Economic Aspects of Migration from Central Asia in Russia', *RUDN Journal of Economics*, 25, 1.

Vosse, W., Drifte, R. & Blechinger-Talcott, V. (2014) *Governing Insecurity in Japan* (Hoboken, NJ, Taylor and Francis).

Ward, C. & Kennedy, A. (1993) 'Where's the "Culture" in Cross-Cultural Transition?' *Journal of Cross-Cultural Psychology*, 24, 2, 221–249.

Wen, L. (2017) 'From International Students to "Permanent Sojourner"—Japanese Institute of Technology Chinese Students' Awareness of Staying in Japan', *International Information Institute (Tokyo). Information*, 20, 7A, 4949–4970.

Wilson, J., Ward, C., Fetvadjiev, V. H. & Bethel, A. (2017) 'Measuring Cultural Competencies: The Development and Validation of a Revised Measure of Sociocultural Adaptation', *Journal of Cross-Cultural Psychology*, 48, 10, 1475–1506.

Yamanaka, K. (1996) 'Return Migration of Japanese-Brazilians to Japan: The Nikkeijin as Ethnic Minority and Political Construct', *Diaspora: A Journal of Transnational Studies*, 5, 1, 65–97.

Yamanaka, K. (1997) 'Return Migration of Japanese Brazilian Women: Household Strategies and Search for the "Homeland"', *Beyond Boundaries: Selected Papers on Refugees and Immigrants. American Anthropological Association*, 5, 11–34.

Yamanaka, K. (2000). '"I Will Go Home, but When?" Labor Migration and Circular Diaspora Formation by Japanese Brazilians in Japan', in Douglass, M & Roberts, G. S. (eds.), *Japan and Global Migration: Foreign Workers and the Advent of a Multicultural Society*, pp. 123–152 (London, Routledge).

Yamanaka, K. (2008) 'Japan as a Country of Immigration: Two Decades After an Influx of Migrant Workers', *Transnational Migration In East Asia*, 77, 187–196.

Yoon I, Rha K, Kim J. (2013) 'Brain Circulation of South Korean Students in Japan and China', *Asian and Pacific Migration Journal*, 22, 4, 501–525.

CHAPTER 5

Gendered Experiences of Uzbekistani Migrants in Japan

Mukaddam Akhmedova

An individual's gender plays a considerable role in the experiences an individual has, and migration experiences are common in Uzbek society. Gendered experiences during migration are also no exception among Uzbek and Uzbekistani communities.

We will examine women's narratives of their experiences with deciding to migrate and with their practices of sojourning to and settling in Japan. The semi-structured interview questions for the project initially did not explicitly consider gender-related topics; nevertheless, the topic of gender naturally became one of the trends in the stories women shared about their lives before coming to Japan, their decision to move to Japan, and their decision to move away from Japan. Although narratives relating to gendered experiences have been continuously raised by women and women's 'proper' role has been mentioned by men, the gendered part of sojourning, caused by the cultural, ethnic, and religious objectives, has gained attention throughout the interviews. The increasing appearance of this topic within the discussion of settlement practices has broadened

M. Akhmedova (✉)
Tokyo, Japan

T. Dadabaev (ed.), *The Grass is Always Greener?*, Politics and History in Central Asia,
https://doi.org/10.1007/978-981-16-2570-1_5

the study of the orientations toward the place of residence within migration studies, which has not been analyzed before within this conceptual framework.

Gender roles and gender equality were not a topic of public discussion in Uzbekistan until the end of the 2010s, although gender within the context of Uzbekistan has been a subject of academic inquiry since the early 2000s vis-à-vis the topics of religious roles (Fathi, 2006; Peshkova 2009, 2014), national narratives and national identity (Koch 2011; Cleuziou and Direnberger 2016), roles in the economy (Bhat 2011; Turaeva 2017; Smagina 2020), sexism and gender inequality (Kane and Gorbenko 2016; Norova 2020), and migration (Kuzibaeva 2011; Piart 2013; Kayumova 2015; Nizamedinkhodjayeva et al. 2017; Jo 2018). In migration studies, while the interrelation of gender and migration has been researched in various contexts utilizing a range of concepts to analyze correlations, gender has not been revealed as a feature affecting the experiences of migrants within studies on sojourners and settlers.

Being a man or being a woman (gender is strictly limited to a binary perception in a broad discussion) in Uzbekistan requires scrupulous navigation. In the Uzbek reality, gender roles and expectations intertwined with religious and ethnic ideology are frequently attached and taught to an individual from birth. Society expects the ordinary Uzbek girl to graduate from school, enter technical college or university, get married halfway through school—between the ages of 20 and 24 (Gender Statistics of Uzbekistan 2019a)—or shortly after graduation, and give birth to a child ideally within the first year of marriage. Deviation from this route is possible but likely requires supportive and similarly minded parents in the best-case scenario and, in a more common scenario, the strong willpower and character necessary to resist conforming to the demands of society and family and endure their criticism.

The ordinary Uzbek boy is also expected to graduate from school, enter technical college or university, and graduate with a degree. Slightly different from girls, marriage follows graduation from the educational institution and/or finding a job; hence, the average age for the first marriage for men is older, at 26 (Gender Statistics of Uzbekistan 2019b). Like women, men are expected to have their first child within the first year of marriage. In addition, men are expected to be the head of household and breadwinner for their own family, including their parents and other in-laws, while women are expected to take on the roles of homemaker, mother, and wife. Mobility practices transform the roles of men and women in families, shifting the distribution of responsibilities accordingly; for example, a son may replace his father in his paternal responsibilities if the father has migrated (Abashin 2015, pp. 145–146).

The pressure to fulfill traditional gender roles is felt by everyone; however, these challenges are commonly accepted as an inevitable part of life. The strict patriarchal societal system and religious background of Uzbeks teach women to endure pressure, toxic relationships with partners and their families, and violence as a part of *sabr*, and men are taught to stay firm in all life situations without showing any indication of weakness. Traditionally, investment in the education of male children and early societal exposure are prioritized—male's upbringing includes practical training as a future head of household:

> There were two girls in the family, and on my father's side, there was only one boy—my father. And he had two sisters. My grandmother prioritised boys. After seeing that ... I think this is the biggest disadvantage of Uzbeks. Girls can achieve the same goals too. I don't know if I was trying to prove it to them, but I was trying hard. This is the first reason, the biggest [for why I am in Japan]. (Osiyo 2018)

Osiyo mentions the prioritization of male children and lack of trust placed in female children compared to that placed in male children in her family. She talks about her family and describes that this treatment is a 'disadvantage of Uzbeks.' However, at the same time, this treatment was itself her strongest motivation to fight against it and to go abroad to prove that females can also be trusted. MOJ statistics of registered Uzbekistani by sex are another indicator of the societal approach to migration (among other parts of an individual's life), with only 20% of female Uzbekistani migrants residing in Japan (MOJ 2019). There are numerous factors for such a phenomenon, including:

- The OVIR stamp. Until 2019, before the introduction of international passports in Uzbekistan, when the OVIR stamp on the passport was the only option for Uzbekistani citizens traveling abroad, Uzbekistani women had different requirements for presenting their documents to the stamp-issuing officials. The conditions included a letter of permission from their father (for a single woman) or husband (for a married woman) along with an in-person interview with a police officer and the husband or father of the woman wishing to travel. Considering these male-gatekeeping conditions in the male-centric culture, it was difficult for women to obtain consent for travel from their fathers and husbands.

- Fear of human trafficking. With the rising numbers of migrants from Uzbekistan to Russia, Kazakhstan, the UAE, Turkey, the Republic of Korea, and other countries, the number of human trafficking cases has also been rising. Additional OVIR stamp conditions were added to combat human trafficking, particularly of women for the global sex industry. Dramatic banners at OVIR offices and social advertisements on state television channels have been used to warn the population about human trafficking. Anti-human trafficking campaigns often utilize images and describe the scenarios of women who are victims of trafficking of all sorts in order to combat the issue.
- Cultural Islam and attachment to conservative traditions. In Uzbek families, sometimes on the basis of the Central Asian interpretation of Islam, the modern perception of Uzbek traditions, or a combination of both, women's status within families is established in such a way that it undermines their participation in family affairs. Thus, while their participation in family matters is broad, women's decision-making power is limited, and final rulings come from men. Women's societal participation is even more limited and is controlled by men both within and outside the family. Within the family, Uzbek women traditionally seek men's (fathers, brothers, husbands) approval before embarking on a new course of action. Outside the family, the decision-making positions in institutions of all levels are dominated by men. For example, women must pass an interview for the OVIR stamp with a male police officer, and the male head of the mahalla committee is the one who issues various certificates. While Uzbekistan is a secular country with corresponding legislation, there is often a second layer to governance—cultural judgment—that affects the legislative transparency of the services citizens have the right to access. It should also be noted that men's dominance in decision-making positions is not the only limiting factor for women's full participation in societal life—women perpetuate the effects of patriarchy and patriarchal rules by applying them to other women and themselves.

The OVIR stamp is mentioned above and in other parts of this work because this entry-exit registration system was in place in Uzbekistan until 2019, and all the respondents, who were interviewed in 2018, were affected by this system.

From the stories of female respondents, we realize that in the case of Uzbekistani migrants, gendered experiences in the homeland, which were not mentioned or simply did not come up contextually in the previous literature, affect sojourning and settling practices and decisions. Tahmina, a Tajik woman from Samarkand whose marriage was arranged, describes her initial plan in Japan:

> So, initially, after arriving in Japan following an arranged marriage, I wanted to find a job in a Japanese company. And because I was married, he didn't let me work, because of all these, you know, religious, cultural stereotypes and imposed social roles. So, I lost, like, three years ... after graduating from university. He [my husband] didn't let me work anywhere. ... Since I liked Japan, I wanted to stay in Japan longer [after divorcing my husband] and I was searching for opportunities to work. So, basically, I divorced that guy and then I started my company, the following month. (Tahmina 2018)

However, as described above, the culture of women's submissiveness held her back from her plans. We cannot generalize this story to the overall image of the institutions of marriage in Uzbekistan. However, such marriages are certainly not rare, especially in smaller towns and conservative parts of larger cities. Such a construct of marriage limits women's decision-making with regard to their migration plans, among other activities. In Tahmina's case, the limitation manifested in her inability to work after graduating from university in Uzbekistan because of her conservative and patriarchal husband. In a sense, leaving Uzbekistan has been an escape from the patriarchal culture and cultural expectations directly affecting her life (Dadabaev and Akhmedova 2022, pp. 18–21). As mentioned above, in Osiyo's family, boys were prioritized. Osiyo, conscious of this differentiated treatment, also chose to escape from the male-dominated reality to a place where she could have more freedom as a woman.

The respondents mentioned the gender-specific roles expected in Uzbek society, which affected the women's experiences in Japan:

> I went to Uzbekistan because my parents wanted me to return to Uzbekistan. The marital situation demanded, 'You're a girl, you need to get married' – that, as a girl, I should get married. The Uzbek mentality still influenced me. Having a career alone is not enough. As a woman, I have to have both family and a career. (Nafisa 2018)

More often than not, Uzbek women are advised and/or pressured to get married before continuing their migrant or immigrant moves. Marriage is perceived as the peak accomplishment in an individual's life in Uzbek society. It is, in theory, voluntary, but it is often a critical checkpoint. As women enter into marriage at an earlier age than men, matrimony is more likely to interrupt single women's sojourns.

> My parents saw the results of my efforts, and they were really supportive. But because I was a woman who was from the valley, a village, my mother was anxious about me: "Will my daughter remain single?" – We have such a thing among Uzbeks, right? My mother was worried that I'd become a spinster. But after I came back from Japan and got married a year later, my husband and I returned to Japan together. (Ilmiyaxon 2018)

Nafisa and Ilmiyaxon talk about how *o'zbekchilik* and its views on women's role affected their mobility decisions after graduating from Japanese universities. While societal views (mainly, and steadily, in the capital city) toward women and their role in the family and society are changing, part of *o'zbekchilik* still begs the question 'What would people say?' in regard to uncommon decisions made by men and women. Usually, making an obligatory marriage is seen as the mission of a successful woman and is advanced by the woman's mother or another woman in the family, as the cases above also show. While men/fathers do not take part in advancing such ideas directly, it is common for them to share this idea:

> In our country, a woman cannot go out until she is an adult. For example, she doesn't leave the house she grew up in until she gets married and becomes a part of her husband's house. But I didn't like that here they [the Japanese] live separately from parents, even when they are not adults. Honestly, I didn't like that. (Bilol 2018)

Bilol, a *musofir* in an alien land, shares his frustration about Japanese women's lifestyle in contrast to the more acceptable, controlled lifestyle of Uzbek women. It should be noted that the life Bilol imagines for women is more frequently practiced in smaller towns and villages and by traditionalist families in larger cities. Once a woman is married, one of her two main missions (the other being childbearing) is accomplished; she is free to go her way with her husband, which is the case for women above—they both moved back to Japan soon after marriage. The situation is different for divorced women—the societal perception of a divorced woman may vary from acceptance to shame depending on the location. Tahmina divorced her husband in order to have freedom to make her own choices and decisions, which initially led her to migrate to Japan.

Another scenario is presented by the case of Tamara—an Uzbekistani woman who decided to stay in Japan permanently after her heterosexual marriage with a Japanese national at 18. Her status as a spouse of a Japanese national gave her more flexibility in the bureaucratic procedures to potentially become a permanent resident in the future, and she later found another reason for not returning to Uzbekistan and staying in Japan permanently:

> Because I'm gay. I want to be free. With the way I live, I don't think I will feel free in Uzbekistan; with the way the women are treated... (Tamara 2018)

LGBTQ+ persons are challenged and discriminated against on the legal and societal levels, and this is reinforced by Islam's homophobic and transphobic views. Article 120 of the Criminal Code of the Republic of Uzbekistan considers homosexual affiliation between men a criminal offense that is punishable with up to 3 years imprisonment. Since the state offers no physical or legal protection and does not respond to the recommendations of INGOs and activists to decriminalize same-sex relations between men, lesbian, bisexual, trans*, and queer persons are influenced by such societal-level indifference. The legal insecurity of homosexual men paves the way for abuse, violence, and homicide against LGBTQ+ persons on a societal level, depriving vulnerable members of the queer community of their basic human rights. Uzbekistan's response to numerous recommendations to reconsider Article 120 has been that the 'country's religious, ethical, cultural traditions and the underpinnings of Uzbek society' (CCPR 2020) construct the unique Uzbek context; in turn, this strengthens the argument that '*O'zbekchilikka to'g'ri kelmaydi*' [It does not fit *o'zbekchilik*] and increases homophobia and transphobia.

Tamara is another example of an escaped settler; however, her case is doubly unique because she is a homosexual woman. The government's failure to protect the queer community from violence, hate speech, and hate crimes helped her decide to settle down in Japan, which does not recognize same-sex marriage but compromises same-sex partnership programs offered by cities and an absence of legal penalties for the LGBTQ+ community. At the time of the interview, Tamara was contemplating obtaining the permanent residency and later exchanging her Uzbek citizenship for Japanese citizenship, which would be possible and uncomplicated as a result of her marriage. Nevertheless, Tamara divorced her husband after coming out as a gay woman. This change has strengthened Tamara's reluctance to return to Uzbekistan, yet it has also weakened her legal chances of quickly becoming a Japanese citizen.

Uzbek migrant communities in Japan are mostly gendered—both online and offline. I will use a celebratory event to demonstrate this point—the celebration of Independence Day. Information about the event was announced at *Yaponiyadagi O'zbek Jamiyati*—the largest group of Uzbekistani on Facebook. The event took place at the Embassy of the Republic of Uzbekistan in Tokyo. I arrived at the embassy 15 minutes before the start. I entered the embassy yard, where approximately 40 people were gathered. I immediately realized I was the only woman among all the attendees (see Fig. 5.1). Many participants were members of the Yaponiyadagi O'zbek Jamiyati group, some of whom brought friends who were not members. I stood in the back of the yard to observe the event and interactions. The event started with an opening speech by the consul. Once the event started, 4–5 women came out of the embassy building. Women and men generally socialized separately throughout the event. Compared to the crowd at Nagoya community events, at the Kanto events, there was an acute difference in the number of women. This is explained by the familiarity of women in the community with the event organizers in Nagoya.

Ilmiyaxon is an event organizer and active member of the Nagoya community. She has gained the experienced and the trusted '*opa*'[1] status among local Uzbeks. Uzbeks arriving in Nagoya are commonly men from the Tashkent State University of Law, which has exchange agreements with Nagoya University and the Ministry of Justice of Uzbekistan. The

[1] In Uzbek language and culture, opa (sister) and aka (brother) are used along with a person's name to recognize that person's experience and to convey respect to the person.

Fig. 5.1 Independence Day event at the Embassy of the Republic of Uzbekistan (*Source* Author)

men bring their wives and children as dependents 5–6 months after their own arrival. These men, women, and their children are sojourners, as men's programs at Nagoya University require them to return to their jobs in Uzbekistan upon completion of the program. Ilmiyaxon discusses their interactions with the female members of the Nagoya community:

> When women come as someone's wife, they, of course, do not know the language [English or Japanese]. And then, in cases where they come with their children, it is often difficult to take them to school, kindergarten, for example, [or] to the hospital for a medical examination. Their husbands come here to study in English, so their knowledge of the Japanese language is not very good either. I try to help with things like that. I translate for them; I take them to places they need to go to. For example, there are times when many of those women can't tell certain things to their husbands. Many women come and get pregnant. In such cases, I definitely help. That's how I help women. I don't expect financial incentives for

these things. As an Uzbek who has lived here for a long time, I can advise and help. (Ilmiyaxon 2018)

Ilmiyaxon, a married woman with children, gained trust among the newcomer sojourners and in the community she built around herself throughout the years she has resided in Japan. Being older than most Uzbekistani in Japan, who are in their twenties when they arrive as students, and having long experience with residing in Japan has enhanced her reputation as a community leader and *opa* for the wives in sojourning families.

Uyat [shameful] or taboo topics (between men and women–even spouses) are approached with the help of people such as Ilmiyaxon, who assist with life situations in Japan. Another option is the Sister to Sister project, which focuses on women's empowerment through women-specific online mentorship seminars regarding the various aspects of living in Japan.

Men, as the heads of families in Uzbek households, tend to have a greater inclination to build cultural networks in Uzbekistan that expand beyond country boundaries, and this tendency is observed among men in Japan as well. Uzbek networks are created between Uzbeks residing in Japan. There are both online and offline Uzbek networks dominated by men: Online groups include the Facebook group *Yaponiyadagi O'zbek Jamiyati* and Telegram groups, and offline groups include *gap*-style[2] gatherings, football games, and meetings at one of the few masjids available.

Legally, women and men in Uzbekistan are not restricted from accessing any sphere. Furthermore, individuals are protected against sex-based discrimination. However, on the societal level, there are certain

[2] Informal meetings for socialization, which can also serve as an economic safety net. For men, *gap* gatherings traditionally took place in *choyxona*—Central Asian teahouses visited by men for *gap* and networking. Women's appearance in *choyxona* was not considered appropriate, so, women traditionally gathered at home for *gap*. Recently, *choyxona* have not been as gender restrictive, yet women still tend to gather at each other's homes and men meet at *choyxona*. Occasionally, there is a loan system for the participants of *gap*. Certain agreed-upon amounts of money are submitted by each participant to the so-called bank of the *gap* every time the group meets. The amount of principle that forms depends on the frequency of the *gap*, the number of participants, and the amount of money agreed upon for submission at every meeting. Money can be requested by any participant as emergency funds.

restrictions for men and women. Traditional notions of motherhood, children, and family are predominant in Uzbekistan, and they are at the core of social practices. However, given their excessive attention, these notions perpetuate gender stereotypes (how a man/woman should look, where they should work, how they should behave based on their gender) by creating a gender-based bias at the individual, communal, and institutional levels. For instance, (labor) migration has been considered a 'male' work, which is a gender bias, and hence, males have dominated the outflow of residents from Uzbekistan. Therefore, Japan is not an exception with regard to the disproportionate sex distribution of Uzbekistani migrants in the country.

The responses from women have demonstrated the gender bias in Uzbekistani sojourning and settling practices that affects the course of women's plans. Uzbekistan's gender-based societal expectations and legal discrimination against certain sexual orientations may serve as motivation for a woman to seek a less limited lifestyle by escaping to another country. During a sojourn, the marital plans parents put before their children may turn sojourner women into reluctant returnees, although they may return to their host country after fulfilling their parents' expectations if their partner shares their interest in migration. In the case of a gay woman, due to the vulnerable situation of the LGBTQ+ community in Uzbekistan, migration may turn into permanent settlement abroad rather than in Uzbekistan. Migrant community practices in Japan are frequently separated by sex both online (social platforms) and offline (various events), perpetuating the limits on discussing topics that are *uyat* in traditional patriarchal Uzbek society.

References

Abashin, S. (2015). Возвращение домой: Семейные и миграционные сценарии в Узбекистане [Returning home: Family and migration scenarios in Uzbekistan]. *Ab Imperio*, 3, 125–165. https://doi.org/10.1353/imp.2015.0064

Bhat, B. A. (2011). Gender earnings and poverty reduction: Post-communist Uzbekistan. *Journal of Asian and African Studies*, 46(6), 629–649. https://doi.org/10.1177/0021909611407584

CCPR. (2020, March 2–27). *Replies of Uzbekistan to the list of issues in relation to its fifth periodic report*. United Nations: International Covenant on Civil and Political Rights. https://documents-dds-ny.un.org/doc/UNDOC/GEN/G20/003/81/PDF/G2000381.pdf?OpenElement

Cleuziou, J., & Direnberger, L. (2016). Gender and nation in post-Soviet Central Asia: From national narratives to women's practices. *Nationalities Papers*, 44(2), 195–206.

Dadabaev, T. & Akhmedova, M. (2022). A home away from home: Migration identity and 'sojourning' in the life of Uzbekistanis in Japan. *Europe-Asia Studies*, 1(28). https://doi.org/10.1080/09668136.2021.2010660

Fathi, H. (2006). Gender, Islam, and social change in Uzbekistan. *Central Asian Survey*, 25(3), 303–317. https://doi.org/10.1080/02634930601022575

Gender Statistics of Uzbekistan. (2019a). *Percentage of women married at the age of 20–24, of the total number of registered marriages*. The State Committee of the Republic of Uzbekistan on Statistics: Gender Statistics of Uzbekistan. https://gender.stat.uz/en/v-group-en/958-percentage-of-women-maried-at-the-age-of-20-24-of-the-total-number-of-registered-marriages

Gender Statistics of Uzbekistan. (2019b). Средний возраст вступления в первый брак женщин и мужчин в 2019 году [*Average age at first marriage of women and men in 2019*]. The State Committee of the Republic of Uzbekistan on Statistics: Gender Statistics of Uzbekistan. https://gender.stat.uz/ru/osnovnye-pokazateli/demografiya/braki-i-razvody/1365-srednij-vozrast-vstupleniya-v-pervyj-brak-zhenshchin-i-muzhchin-v-2019-godu

Jo, M. J. (2018). The intersectionality of gender and ethnicity in (social) mobility: Migration of Koryŏ saram women from Uzbekistan to South Korea. 통일인문학, 4(1), 49–72.

Kane, D., & Gorbenko, K. (2016). Colonial legacy and gender inequality in Uzbekistan. *Current Sociology*, 64(5), 718–735. https://doi.org/10.1177/0011392115599583

Kayumova, M. (2015, March). *Emigration of "Crème de la crème" in Uzbekistan: A gender perspective*. The Central Asia Fellowship Papers. https://centralasiaprogram.org/wp-content/uploads/2015/04/CAF-papers-8-Marina-Kayumova.pdf

Koch, N. (2011). Security and gendered national identity in Uzbekistan. *Gender, Place & Culture*, 18(4), 499–518. https://doi.org/10.1080/0966369x.2011.583346

Kuzibaeva, G. (2011). Uzbek women in the global sex industry. In N. Katjasungkana & S. E. Wieringa (Eds.), *The future of Asian feminisms: Confronting fundamentalisms, conflicts and neo-liberalism* (pp. 417–435). Cambridge Scholars Publishing.

MOJ. (2019, July 11). 在留外国人統計 (旧登録外国人統計) 統計表 [*Statistics of Foreign Residents (Formerly Registered Foreigners)*]. Ministry of Justice. http://www.moj.go.jp/housei/toukei/toukei_ichiran_touroku.html

Nizamedinkhodjayeva, N., Bock, B. B., & Mollinga, P. (2017). Gender, migration and rural livelihoods in Uzbekistan in times of change. In B. B. Bock &

S. Shortall (Eds.), *Gender and rural globalization: International perspectives on gender and rural development* (pp. 34–50). CAB International.

Norova, N. (2020). Sexism in elementary EFL textbooks: Spotted in Uzbekistan. *REiLA: Journal of Research and Innovation in Language*, 2(2), 37–45.

Peshkova, S. (2009). Bringing the mosque home and talking politics: Women, domestic space, and the state in the Ferghana Valley (Uzbekistan). *Contemporary Islam*, 3(3), 251. https://doi.org/10.1007/s11562-009-0093-z

Peshkova, S. (2014). *Women, Islam, and identity: Public life in private spaces in Uzbekistan*. Syracuse University Press.

Piart, L. (2013). Transition, migration, capitalism: Female Uzbek shuttle traders in Istanbul. In *Migration and social upheaval as the face of globalization in Central Asia* (pp. 333–354). Brill.

Smagina, O. (2020). Gender and job satisfaction in higher education institution: Case study from Uzbekistan. *Journal of Eastern European and Central Asian Research (JEECAR)*, 7(2), 219–229. https://doi.org/10.15549/jeecar.v7i2.392

Turaeva, R. (2017). Gender and changing women's roles in Uzbekistan: From Soviet workers to post-Soviet entrepreneurs. In *Constructing the Uzbek state: narratives of post-Soviet years* (pp. 303–318). Lexington Books.

CHAPTER 6

The Role of *O'zbekchilik* and Islam in the Migration Practices of Uzbeks in Japan

Mukaddam Akhmedova

Introduction

This chapter discusses and demonstrates factors related to ethnicity and religion in various manifestations that affect the settlement of Uzbekistanis and other foreigners throughout their journeys and decision-making practices in the processes of migration and immigration. The scholarship on Central Asian migrants rarely takes factors regarding the subjective perception of the self through the lens of ethnic belonging and religious views within the host society into account when conceptualizing settlement practices; instead, such scholarship focuses more on the economic and political contexts of the host country that bring more or less comfort to these migrants. In the case of Uzbeks and Uzbekistanis in Japan, the grounds for decision-making are blurred, as we saw in the previous chapter regarding the temporality of Uzbekistani settlement practices; these justifications are backed up with subjective perceptions, which are elaborated on in this chapter.

M. Akhmedova (✉)
Tokyo, Japan

T. Dadabaev (ed.), *The Grass is Always Greener?*, Politics and History in Central Asia,
https://doi.org/10.1007/978-981-16-2570-1_6

As is the case with the gender, covered in the previous chapter of this volume, the focus on ethnicity or religion was not an initial goal of inquiry. However, as the interview process went further, the narratives about experiencing Japan as an *Uzbek* migrant with *Uzbek* ways kept reoccurring in various forms, such as strengthening the Uzbek identity as self-preservation in a foreign land, teaching Uzbekness to new generations born in Japan in opposition to Japaneseness, using Uzbekness as a way to ease sojourning abroad, and using Uzbekness as a measure for the immersion in and adoption of the host culture.

O`zbekchilik (Uzbekness) as Understanding of 'Self' for Uzbek Migrants

O'zbekchilik, which translates into English as 'Uzbekness,' refers to being Uzbek culturally (rather than Uzbek being an indication of ethnic belonging), while the term practically extends to a wide variety of manifestations. As a relatively new[1] phenomenon shaped in post-Soviet Uzbekistan in the 1990s, the term was a response to the desire to form a nation-state with its own national ideology after the collapse of the Soviet Union. What *o'zbekchilik* connotes at both the personal subjective level and the sociopolitical level remains contested both in academic and public discourse, while it remains widely practiced both consciously and unconsciously by Uzbekistanis both in Uzbekistan and abroad. *O'zbekchilik* was a government-run national policy under Karimov's *Milliy Istiqlol G'oyasi* [National Independence Ideology], which fostered Uzbekness as the most appealing identity; at the same time, it was discriminatory as an idea toward the non-Uzbek minorities in Uzbekistan (Hojaqizi 2008: p. 313).

O'zbekchilik, in a broad sense, is a mindset that, in turn, comprises many components. *O'zbekchilik* can be understood as a particular spirituality that is specific to Uzbeks. It is said to refer back to their cultural heritage, historical roots, and moral values (Sayidov & Umansky 1998). *O'zbekchilik* does not exist separately as an ethnicity-based national ideology; rather, it is sometimes contiguous to Islam because most Uzbekistanis identify as Muslims and observe Islamic traditions and

[1] In the cultural sense.

rituals. However, this combination is treated by the state with caution due to the securitization of Islamic practices in Uzbekistan.

O'zbekchilik consists of and is not limited to the following elements:

- Collective decision-making. Trust in community members, particularly older and more experienced members, by default is the basis for collective decision-making for life events (weddings, funerals, graduations, etc.) and consultations about everyday situations (education advice, relationship consultation, and so on) for the younger community members.
- Hierarchical structure. Younger members demonstrate obedience to the authorities, who are the older members of the community.
- Self-sustaining support system. Being born to an Uzbek family and belonging to the Uzbek ethnicity is a free ticket to growing up to the guarantee of help and support in case of hardships, including by *mahalla*,[2] by neighbors, and so on, due to the semicollectivistic traits of Uzbek society. This system is not only practiced in Uzbekistan but also surpasses the borders of the country due to migrating Uzbek individuals, families, and communities, thereby creating a support system abroad that is based on ethnicity and country identity.
- Compassion—*oqibat*. Extra care toward others, which expresses itself in an observant nature and unsolicited assistance toward everyday matters. For example, psychological compassion can be expressed through enquiring about one's mental well-being, while physical assistance can be expressed through helping share the burden of heavy bags with an acquaintance or a stranger.
- Moral police. Promotion of a set of collective rules that determine recommended behavioral and moral practices, which are directed at improving public morale and reducing criminal thinking.
- Social obligation. Owing to collective decision-making and support, the sentiment of indebtedness to the community and shame in the case of the unfulfillment of societal responsibilities is a natural consequence of *o'zbekchilik*. In an attempt to save one's pride before the community, *'Odamlar nima deydi?'* ['What will other people say?'], as asked by a family member, friend, and a neighbor, is the key question to answer making unconventional life choices.

[2] A neighborhood; a local community built on the neighborship of families as units.

- Tolerance. While Uzbeks may or may not adopt elements of other cultures, *o'zbekchilik* promotes general respect and tolerance toward other cultures. Tolerance is the keyword in this aspect because differences are tolerated by *o'zbekchilik* but are not accepted or adopted in order to preserve the unique Uzbek culture and traditions, as well as to de-escalate culture and identity-based conflicts.

In a less-abstract description, *o'zbekchilik* covers the daily practices and norms of Uzbeks. While essentially well intended, individual interpretations may surpass the personal boundaries to which the practice is directed. Utilizing the moral police element can be utilized to regulate and limit the way that people dress[3] (UzNews 2020); conduct themselves,[4] i.e., what is proper and what is not according to Uzbek morality (Gazeta.uz 2020); gender roles, i.e., what a man is to do and what a woman is to do in given situations; and other aspects. This is one way that the mostly altruistic values of *o'zbekchilik* transform into collectively accepted and advocated discriminatory practices aimed at all members of society.

O'zbekchilik might have been created to empower Uzbekistanis by creating a sense of communal unity and self-identification using unique norms and values (Dadabaev et al. 2017: pp. 20–21) for post-Soviet nation-building in the Karimov era, yet in Mirziyoyev's Uzbekistan, the concept has been gaining criticism (mainly through the use of online platforms such as Facebook and Twitter by residents of Tashkent, followed by dwellers of other large cities). The term *'ma'naviyatchilar,'* i.e., 'spiritualists,' has appeared in the public vocabulary as a reference to promoters of Uzbek cultural and spiritual norms. *Ma'naviyat* [spirituality] and *milliy g'oya* [national ideology] agendas that were fostered in the Karimov era

[3] For instance, when the 'Munosabat' TV program discussed the fashion choices of young people, a historian and celebrities brought up recent trends in hairstyles and the wearing of ripped jeans and short socks by men. The discussants concluded that these fashion trends are signs of homosexuality, and they proposed wearing proper national clothes as opposed to those exported by the West.

[4] In the same TV program, hosts and celebrities condemned ideas of feminism and feminist protests among young women, as these 'inhumane, immoral vices completely contradict the national mentality, customs and religious values.' The protest in question was about raising awareness of violence against women in response to the incident in which a 17-year-old woman was beaten up by a stranger in the street in Fergana for wearing shorts.

as a part of *o'zbekchilik* are now questioned during the Mirziyoyev era. The Mirziyoyev era is more relaxed in terms of media freedom (yet still limited and censored) (HRW 2018) and serves as a basis for individuals to be more vocal on social media platforms. A particular layer of society with specific characteristics opposes and criticizes *o'zbekchilik* and its components; this layer is usually comprised of Russian- and/or English-speaking Uzbekistanis with broader access to alternative information, which is not limited to only being produced in Uzbekistan or the Uzbek language. Some of those in smaller towns and villages who do not have access to the Internet and do not speak Russian or English are limited to the information provided in Uzbek via state-owned and censored newspapers, TV, and radio, which promote ideas of *o'zbekchilik*.

Furthermore, *o'zbekchilik* might not be practiced by non-Uzbek Uzbekistanis such as Russians, Karakalpaks, Koreans, Tajiks, Uyghurs, Kazakhs, and others. It should be noted that 'being' and 'belonging' in terms of Uzbekness are different; the former is passive, i.e., existing as is, and the latter is active, i.e., a conscious choice and the alignment to it (Hojaqizi 2008: p. 314). Therefore, views on *o'zbekchilik* in Uzbekistan differ, which consequently affects Uzbekistanis' ethnicity-based practices in Japan.

Uzbekness and Its Japanese Counterpart

In a country with contrasting (from the Uzbekistani viewpoint) culture, rituals, society, and communication such as Japan, *o'zbekchilik* may serve as a sense of belonging, i.e., the basis for one's identity in the foreign land. The use of Uzbek essentialism in Japan is even more fascinating because Japan itself has a similarly robust essentialist notion of *nihonjinron*,[5] which also uses Japanese culture, nationality, and ethnicity to create a unique sense of Japaneseness. In Japanese, this sense is expressed by using words such as *nihonrashisa*,[6] *nihonteki*,[7] *and nihon bunka*.[8] Similarly, one of *nihonjinron*'s ideas, similar to that of *o'zbekchilik*, is to minimize outside influences on culture, ethnicity, and nationality to preserve

5 日本人論—'theories/discussions about the Japanese'.

6 日本らしさ—(jap.) Japaneseness.

7 日本的—(jap.) Japanese-like, typical Japanese.

8 日本文化—(jap.) Japanese culture; Japanese civilization.

the national identity and keep this identity from being contaminated by the Other (Sugimoto 1999: p. 94). Japaneseness stems from the idea of Japan being a homogenous country and being equally (similar to Uzbekistan) discriminatory on ethnic grounds to Japan's indigenous people, the *burakumin*, the *Ainu*, the *Ryukyuan*, and *zainichi* Koreans (who do not hold Japanese citizenship). Having been created and subsequently developed for centuries, *nihonjinron* became especially active during the post-World War II period when Japan started its economic restoration; the question of the Japanese identity became acute again. Reminiscent of the Uzbek method of identity building, Japanese identity construction took place through publications and national symbols (Burgess 2004). The following summarizes the main points of *nihonjinron* ideology:

- The homogeneity of the Japanese people is what makes them unique and superior to other nations.
- Collectivistic traits in society are viewed as a better option than the individualistic values found in Western nations.
- Features of Japanese society include social obligation, indebtedness, and shame stemming from collectivism.
- Japanese society values harmony over conflict and emotion over rationality (Rear 2017: p. 6).

Specific points, such as a relatively strong collectivist approach in Uzbekistan, the notion of shame, and perceived homogeneity, coincide with *o'zbekchilik*; those similarities possibly help Uzbekistani adapt better to life in Japan compared to their Western counterparts. *O'zbekchilik* has become a translation tool used to understand the concept of Japaneseness for Uzbekistanis. The initial conditions of state policies appear to be similar; thus, from that perspective, living in Japan is nothing new and is instead seen as a change of context with a familiar sociopolitical base. Naima brings up an interesting point on this aspect as follows:

> It's not even the issue of time; it's the issue of cultural differences. The uniqueness of Japanese people, the uniqueness of their culture, is what I cannot adapt to. (Naima 2018)

From Naima's perspective, *nihonjinron* looks similar to the acceptance of yet another form of uniqueness, namely, *o'zbekchilik*, yet in another form. Naima, whose Uzbek identity is not the strongest compared to her identity as a member of the intelligentsia, accepts ***nihonjinron*** as it is without replacing it with ***o'zbekchilik*** for herself.

Uzbekistanis, who adhere to their Uzbek identity, explain their attitude toward Japanese culture and society in the following manner:

> I mean I understand Japanese culture, I respect them but I don't try to be like them. I don't adapt myself to be like Japanese. I have my identity as Uzbekistani, my identity is still Uzbekistani and I'm proud of it, you know. So, yeah, I understand them, but at the same time I don't try to be like them. I maintain my Uzbek identity. (Tahmina 2018)

In this manner, the way in which ***o'zbekchilik*** works in multiethnic Uzbekistan, i.e., keeping the Uzbek identity, practices, and lifestyle separate and unmixed with the lifestyles of other ethnic groups, is adaptable to a Japanese setting and ***nihonjinron***. ***O'zbekchilik*** works as a translation module for Japanese patterns of behavior, which become unquestionably acceptable for many. However, at the same time, as it is in Uzbekistan with cultures other than Uzbek, ***o'zbekchilik*** also works as a barrier to or a barricade against the host society (Dadabaev and Akhmedova 2022):

> Living in Uzbek society is good for me right now. For example, the lifestyle – we cook everything ourselves for now. We do not go out and eat anywhere else. We are just trying to preserve our traditions. (Bilol 2018)

Unlike previous studies of sojourners, this case is different because the Uzbek idea of the self manifests as being culturally preserving rather than an isolation tool. The Uzbekistani experience in Japan is a result of voluntary ***o'zbekchilik***, which tolerates differences, and ***nihonjinron***, which keeps away outside influences, thereby making it an interactive phenomenon and unlike the cases of sojourners who are marginalized by the host society (Siu 1952; Bonacic 1973). The preservation of Uzbek practices serves as a safe sojourn, and such practices occur among those who came to exceptionally sojourn in Japan.

Sojourning as a Religious Practice

Uzbeks, in particular Japanese language students such as Bilol, who strongly associate with their ethnic (Uzbek) and religious (Muslim) identity, practice 'ways of belonging' (Hojaqizi 2008) by creating agencies and practices that produce a safe space for them in the Japanese setting, which are discussed below.

Historically according to the Islamic concept of migration, Islamic migration is divided by territories as follows: *dar al-Islam*, land under Muslim control; *dar al-Harb*, land of war, which will pass to Muslim control and doubles as *dar al-Kufr*, land of infidelity. Here, *dar al-Islam* is considered a homeland for Muslims; therefore, technically, it does not necessarily undermine the concept of a sojourn country. *Dar al-Islam* is a country in which every Muslim is a part of the *ummah*,[9] regardless of their ethnicity, nationality, etc. *Dar al-Harb*, however, is controversial and contested. Sojourning in *dar al-Harb* is acceptable by a stream of Muslim jurists if one can practice Islam while one is sojourning there. On the other hand, other Muslim jurists do not approve of sojourning in *dar al-Harb*, as it is a land of *kufras*—the infidels, and they recommend immigration to *dar al-Islam* at the earliest possibility (Sami 1996, pp. 39–44).

In present-day Uzbekistan, the concept of *musofir*—a wanderer, a sojourner—is based on the Muslim concept of migration. The *musofir*, usually a man, goes through hardships in the alien land and returns mature and more experienced, which then affects his social status:

> I feel that my experience in Japan is greatly enriching. Uzbeks have a saying, 'Without being a musofir, one does not become a Muslim' [that is, without experiencing difficulties, one does not appreciate the faith]. I am learning valuable life lessons here. Life is very disciplined here, even in comparison to other countries, and such lifestyle disciplines me so much [by requiring me to be punctual, precise and responsible]. (Javohir 2018)

The notions of *musofirchilik* and religiosity are articulated by the experiences of a group of Japanese language school students. For this group, the sacrifices made for a trip to Japan as a part of their *musofir* hardships started before they arrived in Japan. These students primarily chose Japan as their destination for labor migration; Japanese studies are an instrumental task in increasing employment chances. Before going to Japan, the students studied Japanese for 2–3 months at their local Japanese language center. After passing an exam at the local Japanese center, the center arranged the students' enrollment in Japanese schools in Japan.

[9] Islamic nation.

Most of the respondents did not have the financial solvency to pay for one-way tickets, apartment deposits, and language school fees, or any of the other initial expenses in Japan; therefore, the local language center offered loans for those in need. The students agreed to take out a significant amount loan from these centers because their local center, along with many others, provided misleading information about the prospects of remunerations for part-time work in Japan.

Thus, these students arrived in Japan with a great deal of debt, only to determine the reality of lower pay, higher expectations from part-time workers in terms of Japanese language knowledge, and the limited working hours for students, which enhanced their idea of being tested for their faith—a *musofir* religious notion. The Uzbek saying, 'Without being a *musofir*, one does not become a Muslim' was what everyone in the group of Japanese language students implied. ***Musofirchilik*** is a sojourn that is viewed as a 'test that one must complete with dignity to be rewarded later after their return home' (Dadabaev and Akhmedova 2022, p. 23). *Musofirchilik* specifically regained its Islamic meaning after Uzbekistan's independence for many reasons, one of which was mass labor migration to Russia. Such migration, which did not sustain mass characteristics, became a common phenomenon in many households that strove to maintain their basic needs (Urinboyev 2017, p. 121). As a concept stemming from Islam, *musofirchilik* brings religious aspects to one's sojourning experience:

> In the beginning, when we had just arrived here, I was curious and took a tour of everybody's room. I couldn't help but notice the praying mats in all the rooms. It comes out, 95% of us pray *namaz*.[10] When I saw that, I was amazed and overjoyed. I pray *namaz* myself. (Javohir 2018)

As Japan is not *dar al-Islam*, *musofirs* seek common religious grounds. In the example of Javohir, the indicator for religiousness is a praying mat, which creates a sense of community, i.e., *ummah*, to overcome hardships together. The notion of patience during difficulties related

[10] Daily obligatory standardized prayers in Islam. *Namaz* is the Persian word used in non-Arab countries.

to *musofirchilik*—*sabr*[11]—is another element used in portraying the experience of *musofirchilik*:

> It is also mentioned in Islam: 'Humans are intolerant, but he will get used to it. After a little *sabr*, they get used to it. They get used to everything. (Said 2018)

These characteristics are a few of several that make up a *musofir*. After a sojourn is completed, the experience is gained, and once the *musofir* returns to the homeland, they acquire the social status of someone who has seen/experienced *musofirchilik* [*musofirchilikni ko'rgan odam*], i.e., one who is much wiser but, thanks to *sabr* and a strong character, is now back to serve his or her family and homeland with a renewed vigor.

In Japan, a *musofir* is cautious of surroundings, similar to a Muslim sojourner in *dar al-Harb* and *dar al-Kufr:*

> Then, we realized that it was tough to adapt—now, for the Muslim people—to the environment here. We have never had a separate shop or a *halal*[12] shop for Muslims in Uzbekistan. Because everything is *halal*, everything can be eaten in Uzbekistan. If you do not see pork in some shops from time to time, you will not see it anywhere else, even that you can find in some regional centers. This is not the case in remote areas. Here, however, [*haram*[13] ingredients] are added even to the water. May God forgive us for these sins. We did not know that. (Bilol 2018)

Bilol mentions the difficulties related to adapting to the Japanese environment for practicing Muslims. The Japanese language level is elementary (greetings and elementary daily conversations for a part-time job at a (food) packing factory) among the Japanese language students. They mention struggling to understand the ingredients of consumer products in their efforts to avoid *haram* consumption. Nevertheless, *haram* does not only appear in narratives in terms of food consumption:

[11] Spiritual concept in Islam that refers to undermining patience, perseverance, endurance in challenging situations and outcomes.

[12] Acceptable in Islamic law.

[13] Forbidden by Islamic law.

> I'm glad I got to be among these guys. God forbad these guys from going astray—they are all on the right path. For example, I saw guys in Tokyo eating *haram*, doing *shōkai* [paid job introductions], feeding off of somebody else's money... that is not *halal*. Our guys are not involved in *haram* work. They earn in a *halal* way and send *halal* money home. (Javohir 2018)

Javohir evaluates his surroundings and community of choice based on *halal* behaviors and deeds. As stated above, he prefers a community of practicing Muslims. Doing paid introductions for jobs, which is a common practice in Japan, is evaluated and rationalized from the religious and *o'zbekchilik* perspectives, where a Muslim and a fellow Uzbek compatriot in need are supported and helped based on their communal and ethnic belonging.

While the Japanese language school students create practices (e.g., praying) and agencies (opposing the idea of *shōkai* jobs) that adhere to the 'way of belonging,' Tahmina, Naima, and others who perceive their Uzbek identity as not being paramount to approaches to the 'way of being' manage to fit into Japanese society without bracing themselves with an Uzbek identity, as it is not the most vital identifying point for them. In this way, they do not feel the need to create a particular Uzbek environment around themselves.

Respondents also pointed out other concerns such as *oqibat*, which helped to identify a clearer picture of *o'zbekchilik* and related perceptions of the Japanese environment:

> I think for children's upbringing, it's good to add a little bit of our *o'zbekchilik*. Respect for parents, respect for siblings... for example, in Japanese families, children seem to be strangers to each other. When I visit many places myself, they do not talk, and they do not get along well during dinners, they do not open the doors of their rooms... I wish they would feel for each other. (Zarina 2018)

Especially through parenthood-based opinions and perceptions, it becomes clear that Uzbekistanis' issues regarding Japanese (the Other) culture do not center around being an element of social isolation. Rather, *o'zbekchilik* and *o'zbekchilik*-fueled mobility practices are focused on ideational blockades of similar practices of Japaneseness compared to their own Uzbekness:

> Because my eldest son is growing up, he should go there [Uzbekistan], go to school, and get used to it – this is my plan. There are good private schools in Uzbekistan, too. If you get your child to go to a private school and get him extra tutoring, you can manage his studies. I want my child to grow up as an Uzbek among Uzbeks. Even though we are working on it [Uzbekness] with my husband now, the Japanese environment influences our child's thinking. This is not a bad thing, but it will be difficult for him to live in Uzbekistan with this [upbringing]. (Kamola 2018)

Kamola demonstrates once again that there is no hostility or avoidance of the Japanese lifestyle and culture. It is a similar situation for her as if her kids went to a Russian school or kindergarten in Uzbekistan; someone with *o'zbekchilik* sentiments would usually perceive this situation in a similar way. Unlike Mizukami's (2007) Japanese sojourners, in this case, Kamola and Zarina do not have a Uzbek community to help expose their children to *o'zbekchilik* and the Uzbek culture in Japan outside of their houses. Parents with weaker Uzbekness associations, such as Naima, find Uzbek communities and gatherings in Tokyo for language purposes. Naima (2018) pointed out that she joins women's gatherings in Tokyo to have her child exposed to the Uzbek and Russian languages so that her child can relate to their parents' cultural background.

Conclusion

This chapter demonstrates that the respondents' rationalization of their experiences and their plans toward residence in Japan and Japanese society correlates with the notion of *o'zbekchilik*. *O'zbekchilik* serves as an instrument by which to understand Japanese society and, at the same time, as a tool to measure if it is time for parents with Japan-born children who lack cultural exposure to leave Japan. Along with ethnic interpretations, the experiences of a group of Japanese language school students from a religiously conservative part of Uzbekistan have demonstrated the religious dimensions of the concept of sojourning. Sojourning is rationalized by *o'zbekchilik* norms in the case of practicing Muslims and is a learning experience that enriches the lives of Muslims and raises individuals' social status due to their overcoming of hardships in alien lands. Since Islamic laws and concepts regulate religious sojourning, it is a challenging test. Surviving the process grants the individual respect in society by his or her return and spiritually, with Allah's blessing.

References

Bonacich, E. (1973). A Theory of Middleman Minorities. *American Sociological Review, 38*(5), 583–594. https://doi.org/10.2307/2094409.

Burgess, C. (2004). Maintaining Identities: Discourses of Homogeneity in a Rapidly Globalizing Japan. *Electronic Journal of Contemporary Japanese Studies,* 4(1). http://www.japanesestudies.org.uk/articles/Burgess.html?pagewanted=all.

Dadabaev, T., & Akhmedova, M. (2022). A home away from home: Migration identity and 'sojourning' in the life of Uzbekistanis in Japan. *Europe-Asia Studies*, 1–28. https://doi.org/10.1080/09668136.2021.2010660.

Dadabaev, T., Ismailov, M., & Tsujinaka, Y. (2017). *Social Capital Construction and Governance in Central Asia: Communities and NGOs in Post-Soviet Uzbekistan*. Tsukuba, Japan: Palgrave Macmillan.

Gazeta.uz. (2020, August 27). На ТВ раскритиковали молодежь за «подражание Западу» [Young people were criticized on TV for "imitating the West"]. *Gazeta.uz* https://www.gazeta.uz/ru/2020/08/27/munosabat/.

HRW. (2018). "You Can't See Them, But They're Always There": Censorship and Freedom of the Media in Uzbekistan. *Human Rights Watch*. https://www.hrw.org/report/2018/03/29/you-cant-see-them-theyre-always-there/censorship-and-freedom-media-uzbekistan.

Mizukami, T. (2007). *The sojourner community*. Leiden: Brill.

Hojaqizi, G. (2008). Citizenship and Ethnicity: Old Propiska and New Citizenship in Post-Soviet Uzbekistan. *Inner Asia, 10*(2), 305–322. http://www.jstor.org/stable/23615099.

Rear, D. (2017). A Critical Analysis of Japanese Identity Discourse: Alternatives to the Hegemony of Nihonjinron. *Asian Studies: Journal of Critical Perspectives on Asia, 53*(2). https://asj.upd.edu.ph/mediabox/archive/ASJ_53_2_2017/Critical_Analysis_Japanese_Identity_Discourse_Alternatives_Nihonjinron_Rear.pdf.

Sami, A. (1996). The Islamic Conception of Migration. *The International Migration Review, 30*(1), 37–57. https://doi.org/10.2307/2547457.

Sayidov, A., & Umansky, Y. (1998). The Factor of Polyethnicity in Uzbekistan, Security Challenges, Human Rights and Development Potential. *Medzinárodné Otázky, 7*(3), 50–71. http://www.jstor.org/stable/44961046.

Siu, P. (1952). The Sojourner. *American Journal of Sociology, 58*(1), 34–44. https://doi.org/10.1086/221070.

Sugimoto, Y. (1999). Making Sense of Nihonjinron. *Thesis Eleven, 57(1), 81–96.* https://doi.org/10.1177/0725513699057000007.

Urinboyev, R. (2017). Establishing an "Uzbek Mahalla" via smartphones and social media: Everyday transnational lives of Uzbek labor migrants in Russia. In Laruelle, M. (ed.), *Constructing the Uzbek state: Narratives of post-Soviet years* (pp. 119–148). Boulder, CO: Lexington Books.

UzNews. (2020, August 27). Эксперты на узбекском ТВ назвали ношение коротких носков признаком гомосексуализма - видео [Experts on Uzbek TV call wearing short socks a sign of homosexuality]. *UzNews*. https://uznews.uz/ru/article/23956.

CHAPTER 7

Choice of Japanese Language Schools

Jasur Soipov

One of the more salient elements of inbound immigration and student mobility in Japan in recent years has been a shift from the educated elite to the middle class. The difficulties that some countries are having in keeping up with educational demand have turned into a gain for Japan as an increased number of students of varying stripes has chosen the country as the destination for their studies. Rather than going directly from the institutions in their home country into the various institutions of higher learning in Japan, recent student migrants to Japan head to Japanese language institutions or specialized training colleges (Kuroda et al. 2018). Among these students, cost is an increasingly challenging factor, with, in one case, slightly more than 70% of students indicating that the cost of living in Japan was a challenge for them. This means that these students, despite having to work part-time, are also dependent to some extent on their families. As Kuroda et al. (2018) highlight, "On average, privately financed international students reported receiving 57% of their monthly expenses from remittances by family members, 55% from part-time work, and 22% from scholarships" (p. 25). While there are scholarships for students studying in Japanese language schools and other

J. Soipov (✉)
Tsukuba, Japan

T. Dadabaev (ed.), *The Grass is Always Greener?*, Politics and History in Central Asia,
https://doi.org/10.1007/978-981-16-2570-1_7

specialized institutions, these are far less than those that are available to students studying in the higher levels of a university.

General Student Mobility in and Around Japan

Chinese students form a large proportion of the student population in countries such as the United Kingdom, the United States, Canada, and Australia. However, even as Chinese students have spread around the world to study, students from a wide variety of countries have also made their way into China to fulfill their educational dreams. In 2001, approximately 75% of students studying in China were from other parts of Asia; by 2016, that number was 60%, but approximately 16% of students came from Europe, another 13% from the Americas, and approximately 8% from Africa (Kuroda et al. 2018). The vast majority of Asian students who choose China as a study destination come from South Korea, which has itself become a popular destination for others. As Kuroda et al. (2018) report, "In 1999, 2,869 students studied abroad in South Korea, with 2,318 from Asia (81%). By 2015, the number of international students studying in South Korea had increased nineteen-fold to 54,540, including 49,230 from Asia (90%)" (p. 17). In an interesting reversal, the vast majority of foreign students in South Korea come from China, followed by students from Japan, the USA, and Southeast Asia.

ASEAN countries have also seen an increase in the number of incoming students. In 1999, there were approximately 9,500 foreign students in the region; by 2015, this figure had grown to almost 64,000 (Kuroda et al. 2018), with the top destinations being Malaysia and Thailand.

In recent years, it seems that student mobility trends, while increasing around the world, have also become prevalent in Asia. A large part of the mobility within Asia is internal; that is, it is "intraregional mobility" (Kuroda et al. 2018, p. 4). Japan and China, as the two economic powerhouses in Asia, have held a certain attraction for students who want to be exposed to the technological and cultural amenities of these two powerful nations. However, interestingly, student mobility in the twenty-first century has not been the province of these two key players only. Rather, countries such as South Korea, Malaysia, and Singapore have also had significant influxes of students from around Asia and indeed from other parts of the world. However, mobility has not been one-sided; between 1986 and 2016, outbound mobility has also increased substantially (Kuroda et al. 2018). In terms of driving forces, Kuroda et al.

(2018) suggest that one of the key factors relates to needs that may not be met locally or domestically.

Going back a few decades to study student mobility trends in Japan, Guruz (2011) reports that there were 2,159 foreign students in Japan in 1950, but by 1985, this figure had grown to 15,009. Then, by 2000, foreign student enrollment in Japan stood at 64,011, a number that did not meet the target that the government had set in 1983, which was to have as many as 100,000 foreign students in the country. The number 100,000, however, was surpassed in 2003, as the figure recorded in was 117,302 and was 123,829 in 2008 (Guruz 2011, p. 268). A further breakdown shows that in 1983, those on Japanese government scholarships composed 20% of the student population, while 74% were financing themselves, and 6% had the support of their home country's government (Guruz 2011). The Japanese government, realizing the paucity of students coming to Japan from less developed countries, made the decision to increase support for students from such backgrounds. Using 2008 figures, 73.3% of the 123,892 foreign students in the country were studying in private institutions, whereas 24.6% were in national institutions and 2.1% were in local establishments (Guruz 2011).

The above figures belie the oft-stated notion that Japan, as well as South Korea, has been reluctant to encourage an influx of migrants (Vargas-Lundius et al. 2008, p. 29), apparently because of a fear "of loss of ethnic homogeneity through immigration" (Castles et al. 2014, p. 3). Successive Japanese governments have balked at admitting refugees or foreign workers with the exception of those who fell into the category of "highly skilled professionals" (Akashi 2014, p. 175). It seems that Japan has been partial to an educated group that supposedly could make important contributions to the country. However, over time, it seems that the country has realized that it is not only the highly educated who can benefit a nation. After all, it takes people from many different backgrounds and with different skillsets to ensure that every part of society is functioning as a part of the whole. Additionally, it does not hurt that people who might have come into the country with a low level of education are able to avail themselves of Japanese education and to learn to fit into society.

Delving deeper, Kuroda et al. (2018) note that as far back as 1978, there was a record of 1,132 international students studying in Japan from backgrounds that included approximately 30% from North America and single-digit %ages from Central and South America, Europe, the Middle

East and Near East Asia, and Africa. By contrast, almost 60% of those students came from other parts of Asia. This situation has not changed. Rather, it has held steady, with the majority of Asian students in Japan being of Chinese and South Korean extraction.

Before 2011, the Japanese government distinguished between "college students" and "pre-college students", both of whom received student visas. Since 2011, however, there has been one category for "college students" qualifying for a student visa. There are indications that, at least since 2010, an increasing number of people have made the decision to study in Japan on a short-term basis, meaning six months or less, and this decision has been made at both the undergraduate and graduate levels (Kuroda et al. 2018).

One group from Central Asia that has found a haven of sorts in Japan is the Tajikistani, some of whom have traveled to Japan for educational purposes. Since the country's independence, Tajikistan has sought opportunities to expand education for its youth. One group of students came to Japan through the efforts of various governmental departments in their home country, while others came through Japanese government scholarships (Sodatsayrova and Waljee 2017). Among the reasons, some of the students cited for choosing Japan were the need to enter a university ranked higher than their homegrown institutions, the need to learn at a deeper level, and professional growth (Sodatsayrova and Waljee 2017).

Japanese Support of Uzbekistani Education Efforts

At the governmental level, Japan has been making efforts to support the education of Uzbekistani students in order to help the country develop much-needed skills, including management. As reported by BBC Monitoring Central Asia on July 5, 2003, the government of Japan had provided 58 million yen "to organize Uzbek students' studies in Japan" for fiscal year 2003. Furthermore, in 2007, Japan allocated 307 million yen to Uzbek students studying in Japan (Japan to allocate nearly 3 m dollars to Uzbek students). While this is very hopeful news, the details on exactly what these students studied in Japan and whether they returned to Uzbekistan or remained in Japan are scant. One assumes that such government support would be going to education at the highest levels, but it would be useful to have a more detailed breakdown of what the funds were for and whom they supported. In recent years, however, when Uzbekistani students have been in the news, it has not always been because of their stellar educational output in Japan, though there are bound to be some who have been successful. The Japanese government has created a whitelist of countries whose nationals are largely compliant with Japan's immigration laws. As Nikkei Asian Review reports, "According to a 2018 survey by the Japan Student Services Organization, foreign students in Japan included approximately 6,200 from Indonesia, 2,300 from the Philippines, and 2,100 from Uzbekistan, all of which are not included in the whitelist." As of February 11, 2020, Uzbekistan was listed as one of 80 countries that are "subject to the immigration agency's tougher screening process for foreign students" (Japan intensifies crackdown on student visa over stayers).

Facilitators of Student Mobility from Uzbekistan to Japan: Agencies and Networking

Once prospective students have determined that Japan has the conditions that they are attracted to, including ease of obtaining a visa, safety, and a high level of civilization and sophistication in the country, it becomes apparent through their conversations with those who have had the benefit of living in Japan that the fastest way to turn their dreams of attaining an education outside of Uzbekistan and making some money in the process is not just by coming to Japan but by coming through a Japanese language school. For this, there is a great deal of help available.

Potential students traveling abroad have the choice of receiving this assistance either at the point of deciding to go abroad or during the process of making the necessary preparations for their travel. In fact, "evidence from the research indicated that prospective international students actively sought information and advice from those around them when they were considering study overseas" (Beech 2015). Within the interview process, interviewees shared their opinions regarding the authority held by each member of their social network (Fawcett 1989). The survey and semi-structured data analyses also confirmed these opinions and suggested that networking had a significant influence on Uzbekistani students choosing Japan. The data analysis also shows that Uzbekistani students who participated in the research study were not only informed about Japan and Japanese educational institutions by their friends, family members, relatives, etc., but were also were assisted with the preparation of their documents before coming to Japan. According to Fig. 7.2, out of 77 participants, 27 received assistance Developmental goals assistance from their relatives, friends, and other close acquaintances in preparing their documents before coming to Japan (see Fig. 7.2). It is worth noting that most Uzbek students have access to indirect sources of information about studying abroad if such is needed. It is slightly strange to state that they trust such forms of information without hesitation. Semi-structured interviews with respondents who agreed to do interviews reveal the extent to which they received assistance from friends, relatives, and their other close acquaintances while filling out the documentation required by Japanese educational institutions before coming to Japan. For example, Farhod—an academic lyceum graduate from Samarqand, Uzbekistan, who arrived in Japan in 2015—was interviewed, and he talked about the ways through which he gained information about traveling to Japan:

> …My friends who are one year older than me and my neighbor's uncle who has been in Japan for many years helped their nephew go to Japan. A year later, I met him and asked if I could go to Japan too. He gave me the necessary information, and consequently, I applied to study in Japan. (Farhod 2019)

Mahmud, who is from the Namangan region, Uzbekistan, arrived in Japan in 2018. Speaking about the ways he obtained information about studying abroad, he shared the following:

> As I told you, my cousin lives here. Before I came, he described and explained. Everything in the smallest detail. That's why I came to Japan to prepare myself. I knew a lot in advance. I was ready for it in advance, and I didn't have a hard time because I have a relative here. (Mahmud 2019)

The data analysis that followed the interviews reveals the fact that personal networks such as family members, relatives, and neighbors play an important role in shaping the decision of an individual in regard to studying abroad. A good example is Hasanboy from the Sirdarya region of Uzbekistan. He has greatly influenced other people who have wanted to study in Japan.

> I can say that I have motivated many people: my brother has already started to act. My relatives, especially my cousin, are also on the move. (Hasanboy 2019)

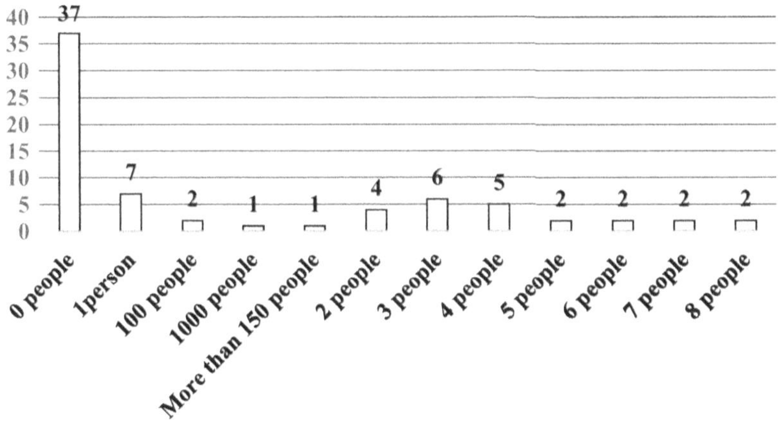

Fig. 7.1 Number of people respondents have helped come to Japan (*Source* Developed for this research)

Figure 7.1 indicates the number of people the respondents have assisted through their migration to Japan. The largest number of respondents—37 people—said that they had not helped anybody with the migration process. Seven respondents had helped one individual each. Only two respondents had helped more than one hundred people move to Japan.

Provision of Supportive Services by Agencies (Mediators or "Enablers")

The evidence collected during this research shows that networking among family members, friends, relatives, or other close neighbors who had lived in Japan before or are living in Japan at the time that a potential international student takes an interest in Japan is essential for students who intend to study abroad. There are several reasons for this. Primarily, networks are popular because they allow for the proliferation and propagation of information quite rapidly. Students who are in need of reliable information mostly appreciate this aspect of the matter. The findings of the survey and semi-structured interviews also show that in addition to networking, there are other facilitators, identified as "educational migration industries/agencies" or "mediators", that assist potential students in

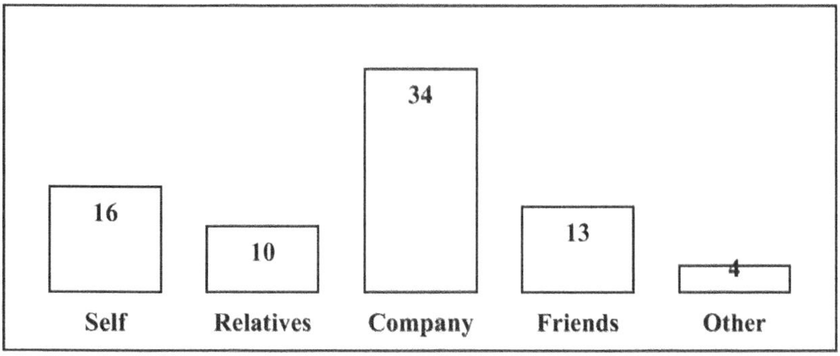

Fig. 7.2 Assistance received in the process of preparing admission documents (*Source* Developed for this research)

coming to Japan. According to the analysis of the survey data, almost half of the respondents (34 of 77) who participated in the research study used an educational migration mediator's (company) services (see Fig. 7.2). The research also demonstrates that these mediator services were used to a large extent by students who came to Japan through Japanese language schools. This raises the question: Why do educational migration mediators assist potential students who are planning to come to Japan? Why do they help students who are planning to come to Japan through Japanese language schools, specifically, rather than other educational institutions in Japan? In the following sections below, this study tries to explain and to answer the two questions above. Before beginning to answer these questions above, the data analysis demonstrates that such educational migration mediators not only help potential students who are planning to go to Japan but also help and work with Japanese language schools in Japan. This raises another question. How and why do such educational mediators work with and help Japanese language schools in Japan? According to the data analysis, effective cooperation with both students and Japanese language schools in Japan is very profitable for such mediators. This is explained by the fact that such mediators charge potential students for the services they provide. At the same time, they receive financial remuneration from language schools for providing them with new Uzbek students.

As a result, educational migration mediators are currently the key agents in marketing Japanese educational services in Uzbekistan. A continual stream of potential students and of Japanese language schools eager for students encourages such educational migration mediators. However, for their services to be lucrative, such mediators require many students to be sent to Japanese language schools. Thus, educational migration mediators use various types of marketing. For instance, they visit numerous educational institutions throughout Uzbekistan to raise public awareness of their services. Interestingly, during such visits, different presentations are held, which are usually received very enthusiastically by the audience. Even the students who might not have had the slightest intention of going abroad are attracted by such presentations. One such student is Alisher from Samarqand. He was very much affected by such a presentation. He recounted the following during the interview:

> In May, during my sophomore year at the Lyceum, there was a Japanese seminar. The Japanese center came and held a festival. Then, they introduced us to Japanese culture and gave us information. Then, I and two other friends became interested. We intended to study abroad. We liked Japan. Therefore, in the second year, in May, I started learning Japanese. The reason we chose Japan was that it is a developed country with high salaries. I was going to study English abroad in the field of computers, and I wanted to go to Britain or America. Later, I became interested in Japan and, fortunately, I came. (Alisher 2019)

The story does not end here. Mediators use active marketing strategies, including spreading numerous brochures among youth to attract an ever-increasing number of potential students. For example, nineteen-year-old Muzaffar became interested in studying in Japan thanks to such promotional brochures. He shared the following about his experiences.

> As I said, at the beginning of the fourth year, I got a flyer. It was written on it that if you want to work in Japan, you can get that much per hour. I was interested. I also searched on the Internet. I knew that Japan was technologically strong, but I did not know much about its culture. After that, I applied to special training centers. When I started this, I dropped out of the institute when problems increased. I took an online exam via Skype and was admitted to a Japanese language school. I got lucky, that's right. It all started after that. (Muzaffar 2019)

Educational agencies exploit the same strategies in relation to both universities and language schools in other countries. However, according to the findings of this research study, the strategies of educational migration mediators in Uzbekistan vary. The statistics exemplify this situation by showing that more students are attracted to language schools than to universities. All respondents who came to Japan through Japanese language schools and received assistance from educational migration mediators in Uzbekistan pointed out that such mediators could assist them in going to Japan only through Japanese language schools rather than universities. As a result, during the period between 2010 and 2018, the number of students attracted to universities increased from 183 to 432 (see Table 7.1).On the other hand, the number for language schools increased from 22 to 1427 for the same period of time (see Table 7.1). It is worth mentioning that this is related only to my research study findings regarding the students who came to Japan and what types of assistance they received before coming to Japan. In addition, this does not suggest that all educational migration agencies in Uzbekistan behave this way. They and their services may be different and varied based on the countries and types of educational institutions where potential Uzbekistani students go to study abroad.

Uzbek students who intend to travel abroad may contact different people within the same network for help. It is possible that a student who wants to study in Japan will initially address his or her direct contacts. Next, he or she may go to mediators, who can provide him or her with more detailed information. As a result, he or she is making use of different levels of contacts within the same network.

Different sources of information about studying in Japan are available. This allows for a huge flow of information. This abundant information in turn causes confusion among those who intend to use it. It also happens that such information is intentionally distorted for marketing purposes. Twenty-year-old Komil experienced such confusion due to the intentional distortion of information. This happened while he was preparing to leave for Japan. The following are his words:

> While living in Uzbekistan, we thought that it would not be difficult to earn $2,000-$3,000 a month in Japan. The people who convinced us all said the same thing. They said you can earn so much per hour in Japan, etc. No, in the beginning, it did not happen at all. A person comes to think that he/she is going to make so much money, but when he/she sees that it is not so, then he/she becomes depressed. Some leave. Therefore, I

Table 7.1 Number of Uzbekistan Students by Institution Type

	2004	*2005*	*2006*	*2007*	*2008*	*2009*	*2010*	*2011*	*2012*	*2013*	*2014*	*2015*	*2016*	*2017*	*2018*
Graduate school	100	106	107	109	125	130	126	117	121	124	117	135	134	125	140
University (undergraduate)	25	132	32	46	50	49	57	60	59	70	121	150	172	200	292
Junior college	0	1	0	0	0	0	0	0	0	0	0	0	2	2	8
College of technology	0	0	0	0	0	0	0	0	0	0	0	0	0	0	0
Professional training college	0	0	0	11	30	44	25	13	22	22	33	50	74	111	258
University preparatory courses	2	0	0	1	0	0	0	1	1	11	3	0	1	3	7
Japanese language institute	-	-	-	-	-	-	22	35	28	54	84	136	258	606	1427
Total	127	139	139	167	205	223	230	226	231	281	358	471	641	1047	2132

would recommend that before coming to Japan, everybody should get to know and consult all its aspects. (Komil 2019)

32-year-old Mirkomil from Samarqand, Uzbekistan, also faced such obstacles prior to his arrival in Japan. He shared the following:

It was a training center in Uzbekistan, located in Samarqand. It also has branches throughout Uzbekistan. ...You know, salaries in Uzbekistan are very low. When they told us that after graduating from Japanese universities, you will get a salary of 4,000-5,000 USD, and during the study period you will earn $15 per hour, we became very interested and began to study Japanese seriously. Then, I came to Japan and found out it wasn't $15. That's right, we were told, there are jobs, there are jobs in bars, nightclubs for up to $40 per hour. I don't know if they meant that. I was interested in the issue of money. (Mirkomil 2019)

It is disturbing to note that such distortions, which are made on the basis of marketing puffery, cause students to make life-changing decisions. Mahmud, from Namangan, Uzbekistan, shared the following experiences.

Yes, also, given that Japan is a developed country, I thought that if I take IELTS, I will enter a prestigious university in Japan. I knew English well. This is my current intention; I will enter when I finish school. When we came to the center, I explained the situation in Japanese and they said, "You don't need English very much. You have been studying Japanese for two years, and you speak Japanese fluently." If you have a high level of knowledge of the Japanese language, you enter and don't need IELTS. (Mahmud 2019)

Sherzod from Samarqand faced obstacles similar to those of Mahmud.

Japanese language schools in Uzbekistan have "poisoned" my brain. I didn't know enough about education in Japan, Japanese language schools. People in Uzbekistan introduced me to Japanese language schools as sub-courses of Japanese universities. It is thought that they have contracts with Japanese universities, which prepare students for two years. Then, yes, for only two years, I chose this path because I had time. I learned the truth when I came to Japan. Before coming, I did not consult with any Japanese, but only with Uzbeks. If I had known earlier, I would have studied English better, obtained a higher IELTS score, and come to a Japanese university at once. The reason for my lack of information in Uzbekistan was that the centers deceived me. (Sherzod 2019)

The Business of Special Training Centers

It has been mentioned above that the individuals who possess information related to studying in Japan do not share it for free. Another point is that such mediators not only provide the necessary information but also help the potential student find a language school and prepare his or her documents. This help also includes translating documents into Japanese. They also assist students during the online interviews carried out by Japanese language schools.

Additionally, future students are obliged to take Japanese language courses specifically in these training centers. From the results of the survey questionnaires, more than half of the respondents (41 of 77) took Japanese language courses in these language training centers before coming to Japan even though there are other options, such as regular courses (through universities or some academic lyceums/colleges) or private tutors, for learning the Japanese language (see Table 7.2).

Table 7.2 Sources of Japanese language instruction

	In Uzbekistan				*In Japan*			
	Regular course	*Training center*	*Tutor*	*None*	*Regular course*	*Japanese language school*	*Vocational school*	*Self-education*
Japanese language school students	1	26	3	4	0	34	0	0
Vocational school students	1	6	3	3	0	10	6	0
University students	6	9	3	0	11	7	0	0
Workers	5	0	4	2	2	7	1	1
Dependent visa	1	0	0	1	0	1	0	1

Source Developed for this research

This table also shows the extent to which the language training centers impact potential students who plan to come to Japan. Surely, the students are charged for each of the abovementioned services. Such language courses at "special training centers" may cost between 200,000 and 300,000 UZS per month (the price depends on the school and its location in Uzbekistan, and even after the student obtains his or her visa, the student is required to continue studying the Japanese language until his or her departure to Japan or be responsible for paying fees for the period [SUM 2,500,000]). The cost of document preparation, translation and preparation for online interviews, including Japanese language courses, varies between 800 and 1,500 US dollars. This difference depends on many factors: the financial condition of the family, their social status, the complexity of the documents, and the region of Uzbekistan where the student lives. According to my findings, the majority of Uzbek students studying in Japan went through these steps. For instance, Abdukamol, who came to Japan in 2019, was assisted by such centers and tells the following about his experiences.

> I paid 2.5 million so'm for 6-9 months of education just to study at the beginning. I did not pay extra for the documents. However, for the visa, I paid $1,000 to translate some of the visa documents. They said that if for some reason the visa is not issued, they will return $700 and take $300 for the paperwork. I paid $1,000. (Abdukamol 2019)

Similarly, nineteen-year-old Jahongir came to Japan in 2019, and he had the following experience:

> I did not prepare anything. They helped me when I went to that center in January. They told me to bring some documents from my parents. They asked for $1,000 to get a visa. They said they would return $700 if the visa was not issued. I paid for it. But I did not interfere in the documents at all, they did it themselves. I paid for all the paperwork. Also, I paid 2 and a half million yen in tuition fees, and another 4 million yen in small amounts before I went to Japan to study at the center. (Jahongir 2019)

Financial Benefits to "Individual Students" Bringing Other Potential Students to Japan

The business of bringing Uzbek students to Japan by charging them fees and receiving remuneration from Japanese language schools is so profitable that not only language centers but also individual students who have had some experience in Japan try to take it up with great enthusiasm.

Such individual students do not provide detailed information to prospective students. Neither do they teach the prospective students Japanese. However, as they charge much less for their assistance, they also attract huge numbers of potential students. Thanks to the increasing number of Uzbek students in Japan, competition has become more intense not only among language centers but also among individual students. Consequently, this has caused the emergence of misinformation regarding studying in Japan. Sardor came to Japan in 2007, and he has helped numerous Uzbek students who wanted to study in Japan. He gave the following account:

> I was not a recruiter when I worked at a Japanese language school. I reviewed the documents provided by the Japanese language school and called Uzbekistan to make a confirmation… I learned to work on documents…. My biggest experience was my brother Bahrom. Before I came to Japan, I corrected his documents and brought them to Japan. When I handed it in, the company saw it and asked me if I had filled it out myself. After I confirmed it, they said that I could work for their company…So, in 2009, I started recruiting students…I was in this business for nine years and then I stopped - I don't do it now, at all…I had a contract with six schools…Maybe I've brought about a thousand students to Japan; I haven't counted yet. Maybe. (Sardor 2019)

However, according to another respondent from the Andijan region of Uzbekistan, his reason for coming to Japan was as follows:

> I said at the beginning that I had tried to study English before, but I could not improve my skills in this language. The Japanese language was easier for me, and the grammar was easier. In addition, after going to Japan [the training center in Uzbekistan], they said that they would teach Japanese, so we went this way without fear. (Shuhrat 2019)

Reasons for Coming to Japan Through Japanese Language Schools

The analysis of the research data shows that more than three-quarters of respondents (62 of 77) came to Japan through Japanese language schools (see Table 7.3). Here, the question of why most Uzbekistani students chose Japanese language schools as their entryway to Japan rather than other educational institutions arises, and it interested me. Based on the analysis of the data, this research study finds the following several reasons why students come to Japan through Japanese language schools.

Low bar for Entry to Japanese Language Schools

According to the data analysis, the first main reason Uzbekistani students come to Japan through Japanese language schools is that it is the easiest and quickest way to come to Japan relative to other Japanese educational institutions. In addition to the survey questionnaires, the semi-structured interviews also confirmed this fact as students described their real experiences. For example, according to one respondent from the Sirdarya region of Uzbekistan who is 29 years old:

> I came to Japan with the assistance of my relative. First, I went to Russia to work and stayed there for 5 years. I was deported because of expired documents. After returning to Uzbekistan, the situation worsened because we had a large family and most of us were not working. Then, my relative, who was studying at a Japanese university, showed me how to come to Japan even though I had not been to university. As a result, I came to Japan through a Japanese language school because it was an easy way.
>
> True, there was a chance to come to Japan through a university, but we looked for a more certain and faster way (a student who had an undergraduate degree and knew English very well before coming to Japan and also worked during his/her time in Japan). (Ganisher 2019)

> There is a lack of knowledge of the language if one comes directly. Without in-depth study, it is impossible to achieve an N4 (lowest level of the Japanese Language Proficiency Test) or have the ability to engage in simple "daily communication". Coming through a Japanese language school is one of the easiest ways. (Feruz 2019)

Table 7.3 Educational channels to come to Japan

Japanese language school							*University*		
62							15		
Japanese language school	Japanese language school	Japanese language school	Japanese language school	Japanese language school	Japanese language school	Japanese language school	University	University	University
	Vocational school	University	Work	Vocational school	University	Vocational school		Work	
				Work	Work	Work			Dependent
						Dependent			
34	13	6	3	4	1	1	12	2	1

Source Developed for this research

Low Educational Qualifications

The second key reason why Uzbekistani students come to Japan through Japanese language schools is their low level of language proficiency in both Japanese and English. The findings and the analysis of the survey questionnaire confirm this and show that the level of language proficiency of Uzbekistani students who came to Japan through Japanese language schools compared to those who come as university students is extremely low, which shows that it would have been impossible for them to enter any higher educational institutions given their language ability level (see Table 7.4). According to Table 7.4, only two (6%) students who came to Japan by means of a Japanese language school had an N2 (Japanese Language Proficiency Level), while the remaining 32 (94%) respondents were at a level lower than an N2 (8 [N3], 6 [N4], 5 [N5], and 13 [lower than N5]). Table 7.4 shows the respondents' real English proficiency levels. According to Table 7.4, only five (15%) of the participants' English language proficiency was intermediate (3) or advanced (2), while the remaining 29 (85%) respondents had an English language proficiency at the beginner level (19 respondents) or did not know English at all (ten respondents). On the other hand, compared to students who came to Japan through a Japanese language school, those who came to Japan directly through a university had the highest language proficiency level in both Japanese and English (10 of 18 were at the N2 or N1 level in Japanese, and similarly, 10 of 18 respondents were at an intermediate (4) or advanced level (6) of English language proficiency.

Similarly, the findings from the semi-structured interviews with students who came to Japan through Japanese language schools also confirm that the main reason Uzbekistani students come to Japan through this route is their low level of foreign language proficiency in both Japanese and English. For instance, a student who had an undergraduate degree and came to Japan through the Japanese language school route described his foreign language proficiency as follows:

> [....]. Now, back to your question, I didn't know the Japanese language well even though I learned Japanese at university for four years. I knew

Table 7.4 Level of Japanese/English language proficiency

Language proficiency level	*Japanese language proficiency level*							*English language proficiency level*			
	N1	*N2*	*N3*	*N4*	*N5*	*Lower than N5*	*Unknown*	*Beginner*	*Intermediate*	*Advanced*	*Unknown*
Japanese language school students	0	2	8	6	5	13	0	19	3	2	10
Vocational school students	0	4	7	2	0	0	0	5	2	2	3
University students	3	7	3	3	2	0	0	5	4	6	3
Workers	2	7	0	0	1	0	0	3	1	5	1
Dependent visa	1	0	0	0	0	0	1	0	0	2	0

Source Developed for this research

English but that was not enough to enter a Japanese university. (Botir 2019)

[…]. To enter the institute... it would take time to learn the language and I don't know English very well. To be honest, I found out later that it is possible to come in this way. I didn't know before (Zohid 2019).

The reason I chose and came through a Japanese language school was that I actually had to do a master's degree, not a bachelor's degree. I did not believe that I could study both a master's degree and Japanese at the same time. That's why I thought it would be good to study the Japanese language at school for two years and study for a master's degree for the next two years (Kamol 2019).

In addition to the above facts, Table 7.5 confirms and shows that the language proficiency of the respondents who came through a Japanese language school could not have been exceptional because their exposure to the Japanese language in Uzbekistan was extremely short. According to the Table, with the exception of one respondent who had learned the Japanese language for more than two years, the rest of the participants spent a relatively short time learning Japanese in Uzbekistan; the maximum was six months: among 33 respondents, eight had studied Japanese for anywhere from six months to one year, nine for between four and six months, 11 for less than three months, and five had no Japanese language training at all (see Table 7.5).

The third most important factor that caused so many Uzbekistani students to come to Japan through Japanese language schools was a lack of information about channels other than Japanese language schools. As a result, many Uzbekistani students were forced to come to Japan in this way rather than by means of higher educational institutions. In the quotations below, some of the respondents reveal their prior lack of information about Japanese educational institutions. For instance, Ali, who had an undergraduate degree in Uzbekistan and at that time was in his second year at a Japanese language school, described his reason for choosing a Japanese language school as his way to come to Japan:

I didn't know much about the possibility of coming to Japan through another route, so I came through a Japanese school. The training center was also a young organization with experience. (Ali 2019)

At that time, I never thought of going to university or college. Initially, the only goal was to learn Japanese, but later, I became interested in

Table 7.5 Extent of Japanese language learning in Uzbekistan

	Less than 3 months	*4–6 months*	*6 months–1 year*	*1 year–18 months*	*18 months–2 years*	*More than 2 years*	*No learning*
Japanese language school students	11	9	8	0	0	1	5
Vocational school students	5	3	1	0	0	0	4
University Students	6	1	2	1	1	5	2
Workers	1	1	1	0	1	4	2
Dependent Visa	0	0	1	0	0	0	1

Source Developed for this research

Japanese schools. I thought it would be difficult to apply to college or university, and I thought the fee was too expensive (Akram 2019).

Then you had the opportunity to come to the university directly because you knew English very well. Would you like to get a bachelor's degree?

Why did you come through the Japanese school? I didn't know that. I didn't know about them. No one told me (Said 2019).

Sources of Financing Prior to Coming to Japan

Even though the prospect of living and studying abroad sounds very attractive to many Uzbekistani who are unsatisfied with their lot in their home country, going through with it requires money that many people simply do not have. However, with all the information they receive from their networks and from Japanese language school agents about the possibility of studying and working and making enough to even send money back home, many people come to believe that it is worth to find the money in any way they can. They might therefore rely on family members to provide them with the funds they need or even go so far as to borrow from relatives or other acquaintances to fulfill their dream of making it to Japan.

This study also collected information on the types of financial assistance that respondents received before coming to Japan as is demonstrated in the Fig. 7.3. First, the largest number of respondents received financial assistance from their families or borrowed the necessary amount of money (20 and 19 people, respectively). The other financing sources

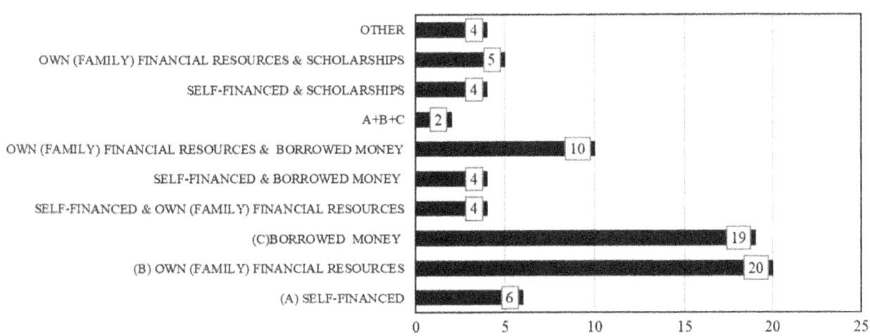

Fig. 7.3 Respondents' sources of financing (*Source* Developed for this research)

included self-finance, family support, and borrowed money in combination, which made up the same number each (four persons). Nine people came to Japan through scholarships, their own money, or family support (see Fig. 7.3).

Life Satisfaction of Respondents in Japan

It is important for this study to determine the extent to which respondents had met the preliminary goals they had set for themselves in terms of being able to study and work in Japan while fulfilling their obligation to send money back to their relatives. The research showed that for the largest share of respondents (42%), their level of satisfaction was neutral. This meant that they could not determine one way or the other whether they had cause to be dissatisfied or not. Just over one-third of the respondents (35%) said that they were very satisfied with their life in Japan. Meanwhile, a tiny minority of respondents replied that they were very very dissatisfied and somewhat dissatisfied (2% and 1%, respectively) (see Fig. 7.4).

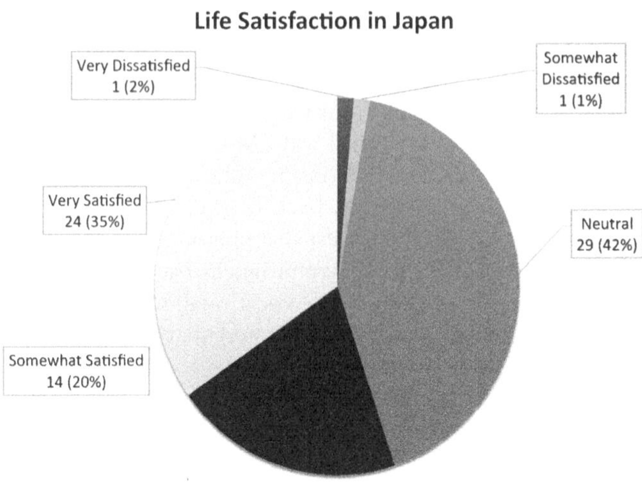

Fig. 7.4 Life satisfaction of respondents in Japan (*Source* Developed for this research)

Importance of Remittances

In many developing countries, remittances received from relatives abroad form a significant part of their income for expenditures on daily living. For many of the families that depend on remittances, the funds received may be used for many different purposes, but according to Kakhkharov et al. (2020), in regard to the South-South remittances of labor migrants, the household expenditure of those remaining is channeled mainly "to consumer goods, limiting their contribution to economic development." This issue affects many labor migrants from many different countries, all of whom feel the need to ensure that those they have left behind are, if not thriving, then at least surviving on whatever funds they are able to remit home. As Yun (2016) has pointed out, remittances are a huge part of the GDP of countries such as Uzbekistan.

As with labor migrants, international students also feel a similar need to ensure that their families back home are doing well. Seeing themselves as being in a more privileged position in which they are able to make enough money to meet their basic expenses and to have a small surplus, they do, in fact, contribute to their families regardless of the amount of money they feel that they can send (Salas 2014). This idea of students' sending remittances might seem strange to some, but research indicates that for those who are engaged in this practice, it is far from being an anomaly. Rather, they feel that the people whom they are caring for had sacrificed for them and that their contributions were going toward helping to build their country, even if in a very small way (Muruthi et al. 2017).

This research shows that a considerable number of Uzbekistani students in Japan send remittances back to their home country. As the results show, in %age terms, the largest share belongs to Japanese language school students, 90% of whom sent remittances back to Uzbekistan. The next largest share—70%—belongs to vocational school students. With university students, as many as 55% indicated that they sent remittances back to their home country (see Fig. 7.5).

There is a wide variety of reasons why labor migrants or students might send money back to their home country. Having grown up in the same circumstances as those that they have left behind, they are able to appreciate how much their new circumstances could be a source of benefits for those left behind. This research sought to determine the various reasons for which the respondents sent money. Across the board, money for saving was the primary reason (35 respondents). Following that, the

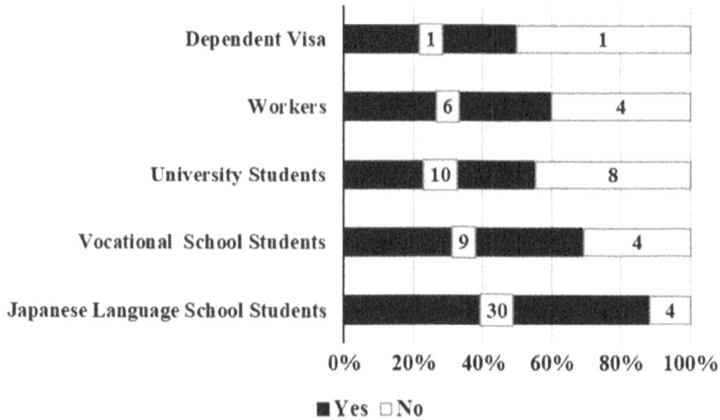

Fig. 7.5 Respondents send remittances to Uzbekistan (*Source* Developed for this research)

money was needed to meet various personal needs (18 respondents), and next was money that the families needed back home to cover their debts (14 respondents). In particular, students from Japanese language schools saw the payment of debts as a significant reason for sending money back home. It must be noted that some of the respondents gave multiple responses regarding the purpose of sending back remittances (see Table 7.6).

Table 7.6 Reasons for sending remittances

	Health	*Education*	*Savings*	*To pay debt*	*For personal needs*	*Other*
Japanese language school students	1	3	16	9	9	3
Vocational school students	0	2	7	3	3	0
University students	1	1	6	2	3	2
Workers	2	3	5	0	3	1
Dependent visa	0	0	1	0	0	0

Source Developed for this research

Table 7.7 Improvement in families' standards of living since respondents' arrival in Japan

	Not well at all	*Not well*	*Fairly well*	*Quite well*	*Extremely well*
Japanese language school students	13	7	8	5	1
Vocational school students	0	1	4	2	6
University students	6	4	4	3	1
Workers	0	2	2	1	6
Dependent visa	0	0	0	0	2

Source Developed for this research

It is natural for people continually sending money back home to wonder about the extent to which the funds are helping to improve conditions there. This, of course, is only a matter of perception and is perhaps based on what the respondents had learned from their relatives as to how the funds had been used. This research sought to determine the extent to which the conditions in the respondents' families' homes back in Uzbekistan had changed since they arrived in Japan. According to the research results, the most significant share of those whose family conditions had changed belongs to workers. Six out of eleven of workers said that their family conditions had improved dramatically. The lowest level of perceived improvement was observed among university students (one out of eighteen) and Japanese language school students (one out of thirty-four). Only one respondent from each group said that their family conditions in Uzbekistan had improved dramatically. Among the vocational school students, six out of thirteen indicated that their families' conditions in Uzbekistan had been significantly improved (see Table 7.7).

Students' Future Plans

Students might go to another country to expand their knowledge with a view of returning home shortly after their studies to contribute to the welfare of their home country. Once they are actually in their destination country, reality may set in that after only one or two years, they do not have enough grounding in their studies to return to their home countries and be successful. They may also realize that there is a large discrepancy between their home countries and their host country and that it would be a mistake for them to return too soon. In some cases, the host country presents a number of inducements that make it harder for foreign students to want to return. This may include the opportunity to access lucrative job opportunities or even to apply for permanent residence. This leads to the common phenomenon of brain drain that has long been associated with the transfer of skills from one country to another (Baruch et al. 2007). This research has indicated that for the Uzbekistani respondents in Japanese language schools, the majority wanted to proceed to university (14), several others wanted to go to vocational school (10), a few wanted to return to Uzbekistan (5), and a small number indicated that they wanted to work (4). Of course, those who wanted to proceed to a vocational school or a university might eventually end up working in Japan as well, but for the moment, their immediate future goals were to further their education. In contrast with students from Japanese language schools, among those in vocational schools, most wanted to get a job (8), a few wanted to proceed to a university (3), and a minority wanted to return to Uzbekistan (2). Finally, among those in university, those who wanted to get a job constituted the majority (8), while the next largest group included those who wanted to study further in the university (6), while the number of those who wanted to return to Uzbekistan was minimal (4). These data show that education is important to the respondents and that they are not necessarily in a rush to enter the job market (see Table 7.8).

Many of the respondents seemed to appreciate the value of the education they were getting in Japan. They were also aware of the contributions that they could make in their country in the future. Few of the respondents wanted to return to Uzbekistan immediately. Most of them expressed a desire to remain in Japan for at least a few years so that they could earn more experience in Japan and save enough money to start some venture back in their home country. As Nodir noted,

> After graduation, I intend to start working for a Japanese company. I want to sign a five-year contract with a Japanese company. After working for a while I will return to Uzbekistan and continue working in one of the developing industries there, for example, in the banking sector. (Nodir 2019)

Table 7.8 Future plans of respondents after finishing their current educational program

Future plan					
	Return to Uzbekistan	*Proceed to vocational school*	*Proceed to a university*	*Get a job*	*Other*
Japanese language school students	5	10	14	4	1
Vocational school students	2	0	3	8	0
University students	4	0	6	8	0

Source Developed for this research

Even though living in Japan over the long term could mean greater financial success, Nodir expressed a desire to return mostly on account of his family; in his words, "I always put my family first. My motherland—we grew up there, and now, I have to return there to serve."

Conclusion

Uzbekistan is a country with a young, restless population of people who are hugely dissatisfied with the limited prospects available to them: difficulty entering institutions of higher education, high cost of education, and low pay even when one has a job. At the same time, thanks to the Internet and information flows through networks comprising family, friends, and even complete strangers, young people are not unaware of the vast differences that lie between their own lives and those of their compatriots who have been able to settle abroad.

While there is an ample number of push factors to motivate those searching for greener pastures to leave, one finds numerous barriers set up in the traditional places that they might consider such as Russia, which has the benefit of a common language but increasingly hostile policies, the United States and the European Union, which boast some of the finest universities in the world but are both expensive and unaccommodating with giving visas to people from Uzbekistan.

In recent years, Asian countries such as Japan and South Korea have found ways to serve their own national needs while also opening up the way for ambitious young people from around the world to achieve their own personal and professional goals. Thus, there is mutual benefit for both the countries and the young people involved.

In addition to information garnered from family and friendship networks, a whole industry has risen to support the dreams of people from all over the world who want to take advantage of such opportunities. In Uzbekistan, in particular, language centers have become ubiquitous, either specializing in Japanese or teaching a slew of other languages. In addition to the language instruction they provide, they have also become conduits for promoting Japanese language schools based in Japan, and thus, steering students to these institutions through various fee arrangements they have with the schools. These same schools offer ancillary services such as helping with the completion of forms that might facilitate the prospective students entry to Japan.

Through the semi-structured interviews conducted for this research, it became clear that most of the respondents very much wanted an opportunity to work in a country where they could attend to their own daily needs and be able to help their family members as well. The fact that it is possible to work part-time in Japan and go to school at the same time and be able to send some remittances home makes Japan such an ideal country for many of the respondents. But this was mostly before they actually set foot in Japan. Once in the country, some discover that they had either been lied to outright regarding how much money they could make or that the ease of the life they had expected was greatly exaggerated. Even so, practical realities determine that they make the most of their Japanese language school studies, further their education at a vocational school or university in order to improve their earning potential or to develop skills that they could deploy back in their home country. In the last two decades, the number of students coming to Japan from Uzbekistan has been increasing steadily, and there has been a monumental shift from most students going to Japan directly to seek undergraduate or graduate degrees to most making Japanese language schools their primary mode of entry, not because of their love for the Japanese language but because it provides the easiest and fastest way by which they can turn their dreams of gainful employment into eventual reality.

References

Akashi, J. (2014). New aspects of Japan's immigration policies: Is population decline opening the doors? *Contemporary Japan, 26*(2), 175–196. http://doi.org/10.1515/cj-2014-0009

Baruch, Y., Budhwar, P. S., & Khatri, N. (2007). Brain drain: Inclination to stay abroad after studies. *Journal of World Business, 42*(1), 99–112.

Beech, S. E. (2015). International student mobility: The role of social networks. *Social & Cultural Geography, 16*(3), 332–350.

Fawcett, J. T. (1989). Networks, Linkages, and Migration Systems. *International Migration Review, 23*(3), 671–680.

Guruz, K. (2011). *Higher education and international student mobility in the global knowledge economy: Revised and updated second edition*. Suny Press.

Kakhkharov, J., Ahunov, M., Parpiev, Z., & Wolfson, I. (2020). South-South Migration: Remittances of Labour Migrants and Household Expenditures in Uzbekistan. *International Migration.*

Kuroda, K., Sugimura, M., Kitamura, Y., & Asada, S. (2018). Internationalization of higher education and student mobility in Japan and Asia. *Background paper prepared for the prepared for the 2019 Global Education Monitoring Report*. Retrieved from https://www.jica.go.jp/jicari/publication/other/l75nbg00001 0mg5u-att/Background_Kuroda.pdf

Muruthi, B., Watkins, K., McCoy, M., Muruthi, J. R., & Kiprono, F. J. (2017). "I feel happy that i can be useful to others": Preliminary study of east African women and their remittance behavior. *Journal of Family and Economic Issues, 38*(3), 315–326.

Salas, V. B. (2014). International Remittances and Human Capital Formation. *World Development*, *59*, 224–237.

Sodatsayrova, N., & Waljee, A. (2017). Re-interpreting cultural values: Tajikistani students abroad. *Cambridge Journal of Eurasian Studies, 1*, 1–22. http://doi.rg/10.22261/CJES.DKC8NT

Vargas-Lundius, R., Lanly, G., Villarreal, M. (2008). *International migration, remittances and rural development*. Rome, Italy: International Fund for Agricultural Development. Retrieved from https://www.fao.org/3/a-ak405e.pdf

Yun, C. (2016). The Russian Economic Crisis and Falling Remittances in Central Asia. *World Economy Brief*, *6*(28), 1–6.

CHAPTER 8

Some Reflections on Students Mobility and Labor Migration

Jasur Soipov

Introduction

Throughout history, people have not been unwilling to leave their home countries for destinations far and near, lured by the opportunity not just to work but also to gain the kind of education that they believe will equip them for reaching the goals they have set for themselves. Whereas traditional migration is associated with settlement of a permanent nature, with uncertainty surrounding whether the migrant will ever return to permanently settle in his or her original homeland, there are also travelers, often from the upper echelons of society, who are able to travel freely, settle abroad for some time, and then return home at some point (Murphy-Lejeune 2003, p. 5). However, this conception may be on the way out in that, increasingly, those individuals on the move are not the elite members of society but people from the middle or even lower rungs of society who, thanks to the Internet and other international networks, have become plugged into information flows that allow them to seek

J. Soipov (✉)
Tsukuba, Japan

T. Dadabaev (ed.), *The Grass is Always Greener?*, Politics and History in Central Asia,
https://doi.org/10.1007/978-981-16-2570-1_8

their own novel pathways in order to become part of the global student mobility phenomenon.

This phenomenon of student mobility is not confined to any one part of the world. For instance, there are historical precedents of students going to Germany to learn about medical advances that were unknown in their own country. Europe was and continues to be a destination for students from Africa and other parts of Asia who acknowledge that the educational system there, honed over many centuries, is in many ways superior to what they have access to in their home countries. The United States of America has also served this role for students from Africa and Europe, and in recent years, vast numbers of students from Asia, in particular South Korea and China, have become a dominant presence in American institutions of higher education. Japan, since World War II, though perhaps to a lesser extent than Europe or the United States, has also served as a target destination for students from various parts of the world, notably China and in recent years, the liberated countries of Eastern Europe and Central Asia.

Key Mechanisms and Main Factors Stimulating Student Mobility

In practice, student mobility is about opportunities that students have to either work or study abroad while pursuing a degree, either at the undergraduate level or at the graduate level. One-way mobility pertains to students from one region or country making their way to another country or territory without a reciprocal agreement with either a corresponding institution or government. On the other hand, many institutions around the world pursue two-way student mobility, recognizing that students from both worlds can expand their horizons to the benefit of not only the student but also the sending institution or nation.

Whether student mobility is pursued as a one-way or two-way endeavor, it often requires a great deal of research to ensure fitness for purpose. It might require assistance from a wide variety of individuals and institutions in supportive roles to assure success. This is because even prior to departure, students have to contend with issues such as financial fitness, visa procurement, disruptions associated with relocation, a lack of time to put all affairs in order, and the impact of their departure on family members who are left behind.

Considering that studying abroad involves a host of challenges, including culture shock, communication challenges, and various feelings of distress, researchers must have wondered what the true motivations behind such endeavors are. Researchers have not been oblivious to the manifold reasons that might underlie the decision to move abroad for study purposes. The constellation of reasons includes push–pull factors, but it has also been noted that friends and family members in the host countries sometimes serve as anchors for the newcomers (Chirkov et al. 2007). Jewish people who moved from Russia to Israel following the collapse of the Soviet Union identified three motives for embarking on that journey back to what they perceived as their ancestral homeland: self-preservation, that is, safeguarding oneself from potential harm; self-development, which includes exploring the limits of one's abilities and capabilities; and materialism, which reflects the natural human desire to enjoy a better quality of life. The reasons for moving abroad have also been found to include considerations of self-determination tied to the intrinsic motivation to do something challenging, something that perhaps not all of one's peers are able to attain.

In addition, there are those who study abroad because of external factors such as pressure from parents (Duan 1997; Jiang and Ashley 2000; Mazzarol et al. 2001; Chinaview 2006; Yang 2007; Tan 2015). Many scholars who focus their studies on the effect that Chinese parents have on their children's higher education abroad highlight that there is a significant positive influence of parents on their children's schooling abroad. For example, Yang (2007) demonstrates Chinese parents' influence on their children's education abroad as follows: "With only one child in most Chinese families, parents are making every effort to endure any financial burden to provide a good education for their children's future" (p. 3). In China, higher education is considered the second major factor in their livelihood after food expenses because Chinese people believe that a good education will guarantee a better future (Duan 1997; Jiang and Ashley 2000). Obtaining a foreign degree leads to more options, e.g., through the development of superior skills and greater employability in the marketplace, than obtaining a higher education degree in China (Zhang 2001; Fam and Gray 2000; Gareth 2005). Tan (2015) argues that in China, parents influence their children's selection of a study-abroad institution. However, according to Mazzarol and Soutar (2002), parents not only influence their children's choice of institution abroad but also, normally, their children's decision to study abroad. These scholars also suggest that parents influence their children's choice of destination country, particularly when their children are planning to pursue a bachelor's degree. Other scholars, such as Findlay et al. (2006) and González et al. (2011), argue that parents' educational backgrounds are also main motivational factors for their children's education abroad.

Challenges and Opportunities

Regardless of the motivation, a student who finds himself or herself abroad has to deal with various challenges, and if the determination to succeed is strong enough, the student will come out of the experience more seasoned and in a better position to tackle the next stage of life, whether this be full entrenchment in the world of work or the resumption of studies at another level.

Despite such challenges, student mobility has continued to increase over the years, with the number of students traveling for educational purposes within the European Union climbing from 1.6 million in 2000 to approximately 3.4 million in 2012 (Sodatsayrova 2018). It must also be noted that the trend in studying abroad is not only for students from developing countries to make their way to more advanced countries. In terms of push factors, certain conditions in a person's home country, such as a deteriorating educational infrastructure or a lack of employment opportunities, might function to accelerate students' decisions to leave. As Sodatsayrova (2018) suggests, however, such decisions are not unconnected to "larger local and global life and ideas" (p. 4), such as the need to be connected to excellence, wherever it may be found. On the other hand, there are some institutions around the world that have distinguished themselves so much that they have developed worldwide reputations, sending a message from Afghanistan to Zimbabwe that anyone who can pass through their halls has an assuredly successful future. One can count among such institutions Harvard University, the University of Oxford, Cambridge University, the Massachusetts Institute of Technology, Stanford University, and others. However, quite apart from these elite institutions, many others lacking such cachet are good enough for aspiring students, who know that the benefits of acquiring an education from even a mid-tier institution in the United States, Canada, or the United Kingdom far surpass any gains they might accrue by attending a domestic institution. Another important factor influencing students is the kind of university or college that they are able to attend in a host country (Moogan et al. 1999; Altbach and Teichler 2001; Mazzarol and Soutar 2002; Jacobson 2005). Based on data analyses of a large set of countries (125) that were available for selection by international students, the United States was the destination country of choice for the majority. Beine et al. (2014) argue that there are two reasons for the selection of the USA by international students, namely, "the skill premium paid in the labor market and... the large number of US universities" (p. 4). Altbach and Teichler (2001) highlight that in terms of the "quality of faculty and the quality of curriculum," the American teaching method is thought to be the best among several countries in the world (p. 3). These opinions are also confirmed and supported by Moogan et al. (1999), Mazzarol and Soutar (2002), and Jacobson (2005). However, Marginson's (2006) view is slightly different from that of the other scholars mentioned above. In considering the movement of international students into developed countries and the reasons for their selection of highly ranked schools in those countries, Marginson (2006) observes that "international students were not currently studying at their current institutions because of the ranking but because of the ease of the admission and acceptance processes. Students believed that they could not get acceptance from a higher-ranking institution and the ease of the admissions process was the second most important factor (recommendation from family and friends is the most important factor) in making the decision to study at their current institution" (p. 8). As academic offerings, campus life considerations, facilities, research funding, the pursuit of research excellence, and the opportunity to become fluent in English are better at higher-ranking institutions in developed countries than at institutions in developing or less-developed countries, and many international students prefer to study at institutions of higher learning abroad (OECD 2001; Benzie 2010; González et al. 2011; Matthews 2016; Choudaha 2017; Beech 2018).

Government and Political Factors Affecting Student Mobility

Whether in developed, developing, less-developed, or least-developed countries, the role of governments in sending students abroad to study or receiving students from other countries is considerable; it cannot be measured or explained in a few words because it affects every state sector (the economy, policy, socioculture, education, etc.). Both sending and receiving countries receive substantial benefits from the movement of students in or out of their countries for study purposes. As a result, international student mobility has become one of the most important topics and has touched many fields of research since the 1990s. Undoubtedly, the rapid globalization and internationalization of countries, institutions, and people have played a part in this acceleration.

As a result, international student mobility in both sending and receiving countries is a public policy issue, so governments try to exert as much influence in this area as they can. Yang (2007) argues that pursuing education abroad was the primary motivation for Chinese students in the twentieth century. Currently, China is the largest exporter of international students, providing 15.2% of the total number of international students. In addition, according to Hui (2005) and Wang (2003), it has been more than 100 years since China first sent students and scholars to study abroad.

It is clear that a principal factor that encourages students to migrate abroad is the pursuit of better education. However, we should also take into consideration factors such as a country's favorable political conditions. In the second half of the twentieth century, the geopolitical situation in the world began to change. Gareth (2005) maintains that in the 1960s, with the change in the international political climate, the central government of China began to make adjustments to its policies related to sending students and scholars abroad. Later, in 1978, the late Chinese leader Deng Xiaoping decided to expand the scope of the ability of students and scholars to study abroad (Gareth 2005). This might have been totally unthinkable in the years when China and the West seemed to be at loggerheads and expressed quiet disdain for each other.

Recently, the central government of China has supported the idea of student migration abroad not only for government projects but also for students' personal initiatives. According to studies by Mazzarol (2002) and Marginson (2001), the Chinese government's policy on studying abroad has had a strong influence on the flow of Chinese students going abroad to study (Mok 2003).

Another study, carried out by the Department of Foreign Affairs and Trade, Australia (DFAT), found that among other influential factors, skilled migration policies have had a great impact on students' destination and program selections. Among the students interviewed, the main reason for choosing accounting and information technology programs was their link to the prospect of future migration opportunities. The export of international education is also policy-driven (DFAT 2005).

Regarding the effect of migration policies on international students in host countries, Beine et al. (2014) maintain that destination countries' policies related to the management of international students can have two complementary goals. First, they can focus on attracting foreign students. Second, they can attempt to influence the retention of students once the students have graduated to ensure a highly skilled workforce.

Brain Drain and Brain Gain

Haupt et al. (2010) study the migration of students from the perspective of brain gain and show that brain drain is not only due to incentives to acquire human capital by individuals from developing countries but also by incentives in rich countries to improve their education policies. The need for host countries to retain foreign students indeed leads them to increase the quality of their educational systems to benefit from the externalities of human capital accumulation. This enhances the human capital of all students, including those who return home. As such, it can generate brain gain.

The international mobility of students and its effects are also studied by Dreher and Poutvaara (2005), who find a positive correlation between flows of students and international migration as a whole.

In recent years, Western economies have increasingly sought to both recruit international students and retain them after graduation because in an era of globalization, international students provide several short- and long-term advantages for institutions and countries. In the first instance, with public per-student funding for higher education decreasing in many countries, universities and colleges are looking to diversify their income sources, and obtaining revenue from overseas student tuition has become one important way of doing so. In the long term and the wider socioeconomic context, developed countries are looking to attract foreign skilled labor to supplement their rapidly decreasing and aging populations. According to its national immigration authorities, Australia will have 200,000 more jobs than people to fill them in five years. With one of the lowest birth rates in the Organization for Economic Co-operation and Development (OECD), Canada is expected to become increasingly reliant on skilled immigrants to boost its labor force. Currently, close to 20% of Canadian citizens were born abroad, an indication that the country is arguably already reliant on the skills of the more than 130,000 international students who annually enroll in schools there. Tan (2015) maintains that some dynamics affecting the number of students studying abroad include flexible immigration systems, better research opportunities, and support services for international students at the university level.

Reasons for Choice of Educational Destination

Among the factors that influence international student mobility (ISM), destination is the most important factor for international students compared to other factors. There are many studies regarding the effect of destination, and almost all of them suggest a positive impact of destination country on ISM (Sandhu and Asrabadi 1994; Mazzarol and Soutar 2002; IIE 2004; Chen 2006; Verbik and Lasanowski 2007; Li and Bray 2007; Kondakci et al. 2008). Additionally, scholars have argued that there are many factors that influence the choice of study destination for international students. For example, Stewart & Felicetti (1991), who studied the reason for international students' choice of the USA as their study destination place, finds that four main factors influence their selection, namely "living cost, availability of financial aid from the school, opportunities for employment and academic requirements of the prospective department" (p. 73). However, the analysis of Mazzarol et al. (1996), who are the main scholars on student mobility in higher education and have contributed enormously to the international student mobility literature, finds fifteen factors that have possible effects on student choice of study destination: "Reputation of the host country; Reputation of the host institution; Safety (e.g., crime rate); Cost/fees; Availability of scholarships or work; Ease of visa processing and visa cost; Historical or economic links between host country and home country; Availability of specific teaching programs (e.g., science and technology); Geographic proximity of host country; Lifestyle in host country; Climate in host country; Recognition of qualifications; Family and friends in host country; Plans for immigration; Overall value for money" (pp. 29–30). However, this does not mean that all international students abroad choose all of these fifteen factors during the process of selecting a destination country. The factors that students who are planning to study abroad consider may differ country by country based on the students' backgrounds, family, host and home country conditions, or other reasons, that is, there may be two, five, six, eight, or even more than ten influencing factors. These views are confirmed and supported by other educational mobility scholars (Sandhu and Asrabadi 1994; Altbach and Teichler 2001; DFAT 2005; Ziguras and Law 2006; Marginson 2006; Verbik and Lasanowski 2007; Yang 2007; UNESCO 2008; OECD 2009; Kondakci 2011).

It is well known that the Australia, New Zealand, the USA, Canada, and the UK (ANUCU) are considered the core educational destination countries and are the countries most visited by international students from around the world for the purpose of studying. Two opinions are presented by educational mobility scholars regarding the reason for the selection of these countries by international students. The first group of scholars argues that international students' preference for these destinations is because of the kind of higher education provided by these countries' institutions (Altbach and Teichler 2001; Yang 2007; UNESCO 2008; OECD 2009). According to the second group of scholars, the selection of these countries by international students is due not only to the higher education offered but also to other reasons, such as the variety of academic programs, excessive capacity, financial aid availability, use of the English language, ease of access, safety, and the prospect of remaining in the host country (Sandhu and Asrabadi 1994; DFAT 2005; Ziguras and Law 2006; Marginson 2006; Verbik and Lasanowski 2007). Recently, however, in light of the availability of excess research capacities, competitive lower tuition fees compared to traditional destination institutions, and their capacity to provide English-medium programs, some industrialized and highly developed countries, such as Germany, France, Japan, Korea, Singapore, Malaysia, and China, which are non-Anglophone countries, have also begun to receive ISs and have become attractive destinations for IS around the world.

The Importance of Climate

The climate in a host country plays an important role for international students during the process of selecting a host country before moving away from their homeland. Although there is a lack of research about the influence of climate on international student mobility, some scholars argue that the climate in host destinations is also one of the main factors that influence international students' decisions when choosing a potential country in which to study abroad (Mazzarol et al. 1996; Mazzarol and Soutar 2002; González et al. 2011). For example, according to Mazzarol and Soutar (2002), the "local environment" of the host country is one of the major factors that influence ISs; they describe the effect of climate on international student mobility as follows:

> The climate, the lifestyle and whether the country is viewed as being quiet or 'studious' were seen as aspects of this 'environment.' Focus group discussions with students suggested that this environment could be a significant influence. Many students from South East Asia viewed Australia as a preferred destination to the United Kingdom, New Zealand or Canada because the weather was warmer. (Mazzarol and Soutar 2002, p. 17)

Similarly, for international students from the United States and Japan who had gone to Australia to obtain higher education, the climate of Australia was found to be a place of "beaches and fun" (AGB 1992). González et al. (2011), who conducted research under the title "The determinants of international student mobility flows: an empirical study on the Erasmus programme," also argue that the climate of a host country plays a significant role for international students. Europe is divided into two broad climate types: Mediterranean and continental/oceanic. According to these scholars, many international students choose Mediterranean countries as their destination because the Mediterranean climate is warm and provides "a means of easily accessing leisure activities by students" (p. 427).

The Cost of Living

Another very important factor for international students is cost (Bornsztein 1987; Mazzarol et al. 1996; Yang 2007; Beine et al. 2014). Based on a study of four countries (Taiwan, India, China, and Indonesia) conducted between 1996 and 2000, Mazzarol and Soutar (2002) found six factors (knowledge and awareness, recommendation, cost, environment, geographical proximity, and social links) to be vital to students' choice of host country, and they explain the cost factor as follows:

> The third factor is related to cost issues, including the cost of fees, living expenses, travel costs and social costs, such as crime, safety and racial discrimination. The presence of students from the student's country (social cost) and the availability of part-time work (financial costs) also formed part of this factor. (p. 83)

Yang (2007), who studied Chinese students' choice of Australia as their destination country, argues that in addition to future migration prospects, the key factors that motivate Chinese students to choose Australia as a destination country are high-quality education; competitive, lower tuition fees; and the cost of living. For international students who study in the 13 OECD countries, cost factors, such as housing prices, have been found to be a significant factor, while registration or university tuition fees have not (Beine et al. 2014). Additionally, for Chinese international students, who traditionally compose the largest portion of New Zealand's overseas students, cost has been found to be a key factor (Verbik and Lasanowski 2007). Cost is considered a major factor for an IS not only during the process of selecting a specific country but also when choosing a college or university. According to Agarwal and Winkler (1985) and Bornsztein (1987), many transnational students cannot enter the college or university they desire because the target institutions do not provide financial assistance and the tuition fees at these colleges and universities are high.

Colonialism and Student Mobility

Despite the lack of extensive studies regarding the effect of colonial ties on international student mobility, some scholars argue that international student mobility is also significantly influenced by colonial route factors (Cummings and So 1985; Rivza and Teichler 2007; Chan, 2012; Madge et al. 2015). For instance, according to Khadria (2001) and Raghuram (2009), many students from the countries of Cape Verde and India travel and migrate to study abroad, especially to countries where they have colonial ties. Madge et al. (2009) suggest that political issues, inequalities, and injustices that occurred during the period of colonialism significantly influenced the shaping of the modern neo-colonial relations of education. This is also highlighted by Lahiri (2000) and Clover (2005). Before the 1990s, many Asian international students studied abroad, specifically in Japan. Chan (2012) explains the movement of Asian students into Japan as follows: "There are two major explanations for Japan's dominant position: its developmental level and its colonial history" (p. 3). This is the same for the movement of students from Central Asian countries, including Uzbekistan. Despite the rapid increase in the number of Central Asian students who study abroad, most of them go to study in Russia, particularly because of colonial ties (Brunner and Tillett 2007; Perna et al. 2015; Nazira 2018).

The Language Factor

Language, mainly the English language, is also one of the major factors that influence international student mobility. González et al. (2011) describe the relationship between language and international student mobility as follows: "In terms of the results in relation to language, it seems that ESM, instead of being discouraged by the lack of knowledge of foreign languages, is actually used by mobile students as an opportunity to learn or improve a major spoken foreign language" (p. 15). In terms of ISM, language plays an important role, specifically during the process of selecting a country as a study destination. According to Mazzarol and Soutar (2002), on the one hand, the major direction of much of the international student stream is based on the historical or colonial links between host countries and homelands. On the other hand, this colonial connection, rather than just being a matter of sentiment, has a practical element, namely the language that the aspiring student from the homeland shares with the former colonial power is now dressed up in the cloaks of a benevolent mentor willing to share knowledge and technology through an educational institution. Over the last two decades, language has had a considerable effect on the changing patterns of educational mobility. In the past, a large number of international students went to study in countries such as the USA, the United Kingdom, Australia, and Canada because of the higher quality of education available; the strength of the quality of their institutions; the variety of academic programs provided by the universities; the commonality of the English language, which was considered a "mobility barrier" to other countries; and other opportunities provided by these destination countries (Mazzarol and Soutar 2002; Rosenzweig et al. 2006; Marginson 2006, 2008; Verbik and Lasanowski 2007; Yang 2007; OECD 2009). However, in recent years, with the significant increase in the total number of international students, the number of destination countries has increased, and the students' selections have diversified. The new destinations appear to have received some benefits from hosting international students. As a result, to attract more international students, they have changed their migration policies for international students and have begun to provide them with more opportunities, such as lower tuition fees and living costs compared to the USA, the UK, and Australia, and to introduce English as a medium of instruction (McMahon 1992; Chen and Barnett 2000; Chen 2006; UNESCO 2008; Cantwell et al. 2009; Choudaha 2017). Verbik and Lasanowski

(2007) demonstrate the influence of the use of the English language on the selection of a destination country by noting that "the increasing use of English as a language of instruction is contributing to their growing popularity as an overseas student destination" (p.7). Recently, many countries, such as Germany, France, Japan, Korea, China, Malaysia, Singapore, Egypt, and Saudi Arabia, have become main destinations for international students from around the world (Collins and Ho 2014; Ma 2014; Universities UK 2014; Asian Development Bank Institute 2014; Choudaha 2017).

Intellectual Migration

In their research, Samanchina and Elebaeva (2015) observe an explosion of migration tied to education, that is, intellectual migration, toward the end of the twentieth century. They discuss scientists and other experts and various students and interns who are able to benefit from "new socially economic opportunities" (Samanchina and Elebaeva 2015, p. 135) while serving the labor needs of their host countries. One example they cite is that of Kyrgyzstan, whose young people have taken advantage of educational opportunities available to them from foreign governments such as Turkey. Turkey has made immense investments in its higher education sector, thus raising the profiles of its institutions and making them attractive to students from countries that do not have access to top-notch educational infrastructures and training. On the one hand, regarding the individuals who choose to return to Kyrgyzstan, the nation benefits from their enhanced professional and scientific attainments, their expanded horizons, and their acquisition of new language skills and cultural experiences. On the other hand, as an increasing number of such students decide to extend their stays in Turkey or elsewhere, Kyrgyzstan is deprived of the potential contributions of those students. Those who return and join the ranks of the elite are able to bridge the gap between their country and the countries where they obtained their training, thus potentially contributing to better human relationships and regional stability.

Benefits of Student Mobility

According to scholars of international student mobility, there are diverse and plentiful benefits from students studying abroad (Williams 2005; Agarwal et al. 2007; Spilimbergo 2009; Collins 2010; Knight 2012;

Waters 2012; Raghuram 2013). Tan (2015) argues that the benefits of international student mobility occur at three diverse levels: institutional, national, and international (p. 2). At the institutional level, international students are sources of income, research, and teaching talent (Tysome 2004; Bolsmann and Miller 2008; Lasanowski 2009). In addition, Galway (2000) suggests that there are three significant benefits of international students for universities in host countries. According to Galway, international students abroad produce economic revenue, increase heterogeneity, and enhance international trade links. For example, in the USA, international students "provide revenue to the U.S. economy and individual host states for living expenses, including room and board, books and supplies, transportation, health insurance, support for accompanying family members, and other miscellaneous items" (IIE 2012, p. 16). According to Open Doors 2013, the contribution of international students to the overall United States economy was nearly US$ 24 billion (IIE 2013). Verbik and Lasanowski (2007), however, highlight that in addition to the universities, the host countries also benefit from international students, and these scholars divide these benefits into short- and long-term benefits. In the short term, international students bring several benefits to the host countries' universities, while in the long term, the students replace the declining and aging population of the host countries' skilled labor force. Based on national immigration data from Australia and Canada, Verbik and Lasanowski (2007) describe these countries' situations as follows: Australia will have 200,000 more jobs than people to fill them in five years. With one of the lowest birth rates in the OECD, Canada is expected to become increasingly reliant on skilled immigrants to boost its labor force. Currently, close to 20% of Canadian citizens were born abroad, an indication that the country is arguably already dependent on the skills of the more than 130,000 international students who annually enroll in schools there (p. 3). Conversely, home countries also acquire substantial benefits by sending their students abroad to study, including the expertise that foreign students are able to bring in if they build a business back home while traveling back and forth between their new abode and their original homeland. In recent years, Indian and Chinese professionals who are well established in the United States have also built businesses in their home countries and are able to travel back and forth and share their expertise, technological and otherwise, with their home countries.

Another benefit that accrues to host countries, in particular the United States, which attracts some of the best and brightest students from around the world, is the students' contribution to research capacity. According to Goodwin (1993) and Rosenzweig et al. (2006), developing nations send their students to industrialized countries to study in order to acquire the most recent and advanced knowledge and experience and bring that knowledge and experience back to contribute to and develop investments in education in their homelands. For example, Wang (2003) and Hui (2005) suggest that more than one hundred years ago, China sent its first students and scholars to study abroad to bring home new knowledge. According to these scholars, at that time, the Chinese government believed that international education (new knowledge and skills) could assist in development and make the motherland a strong country. Foreign education that is acquired by international students can contribute "to faster creation of new knowledge and help other people acquire skills without any direct costs" (Kim 1998, p. 338). Students also acquire substantial benefits from receiving an education abroad. In addition to the acquisition of new knowledge, studying abroad can provide them with better skills, work in the destination country, career enhancement and, in general, an opportunity to become more employable in the marketplace (Jiang and Ashley 2000; Zhang 2001; Gareth 2005; Teichler 2007; Franklin 2010). There are also other benefits from international students' foreign educations. In addition to raising national economic growth and productivity (Kim 1998), such education can assist in increasing the internationalization of democratic values (Spilimbergo 2009) and the advancement of human rights practices (Atkinson 2010).

Though some of the students who migrate to more advanced societies for their education might have the goal of returning to their home countries to further the countries' development, the lure of better jobs, better facilities, and a generally higher quality of life often intervenes to turn what might have been a temporary sojourn into a long-term residence. In recent years, many of the advanced countries that have hosted these "foreign" students have come to discover that the skills and expertise that the host countries impart might also be used to continue to advance their societies. Thus, the push to force students to return to their home countries has been replaced in recent years with incentives for them to stay and make contributions. It is notable that approximately 80% of the students from India and China who obtained science and engineering degrees at the highest level from United States universities were still working there in 1995 (Liu-Farrer 2009). An example of a country that has taken full advantage of this opportunity to benefit from migrant labor and skills is Australia. The so-called student-switching pathway has made it easier for international students to switch from student status to permanent residence status. Not surprisingly, with such policies in place, "migration options have clearly become both a key motivation and a key outcome for many international students who undertake degrees in Australia" (Robertson 2011, p. 103).

Japan as a Host to International Students

Some advanced countries, noting the benefits that accrue to them through this educational channel of migration, have sought to take full advantage of it. One such country that has benefited from the skills of students is Japan. While Japan was able to depend on its domestic labor for many years following World War II, in the 1980s, the juxtaposition of a declining population and a galloping economy opened the way for discussions to begin on whether migrants could fill the gap. As noted earlier, there was a great deal of resistance on the part of the Japanese government to directly import foreign labor. However, a "side-door" strategy was enacted in the form of the Japanese Industrial Training Program (ITP), which ostensibly was "for the purposes of international transfer of skills, technology, and knowledge" (Liu-Farrer 2009, p. 180) to developing countries but came to be criticized as a way for the nation to import unskilled or semiskilled labor. The impact of this program can be seen from the fact that as of 2006, over 90,000 people in the "trainee" category stood "as the most populous entry category of long-term immigration in Japan" (Liu-Farrer 2009, p. 180). One of the largest groups to take advantage of this program was composed of the second- and third-generation descendants of Japanese people who had emigrated to Brazil. The so-called *Nikkejin* came to support Japan as manual laborers and semiskilled workers in factories across Japan.

A less well-known program that triggered a new wave of "migrants" was the Japanese government's "Plan to Accept 100,000 Foreign Students before the Beginning of the 21st Century." This program was initiated in the middle of the 1980s and became the impetus for a large number of students from all over the world to come to Japan, seeking a place where their own dreams of prosperity and good life might be found. The students who come through language schools have also made it possible for Japan to continue to benefit from a low-wage workforce.

In recent years, recruitment agencies have become quite a force in helping to guide students to the destinations of their choice. The growth in such businesses can be seen in their growth in China, which went from having only four recruitment agencies in 1979 to "about 3,000 licensed recruitment companies that dispatched around 600,000 workers" (Xiang and Lindquist 2014, S123) a couple of decades later. Data from Australia show similar growth, with migration advisory services "experiencing continual growth at an annualized rate of 6.2 percent with over 7000 professionals and an industry revenue of AU$ 887 million" (Khan 2019, p. 298). In the Philippines, for example, recruitment agents, both legal and otherwise, have played a significant part in the very large number of Filipinos residing in other countries. In Uzbekistan, as well, the influence of recruitment agencies is substantial. These organizations make outlandish claims and promise to entice potential recruits. For those who might be considering leaving Uzbekistan, it is difficult to resist the lure of information indicating that one could potentially make $3,000 to $5,000 a month in Japan. Because of competition among recruiters, each of them has to make a claim that surpasses that of their competitors, thus leading to a situation in which potential recruits find themselves flooded with fake news that they truly have no way of directly ascertaining for themselves, except to travel and see for themselves.

Culture also plays an important role in the popularity of studying abroad and the growth of the number of international students around the world. Despite the lack of widespread studies regarding the effect of culture on international student mobility, some researchers claim that international student mobility is also influenced by cultural aspects (Bhugra and Becker 2005; Chirkov et al. 2007; Stephens 2007). Their views are confirmed and supported by Nazira (2018), who describes the influence of culture on educational mobility as follows: "Educational mobility is influenced by various factors before, during, and after mobility, and culture becomes an important factor in the process of mobility. Cultural beliefs can sometimes become motivating factors for mobility or at the same time can limit it" (p. 4). While the lure of top-notch schools in advanced countries continues to draw a myriad of students from all over the world, students from countries such as the United States have discovered this other dimension of studying abroad, which has put the matter of culture on the upward trajectory. For example, it has been reported that the number of American students who chose to study abroad rose from less than 100,000 in 1997 to almost 250,000 in 2007 (Stroud, 2010). International students are often backed by their own institutions, who obtain the benefit of making themselves much better known around the world and using the program as a recruiting tool. There are large benefits to international studies for students. Studying abroad, students can develop their intercultural competence and linguistic skills. It also gives opportunities for them to think and understand global issues and work with people from other cultures (Stebleton et al. 2013). Sodatsayrova (2018) undertook a study of Tajikistani students in Japan to unearth the motivations behind the students' choice of Japan as a study destination. The attraction for Japan among the Tajikistani students seems to have been the twin benefits of receiving an education that is as advanced as what one might obtain in Western nations such as the United Kingdom, Australia, the United States, or France and learning Asian cultural values. Moreover, "the attraction of international students is not as much about Western or Eastern education systems as it is about opportunities and recruitment policies" (Sodatsayrova 2018, p. 10).

References

Agarwal, P., Said, M., Sehoole, M., Sirozi, M., & de Wit, H. (2007). The dynamics of international student circulation in a global context. In *Higher education in the new century* (pp. 109–144). Brill Sense.

Agarwal, V. B., & Winkler, D. R. (1985). Foreign demand for United States higher education: A study of developing countries in the eastern hemisphere. *Economic Development and Cultural Change, 33*(3), 623–644.

AGB (1992). *International competitiveness study*. Canberra: IDP Ltd.

Akashi, J. (2014). New aspects of Japan's immigration policies: Is population decline opening the doors? *Contemporary Japan, 26*(2), 175–196. https://doi.org/10.1515/cj-2014-0009.

Asian Development Bank Institute. (2014). Labor migration, skills & student mobility in Asia. http://hdl.handle.net/11540/174.

Altbach, P. G., & Teichler, U. (2001). Internationalization and exchanges in a globalized university. *Journal of Studies in international Education, 5*(1), 5–25.

Atkinson, C. (2010). Does soft power matter? A comparative analysis of student exchange Programs 1980–2006. *Foreign Policy Analysis, 6*(1), 1–22.

Beech, S. E. (2018). Adapting to change in the higher education system: International student mobility as a migration industry. *Journal of Ethnic and Migration Studies, 44*(4), 610–625.

Beine, M., Noël, R., & Ragot, L. (2014). Determinants of the international mobility of students. *Economics of Education Review, 41*(C), 40–54.

Benzie, H. J. (2010). Graduating as a 'native speaker': International students and English language proficiency in higher education. *Higher Education Research & Development, 29*(4), 447–459.

Bhugra, D., & Becker, M. A. (2005). Migration, cultural bereavement and cultural identity. *World Psychiatry, 4*(1), 18.

Bolsmann, C., & Miller, H. (2008). International student recruitment to universities in England: Discourse, rationales and globalisation. *Globalisation, Societies and Education, 6*(1), 75–88.

Bornsztein, B. (1987). Why did they come?: A study of the major factors which influence the foreign student's decision to apply for admission to selected graduate schools of education in the United States (Doctoral dissertation, University of Minnesota).

Brunner, J. J., & Tillett, A. (2007). *Higher Education in Central Asia: The challenges of modernization—An overview*. Washington, DC: World Bank.

Cantwell, B., Luca, S. G., & Lee, J. J. (2009). Exploring the orientations of international students in Mexico: Differences by region of origin. *Higher Education, 57*(3), 335–354.

Castles, S, De Haas, H., & Miller, M. J. (2014). *The age of migration* (5th ed.). New York: Palgrave Macmillan.

Chan, S. J. (2012). Shifting patterns of student mobility in Asia. *Higher Education Policy, 25*(2), 207–224.

Chen, L. H. (2006). Attracting East Asian students to Canadian graduate schools. *Canadian Journal of Higher Education, 36*(2), 77–105.

Chen, T. M., & Barnett, G. A. (2000). Research on international student flows from a macro perspective: A network analysis of 1985, 1989 and 1995. *Higher Education, 39*(4), 435–453.

Chinaview. (2006). More Chinese students studying overseas. Released October 16, 2006. Retrieved from http://news.xinhuanet.com/english/2006-10/content_5206549.htm.

Chirkov, V., Vansteenkiste, M., Tao, R., & Lynch, M. (2007). The role of self-determined motivation and goals for the study abroad in the adaptation of international students. *International Journal of Intercultural Relations, 31*(2), 199–222.

Choudaha, R. (2017). Three waves of international student mobility (1999–2020). *Studies in Higher Education, 42*(5), 825–832

Clover, D. (2005). Dispersed or destroyed: Archives, the West Indian Students' Union, and public memory. In *Society for Caribbean studies annual conference papers* (Vol. 6). The Society for Caribbean Studies (UK).

Collins, F. L. (2010). International students as urban agents: International education and urban transformation in Auckland, New Zealand. *Geoforum, 41*(6), 940–950.

Cummings, W. K., & So, W. C. (1985). The preference of Asian overseas students for the United States: An examination of the context. *Higher Education, 14*(4), 403–423.

DFAT. (2005). Education without borders: International trade in education. Released September 7, 2005. Retrieved January 15, 2006, from http://www.dfat.gov.au/publications/eau_education/index.html.

Dreher, A., & Poutvaara, P. (2005). Student flows and migration: An empirical analysis. CESifo Working Paper Series 1490, CESifo.

Duan, J. P. (1997). The influence of various factors on International students in selecting universities: A South Australian study of Chinese students from Hong Kong and Malaysia (Doctoral dissertation). (Unpublished doctoral dissertation). University of South Australia, Adelaide, Australia.

Fam, K. S., & Gray, B. (2000). Asian values and education promotion: An empirical study. Marketing in a Global Economy Proceedings, 431–438. Retrieved April 24, 2006, from http://www.utdt.edu/congresos/empresarial/papers-ama/100.PDF.

Franklin, K. (2010). Long-term career impact and professional applicability of the study abroad experience. *Frontiers: The Interdisciplinary Journal of Study Abroad, 19*, 169–190.

Findlay, A., King, R., Stam, A., & Ruiz-Gelices, E. (2006). Ever reluctant Europeans: The changing geographies of UK students studying and working abroad. *European Urban and Regional Studies, 13*(4), 291–318.

Galway, A. D. (2000). Going global, Ontario colleges of applied arts and technology, international student recruitment and the export of education (Doctoral dissertation, National Library of Canada = Bibliothèque nationale du Canada).

Gareth, D. (2005). Chinese students' motivations for studying abroad. *International Journal of Private Higher Education, 2*,16–21.

Gareth, X. (2003). *Education in China since 1976*. Jefferson, NC: McFarland & Company.

González, C. R., Mesanza, R. B., & Mariel, P. (2011). The determinants of international student mobility flows: An empirical study on the Erasmus programme. *Higher education, 62*(4), 413–430.

Goodwin, C. D. (1993). *International investment in human capital: Overseas education for development*. Institute of International Education.

Guruz, K. (2011). *Higher education and international student mobility in the global knowledge economy: Revised and updated second edition*. Suny Press.

Haupt, A., Krieger, T., & Lange, T. (2010). A note on brain gain and brain drain: Permanent migration and education policy. CESifo Working Paper Series No. 3154.

Ho, K. C. (2014). *Globalising higher education and cities in Asia and the Pacific*. F. L. Collins (Ed.). Wiley-Blackwell.

Hui, L. (2005). Chinese cultural schema of education: Implications for communication between Chinese students and Australian educators. *Issues in educational Research, 15*(1), 17–36.

Institute of International Education. (2004). Open doors 2004 report on international education exchange. New York, NY: Author.

Institute of International Education. (2012). Open doors 2012 report on international education exchange. New York, NY: Author.

Jacobson, F. R. (2005). *Factors influencing choice by foreign nationals to attend small private colleges and universities in the United States*. San Diego: Alliant International University.

Jiang, Y., & Ashley, D. (2000). *Mao's children in the new China: Voices from the Red guard generation* (Vol. 3). Psychology Press.

Khadria, B. (2001). Shifting paradigms of globalization: The twenty-first century transition towards generics in skilled migration from India. *International Migration, 39*(5), 45–71.

Khan, M. (2019). Contested ground: Network governance in Australia's migration industry. *International Migration, 57*(3), 295–309.

Kim, J. (1998). Economic analysis of foreign education and students abroad. *Journal of Development Economics, 56*(2), 337–365.

Knight, J. (2012). Student mobility and internationalization: Trends and tribulations. *Research in Comparative and International Education, 7*(1), 20–33.

Kondakci, Y. (2011). Student mobility reviewed: Attraction and satisfaction of international students in Turkey. *Higher Education, 62*(5), 573.

Kondakci, Y., Van den Broeck, H., & Yildirim, A. (2008). The challenges of internationalization from foreign and local students' perspectives: The case of management school. *Asia Pacific Education Review, 9*(4), 448–463.

Kuroda, K., Sugimura, M., Kitamura, Y., & Asada, S. (2019). Internationalization of higher education and student mobility in Japan and Asia. Background paper prepared for the prepared for the 2019 Global Education Monitoring Report. Retrieved from https://www.jica.go.jp/jica-ri/publication/other/l75nbg000010mg5u-att/Background_Kuroda.pdf.

Lahiri, S. (2000). *Indians in Britain: Anglo-Indian encounters, race and identity, 1880–1930* (Vol. 1). Psychology Press.

Lasanowski, V. (2009). International student mobility: Status report 2009. *The Observatory on Borderless Higher Education*.

Li, M., & Bray, M. (2007). Cross-border flows of students for higher education: Push–pull factors and motivations of mainland Chinese students in Hong Kong and Macau. *Higher Education, 53*(6), 791–818.

Liu-Farrer, G. (2009). Educationally channeled international labor mobility: Contemporary migration from China to Japan. *International Migration Review, 43*(1), 178–204.

Ma, A. H. S. (2014). Social networks, cultural capital and attachment to the host city: Comparing overseas Chinese students and foreign students in Taipei. *Asia Pacific Viewpoint, 55*(2), 226–224.

Madge, C., Raghuram, P., & Noxolo, P. (2009). Engaged pedagogy and responsibility: A postcolonial analysis of international students. *Geoforum, 40*(1), 34–45.

Madge, C., Raghuram, P., & Noxolo, P. (2015). Conceptualizing international education: From international student to international study. *Progress in Human Geography, 39*(6), 681–701.

Marginson, S. (2001, December). Global enterprise and local squalor: Australian higher education and the international student market. In *Proceedings of the International Education Research Conference*. Perth.

Marginson, S. (2006). Dynamics of national and global competition in higher education. *Higher Education, 52*(1), 1–39.

Marginson, S. (2008). Global field and global imagining: Bourdieu and worldwide higher education. *British Journal of Sociology of Education, 29*(3), 303–315.

Matthews, D. (2016). Chinese student market: Can the West weather a perfect storm. *Times Higher Education*.

Mazzarol, T., Soutar, G., Smart, D., & Choo, S. (2001). Perceptions, information and choice: Understanding how Chinese students select a country for overseas study. https://research-repository.uwa.edu.au/en/publications/perceptions-information-and-choice-understanding-howchinese-stud.

Mazzarol, T., & Soutar, G. N. (2002). "Push-pull" factors influencing international student destination choice. *International Journal of Educational Management, 16*(2), 82–90.

Mazzarol, T., Savery, L. K., & Kemp, S. (Eds.). (1996). International students who choose not to study in Australia: An examination of Taiwan and Indonesia. *AEIF Policy, Research and Analysis Section*.

McMahon, M. E. (1992). Higher education in a world market. *Higher Education, 24*(4), 465–482.

Mok, K. H. (2003). Globalisation and higher education restructuring in Hong Kong, Taiwan and Mainland China. *Higher Education Research & Development, 22*(2), 117–129.

Moogan, Y. J., Baron, S., & Harris, K. (1999). Decision-making behaviour of potential higher education students. *Higher Education Quarterly, 53*(3), 211–228.

Murphy-Lejeune, E. (2003). *Student mobility and narrative in Europe: The new strangers*. Routledge.

Nazira, S. O. D. A. T. S. A. Y. R. O. V. A. (2018). Expanding education through local and international borders: Tajikistani students in Japan. *Journal of International and Advanced Japanese Studies, 10*, 1–22.

OECD. (2001). *International mobility of the highly skilled*. Paris: OECD. https://doi.org/10.1787/9789264196087-en.

OECD. (2009). Education at glance 2009: OECD indicators. Paris: OECD. http://www.oecd.org/edu/eag.

Organisation for Economic Co-operation and Development (OECD). (2010). *Education at a glance 2010: OECD indicators*. Paris: OECD.

Perna, L. W., Orosz, K., & Jumakulov, Z. (2015). Understanding the human capital benefits of a government-funded international scholarship program: An exploration of Kazakhstan's Bolashak program. *International Journal of Educational Development, 40*, 85–97.

Raghuram, P. (2009). Caring about 'brain drain' migration in a postcolonial world. *Geoforum, 40*(1), 25–33.

Raghuram, P. (2013). Theorising the spaces of student migration. *Population, Space and Place, 19*(2), 138–154.

Rivza, B., & Teichler, U. (2007). The changing role of student mobility. *Higher Education Policy, 20*(4), 457–475.

Robertson, S. (2011). Student switchers and the regulation of residency: The interface of the individual and Australia's immigration regime. *Population, Space and Place, 17*(1), 103–115.

Rosenzweig, M. R., Irwin, D. A., & Williamson, J. G. (2006, January). Global wage differences and international student flows [with comments and discussion]. In *Brookings trade forum* (pp. 57–96). Brookings Institution Press.

Samanchina, Z. & Elebaeva, A. (2015). The prospects for educational migration from Kyrgyzstan to Turkey. *Central Asia & the Caucasus, 16*(1), 135–148.

Sandhu, D. S., & Asrabadi, B. R. (1994). Development of an acculturative stress scale for international students: Preliminary findings. *Psychological Reports, 75*(1), 435–448.

Sodatsayrova, N., & Waljee, A. (2017). Re-interpreting cultural values: Tajikistani students abroad. *Cambridge Journal of Eurasian Studies, 1*, 1–22. https://doi.org/10.22261/CJES.DKC8NT.

Spilimbergo, A. (2009). Democracy and foreign education. *American Economic Review, 99*(1), 528–543.

Stebleton, M., Soria, K., & Cherney, B. (2013). *The high impact of education abroad: College students' engagement in international experiences and the development of intercultural competencies.*

Stephens, D. (2007, May). *Culture in education and development: Principles, practice and policy.* Symposium Books Ltd.

Stewart, K., & Felicetti, L. (1991). Marketing a public university to international students. *Journal of Professional Services Marketing, 7*(1), 67–74.

Stroud, A., (2010). Who Plans (Not) to Study Abroad? An Examination of U.S. Student Intent. *Journal of Studies in International Education, 14*(5), 491–507.

Tan, A. (2015). College choice behaviors of international students. *Sage Open, 5*(4), 1–14.

Teichler, U. (2007). International dimensions of higher education and graduate employment, REFLEX report. *REFLEX, The flexible professional in the knowledge society. New demands on higher, project supported by the VI framework programme of the EU, 199220.*

The Institute for International Education. (2013). Open Doors Report. Retrieved from www.iie.org/Research-and-Publications/Open-Doors/Data/US-Study-Abroad.

Tysome, T. (2004). UK market worth£ 10 billion. Times Higher Education Supplement, 23.

UNESCO. (2008). *Global education digest 2008: Comparing education statistics across the world.* Montreal: UNESCO Institute for Statistics. http://www.uis.unesco.org/publications/GED2008.

Universities UK. (2014). *International students in higher education: The UK and its competition.*

Vargas-Lundius, R., Lanly, G., & Villarreal, M. (2008). *International Migration, remittances and rural development.* Rome, Italy: International Fund for Agricultural Development. Retrieved from http://www.fao.org/3/a-ak405e.pdf.

Verbik, L., & Lasanowski, V. (2007). International student mobility: Patterns and trends. *World Education News and Reviews, 20*(10), 1–16.

Wang, X. (2003). Education in China since 1976. Jefferson, NC: McFarland & Company.

Waters, J. L. (2012). Geographies of international education: Mobilities and the reproduction of social (dis)advantage. *Geography Compass, 6*(3), 123–136.

Williams, T. R. (2005). Exploring the impact of study abroad on students' intercultural communication skills: Adaptability and sensitivity. *Journal of Studies in International Education, 9*(4), 356–371.

Xiang, B., & Lindquist, J. (2014). Migration Infrastructure. *International Migration Review, 48(S1)*, S122–S148.

Yang, M. (2007). What attracts mainland Chinese students to Australian higher education. *Studies in Learning, Evaluation, Innovation and Development, 4*(2), 1–12.

Zhang, X. (2001). 'China Today: Chinese families spend heavily on children's education'. Released November, 23, 2001.

Ziguras, C., & Law, S. F. (2006). Recruiting international students as skilled migrants: the global 'skills race' as viewed from Australia and Malaysia. *Globalisation, Societies and Education, 4*(1), 59–76.

Index

T. Dadabaev (ed.), *The Grass is Always Greener?*, Politics and History in Central Asia,
https://doi.org/10.1007/978-981-16-2570-1

The manufacturer's authorised representative in the EU is Springer Nature Customer Service Centre GmbH, Europaplatz 3, 69115 Heidelberg, Germany. If you have any concerns regarding our products, please contact ProductSafety@springernature.com

Printed and bound by CPI Group (UK) Ltd, Croydon, CR0 4YY
30/09/2026
02225326-0003